DECEIT, DESIRE, AND THE NOVEL

DECEIT, DESIRE, AND THE NOVEL

Self and Other in Literary Structure

BY RENÉ GIRARD

TRANSLATED BY YVONNE FRECCERO

THE JOHNS HOPKINS UNIVERSITY PRESS

BALTIMORE AND LONDON

TRANSLATOR'S NOTE

The quotations of Proust's *Remembrance of Things Past* are from the C.K. Scott Moncrieff translation (The *Past Recaptured* by Frederick A. Blossom), published in New York by Random House in 1934, and those of *Jean Santeuil* are from the Gerard Hopkins translation, published in New York by Simon and Schuster in 1956. For Dostoyevsky's works I have used the Constance Garnett translations: *Notes from the Underground* (New York: Dial Press, 1945), and *The Brothers Karamazov* and *The Possessed* (New York: Macmillan, n.d.). I have translated all other quotations from the French edition of this book, except where footnotes indicate otherwise.

Y. F.

© 1961 by Éditions Bernard Grasset
Translation © 1965 by The Johns Hopkins Press
All rights reserved
Printed in the United States of America on acid-free paper

Originally published in Paris in 1961 as
Mensonge romantique et vérité romanesque

Originally published in English, 1966
Johns Hopkins Paperbacks edition, 1976
03 02 01 00 99 98 97 96 95 94   10 9 8 7 6

The Johns Hopkins University Press
2715 North Charles Street, Baltimore, Maryland 21218-4319
The Johns Hopkins Press Ltd., London

ISBN 0-8018-1830-3 (paperback)

A catalog record for this book is available from the British Library.

Acknowledgments

The author expresses his deep gratitude to Yvonne Freccero. He also wants to acknowledge the contributions of Steven F. Rendall, who helped prepare this English edition, and Michael S. Koppisch, who compiled the index.

R. G.

Contents

DECEIT, DESIRE, AND THE NOVEL

CHAPTER I

"TRIANGULAR" DESIRE

"I want you to know, Sancho, that the famous Amadis of Gaul was one of the most perfect knight errants. But what am I saying, one of the most perfect? I should say the only, the first, the unique, the master and lord of all those who existed in the world. . . . I think . . . that, when a painter wants to become famous for his art he tries to imitate the originals of the best masters he knows; the same rule applies to most important jobs or exercises which contribute to the embellishment of republics; thus the man who wishes to be known as careful and patient should and does imitate Ulysses, in whose person and works Homer paints for us a vivid portrait of carefulness and patience, just as Virgil shows us in the person of Aeneas the valor of a pious son and the wisdom of a valiant captain; and it is understood that they depict them not as they are but as they should be, to provide an example of virtue for centuries to come. In the same way Amadis was the pole, the star, the sun for brave and amorous knights, and we others who fight under the banner of love and chivalry should imitate him. Thus, my friend Sancho, I reckon that whoever imitates him best will come closest to perfect chivalry."

DON QUIXOTE has surrendered to Amadis the individual's fundamental prerogative: he no longer chooses the objects of his own desire—Amadis must choose for him.

The disciple pursues objects which are determined for him, or at least seem to be determined for him, by the model of all chivalry. We shall call this model the *mediator* of desire. Chivalric existence is the *imitation* of Amadis in the same sense that the Christian's existence is the imitation of Christ.

In most works of fiction, the characters have desires which are simpler than Don Quixote's. There is no mediator, there is only the subject and the object. When the "nature" of the object inspiring the passion is not sufficient to account for the desire, one must turn to the impassioned subject. Either his "psychology" is examined or his "liberty" invoked. But desire is always spontaneous. It can always be portrayed by a simple straight line which joins subject and object.

The straight line is present in the desire of Don Quixote, but it is not essential. The mediator is there, above that line, radiating toward both the subject and the object. The spatial metaphor which expresses this triple relationship is obviously the triangle. The object changes with each adventure but the triangle remains. The barber's basin or Master Peter's puppets replace the windmills; but Amadis is always present.

The triangle is no *Gestalt*. The real structures are intersubjective. They cannot be localized anywhere; the triangle has no reality whatever; it is a systematic metaphor, systematically pursued. Because changes in size and shape do not destroy the identity of this figure, as we will see later, the diversity as well as the unity of the works can be simultaneously illustrated. The purpose and limitations of this structural geometry may become clearer through a reference to "structural models." The triangle is a model of a sort, or rather a whole family of models. But these models are not "mechanical" like those of Claude Lévi-Strauss. They always allude to the mystery, transparent yet opaque, of human relations. All types of structural thinking assume that human reality is intelligible; it is a *logos* and, as such, it is an incipient *logic,* or it degrades itself into a logic. It can thus be systematized, at least up to a point, however unsystematic, irrational, and chaotic it may appear even to those, or rather especially to those who operate the system. A basic contention of this essay is that the great writers apprehend intuitively and concretely, through the medium of their art, if not formally, the system in which they were first imprisoned together with their contemporaries. Literary interpretation must be systematic because it is the continuation of literature. It should formalize implicit or already half-explicit systems. To maintain that criticism will never be systematic is to maintain that it will never be real knowledge. The value of a critical thought depends not on how cleverly it manages to disguise its own systematic nature or on how many fundamental issues it manages to shirk or to dissolve but on how much literary substance it really embraces, comprehends, and makes articulate. The goal may be too ambitious but it is not outside the scope of literary criticism. It is the very essence of literary criticism. Failure to reach it should be condemned but not the attempt. Everything else has already been done.

Don Quixote, in Cervantes' novel, is a typical example of the victim of triangular desire, but he is far from being the only one. Next to him the most affected is his squire, Sancho Panza. Some of Sancho's desires are not imitated, for example, those aroused by the sight of a piece of cheese or a goatskin of wine. But Sancho has other ambitions besides filling his stomach. Ever since he has been with Don Quixote he has been dreaming of an "island" of which he would be governor, and he wants the title of duchess for his daughter. These desires do not come spontaneously to a simple man like Sancho. It is Don Quixote who has put them into his head.

This time the suggestion is not literary, but oral. But the difference has little importance. These new desires form a new triangle of which the imaginary island, Don Quixote, and Sancho occupy the angles. Don Quixote is Sancho's mediator. The effects of triangular desire are the same in the two characters. From the moment the mediator's influence is felt, the sense of reality is lost and judgment paralyzed.

Since the mediator's influence is more profound and constant in the case of Don Quixote than in that of Sancho, romantic readers have seen in the novel little more than the contrast between Don Quixote the *idealist* and the *realist* Sancho. This contrast is real but secondary; it should not make us overlook the analogies between the two characters. Chivalric passion defines a desire *according to Another*, opposed to this desire *according to Oneself* that most of us pride ourselves on enjoying. Don Quixote and Sancho borrow their desires from the Other in a movement which is so fundamental and primitive that they completely confuse it with the will to be Oneself.

One might object that Amadis is a fictitious person— and this we must admit, but Don Quixote is not the author of this fiction. The mediator is imaginary but not the mediation. Behind the hero's desires there is indeed the suggestion of a third person, the inventor of Amadis, the author of the chivalric romances. Cervantes' work is a long meditation on the baleful influence that the most lucid minds can exercise upon one another. Except in the realm of chivalry, Don Quixote reasons with a great deal of common sense. Nor are his favorite writers mad: perhaps they do not even take their fiction seriously. The illusion is the fruit of a bizarre marriage of two lucid consciousnesses. Chivalric literature, ever more widespread since the invention of the printing press, multiplies stupendously the chances of similar unions.

DESIRE according to the Other and the "seminal" function of literature are also found in the novels of Flaubert. Emma Bovary desires through the romantic heroines who fill her imagination. The second-rate books which she devoured in her youth have destroyed all her spontaneity. We must turn to Jules de Gaultier for the definition of this "bovarysm" which he reveals in almost every one of Flaubert's characters: "The same ignorance, the same inconsistency, the same absence of individual reaction seem to make them fated to obey the suggestion of an external milieu, for lack of an auto-suggestion from within." In his famous essay, entitled *Bovarysm,* Gaultier goes on to observe that in order to reach their goal, which is to "see themselves as they are not," Flaubert's heroes find a "model" for themselves and "imitate from the person they have decided to be, all that can be imitated, everything exterior, appearance, gesture, intonation, and dress."

The external aspects of imitation are the most striking; but we must above all remember that the characters of Cervantes and Flaubert are imitating, or believe they are imitating, the *desires* of models they have freely chosen. A third novelist, Stendhal, also underscores the role of suggestion and imitation in the personality of his heroes. Mathilde de la Mole finds her models in the history of her family; Julien Sorel imitates Napoleon. *The Memoirs of Saint-Helena* and the *Bulletins* of the Grand Army replace the tales of chivalry and the romantic extravagances. The Prince of Parma imitates Louis XIV. The young Bishop of Agde practices the benediction in front of a mirror; he mimics the old and venerable prelates whom he fears he does not sufficiently resemble.

Here history is nothing but a kind of literature; it suggests to all Stendhal's characters feelings and, especially, desires that they do not experience spontaneously. When he enters the service of the Rênal family, Julien borrows from Rousseau's *Confessions* the desire to eat at his master's table rather than at that of the servants. Stendhal uses the word "vanity" (*vanité*) to indicate all these forms of "copying" and "imitating." The *vaniteux*—vain person—cannot draw his desires from his own resources; he must borrow them from others. Thus the *vaniteux* is brother to Don Quixote and Emma Bovary. And so in Stendhal we again find triangular desire.

In the first pages of *The Red and the Black* we take a walk through Verrières with the mayor of the village and his wife. Majestic but tormented, M. de Rênal strolls along his retaining walls. He wants to make Julien Sorel the tutor of his two sons, but not for their sake nor from love of knowledge. His desire is not spontaneous. The conversation between husband and wife soon reveals the mechanism: "Valenod has no tutor for his children—he might very well steal this one from us."

Valenod is the richest and most influential man in Verrières, next to M. de Rênal himself. The mayor of Verrières always has the image of his rival before his eyes during his negotiations with old M. Sorel. He makes the latter some very favorable propositions but the sly peasant invents a brilliant reply: "We have a better offer." This time M. de Rênal is completely convinced that Valenod wishes to engage Julien and his own desire is redoubled. The ever-increasing price that the buyer is willing to pay is determined by the imaginary desire which he attributes to his rival. So there is indeed an imitation of this imaginary desire, and even a very scrupulous imitation, since everything about the desire which is copied, including its intensity, depends upon the desire which serves as model.

At the end of the novel, Julien tries to win back Mathilde de la Mole and, on the advice of the dandy Korasof, resorts to the same sort of trick as his father. He pays court to the Maréchale de Fervacques; he wishes to arouse this woman's desire and display it before Mathilde so that the idea of imitating it might suggest itself to her. A little water is enough to prime a pump; a little desire is enough to arouse desire in the creature of vanity.

Julien carries out his plan and everything turns out as expected. The interest which the Maréchale takes in him reawakens Mathilde's desire. And the triangle reappears —Mathilde, Mme de Fervacques, Julien—M. de Rênal, Valenod, Julien. The triangle is present each time that Stendhal speaks of vanity, whether it is a question of ambition, business, or love. It is surprising that the Marxist critics, for whom economic structures provide the archetype of all human relations, have not as yet pointed out the analogy between the crafty bargaining of old man Sorel and the amorous maneuvers of his son.

A *vaniteux* will desire any object so long as he is convinced that it is already desired by another person whom he admires. The mediator here is a *rival*, brought into existence as a rival by vanity, and that same vanity demands his defeat. The rivalry between mediator and the person who desires constitutes an essential difference between this desire and that of Don Quixote, or of Emma Bovary. Amadis cannot vie with Don Quixote in the protection of orphans in distress, he cannot slaughter giants in his place. Valenod, on the other hand, can steal the tutor from M. de Rênal; the Maréchale de Fervacques can take Julien from Mathilde de la Mole. In most of Stendhal's desires, the mediator himself desires the object, or could desire it: it is even this very desire, real or presumed, which makes this object infinitely desirable in the eyes of the subject. The mediation begets a second desire exactly the same as the mediator's. This means that one is always confronted with two *competing* desires. The mediator can no longer act his role of model without also acting or appearing to act the role of obstacle. Like the relentless sentry of the Kafka fable, the model shows his disciple the gate of paradise and forbids him to enter with one and the same gesture. We should not be surprised if the look cast by M. de Rênal on Valenod is vastly different from that raised by Don Quixote toward Amadis.

In Cervantes the mediator is enthroned in an inaccessible heaven and transmits to his faithful follower a little of his serenity. In Stendhal, this same mediator has come down to earth. The clear distinction between these two types of relationship between mediator and subject indicates the enormous spiritual gap which separates Don Quixote from the most despicably vain of Stendhal's characters. The image of the triangle cannot remain valid for us unless it at once allows this distinction and measures this gap for us. To achieve this double objective, we have only to vary the *distance*, in the triangle, separating the mediator from the desiring subject.

Obviously this distance is greatest in Cervantes. There can be no contact whatsoever between Don Quixote and his legendary Amadis. Emma Bovary is already closer to her Parisian mediator. Travelers' tales, books, and the press bring the latest fashions of the capital even to Yonville. Emma comes still closer to her mediator when she goes to the ball at the Vaubyessards'; she penetrates the holy of holies and gazes at the idol face to face. But this proximity is fleeting. Emma will never be able to desire that which the incarnations of her "ideal" desire; she will never be able to be their rival; she will never leave for Paris.

Julien Sorel does all that Emma cannot do. At the beginning of *The Red and the Black* the distance between the hero and his mediator is as great as in *Madame Bovary*. But Julien spans this distance; he leaves his province and becomes the lover of the proud Mathilde; he rises rapidly to a brilliant position. Stendhal's other heroes are

also close to their mediators. It is this which distinguishes
Stendhal's universe from those we have already considered. Between Julien and Mathilde, between Rênal and
Valenod, between Lucien Leuwen and the nobles of
Nancy, between Sansfin and the petty squires of Nor-
mandy, the distance is always small enough to permit the
rivalry of desires. In the novels of Cervantes and Flaubert,
the mediator remained beyond the universe of the hero;
he is now within the same universe.

Romantic works are, therefore, grouped into two fundamental categories—but within these categories there
can be an infinite number of secondary distinctions. We
shall speak of *external mediation* when the distance is
sufficient to eliminate any contact between the two
spheres of *possibilities* of which the mediator and the subject occupy the respective centers. We shall speak of *internal mediation* when this same distance is sufficiently
reduced to allow these two spheres to penetrate each
other more or less profoundly.

Obviously it is not physical space that measures the gap
between mediator and the desiring subject. Although geo-
graphical separation might be one factor, the *distance* between mediator and subject is primarily spiritual. Don
Quixote and Sancho are always close to each other physically but the social and intellectual distance which separates them remains insuperable. The valet never desires
what his master desires. Sancho covets the food left by the
monks, the purse of gold found on the road, and other objects which Don Quixote willingly lets him have. As for
the imaginary island, it is from Don Quixote himself that
Sancho is counting on receiving it, as the faithful vassal
holds everything in the name of his lord. The mediation of
Sancho is therefore an external mediation. No rivalry with
the mediator is possible. The harmony between the two
companions is never seriously troubled.

THE HERO of external mediation proclaims aloud the true nature of his desire. He worships his model openly and declares himself his disciple. We have seen Don Quixote himself explain to Sancho the privileged part Amadis plays in his life. Mme Bovary and Léon also admit the truth about their desires in their lyric confessions. The parallel between *Don Quixote* and *Madame Bovary* has become classic. It is always easy to recognize analogies between two novels of external mediation.

Imitation in Stendhal's work at first seems less absurd since there is less of that divergence between the worlds of disciple and model which makes a Don Quixote or an Emma Bovary so grotesque. And yet the imitation is no less strict and literal in internal mediation than in external mediation. If this seems surprising it is not only because the imitation refers to a model who is "close," but also because the hero of internal mediation, far from boasting of his efforts to imitate, carefully hides them.

The impulse toward the object is ultimately an impulse toward the mediator; in internal mediation this impulse is checked by the mediator himself since he desires, or perhaps possesses, the object. Fascinated by his model, the disciple inevitably sees, in the mechanical obstacle which he puts in his way, proof of the ill will borne him. Far from declaring himself a faithful vassal, he thinks only of repudiating the bonds of mediation. But these bonds are stronger than ever, for the mediator's apparent hostility does not diminish his prestige but instead augments it. The subject is convinced that the model considers himself too superior to accept him as a disciple. The subject is torn between two opposite feelings toward his model—the most submissive reverence and the most intense malice. This is the passion we call *hatred*.

Only someone who prevents us from satisfying a desire which he himself has inspired in us is truly an object of hatred. The person who hates first hates himself for the secret admiration concealed by his hatred. In an effort to hide this desperate admiration from others, and from himself, he no longer wants to see in his mediator anything but an obstacle. The secondary role of the mediator thus becomes primary, concealing his original function of a model scrupulously imitated.

In the quarrel which puts him in opposition to his rival, the subject reverses the logical and chronological order of desires in order to hide his imitation. He asserts that his own desire is prior to that of his rival; according to him, it is the mediator who is responsible for the rivalry. Everything that originates with this mediator is systematically belittled although still secretly desired. Now the mediator is a shrewd and diabolical enemy; he tries to rob the subject of his most prized possessions; he obstinately thwarts his most legitimate ambitions.

All the phenomena explored by Max Scheler in *Ressentiment* [1] are, in our opinion, the result of internal mediation. Furthermore, the word *ressentiment* itself underscores the quality of reaction, of repercussion which characterizes the experience of the subject in this type of mediation. The impassioned admiration and desire to emulate stumble over the unfair obstacle with which the model seems to block the way of his disciple, and then these passions recoil on the disciple in the form of impotent hatred, thus causing the sort of psychological self-poisoning so well described by Scheler.

As he indicates, *ressentiment* can impose its point of view even on those whom it does not dominate. It is *ressentiment* which prevents us, and sometimes prevents

[1] The author quotes from the French translation, *L'Homme du Ressentiment*. There is an English translation by William H. Holdheim, *Ressentiment* (New York: Free Press, 1960). The word *ressentiment* is used by Scheler in the original German text as the most accurate term for the feeling described. (*Translator's note.*)

Scheler himself, from recognizing the part played by imitation in the birth of desire. For example, we do not see that jealousy and envy, like hatred, are scarcely more than traditional names given to internal mediation, names which almost always conceal their true nature from us.

Jealousy and envy imply a third presence: object, subject, and a third person toward whom the jealousy or envy is directed. These two "vices" are therefore triangular; however we never recognize a model in the person who arouses jealousy because we always take a jealous person's attitude toward the problem of jealousy. Like all victims of internal mediation, the jealous person easily convinces himself that his desire is spontaneous, in other words, that it is deeply rooted in the object and in this object alone. As a result he always maintains that his desire preceded the intervention of the mediator. He would have us see him as an intruder, a bore, a *terzo incomodo* who interrupts a delightful tête-à-tête. Jealousy is thus reduced to the irritation we all experience when one of our desires is accidentally thwarted. But true jealousy is infinitely more profound and complex; it always contains an element of fascination with the insolent rival. Furthermore, it is always the same people who suffer from jealousy. Is it possible that they are all the victims of repeated accidents? Is it *fate* that creates for them so many rivals and throws so many obstacles in the way of their desires? We do not believe it ourselves, since we say that these chronic victims of jealousy or of envy have a "jealous temperament" or an "envious nature." What exactly then does such a "temperament" or "nature" imply if not an irresistible impulse to desire what Others desire, in other words to imitate the desires of others?

Max Scheler numbers "envy, jealousy, and rivalry" among the sources of *ressentiment*. He defines envy as "a feeling of impotence which vitiates our attempt to acquire something, because it belongs to another." He observes, on the other hand, that there would be no envy, in the strong sense of the word, if the envious person's imagination did not transform into concerted opposition the passive obstacle which the possessor puts in his way by the mere fact of possession. "Mere regret at not possessing something which belongs to another and which we covet is not enough in itself to give rise to envy, since it might also be an incentive for acquiring the desired object or something similar. . . . *Envy* occurs only when our efforts to acquire it fail and we are left with a feeling of impotence."

The analysis is accurate and complete; it omits neither the envious person's self-deception with regard to the cause of his failure, nor the paralysis that accompanies envy. But these elements remain isolated; Scheler has not really perceived their relationship. On the other hand everything becomes clear, everything fits into a coherent structure if, in order to explain envy, we abandon the object of rivalry as a starting point and choose instead the rival himself, i.e., the mediator, as both a point of departure for our analysis and its conclusion. Possession is a merely passive obstacle; it is frustrating and seems a deliberate expression of contempt only because the rival is secretly revered. The demigod seems to answer homage with a curse. He seems to render evil for good. The subject would like to think of himself as the victim of an atrocious injustice but in his anguish he wonders whether perhaps he does not deserve his apparent condemnation. Rivalry therefore only aggravates mediation; it increases the mediator's prestige and strengthens the bond which links the object to this mediator by forcing him to affirm openly his right or desire of possession. Thus the subject is less capable than ever of giving up the inaccessible object: it is on this object and it alone that the mediator confers his prestige, by possessing or wanting to possess it. Other objects have no worth at all in the eyes of the envious person, even though they may be similar to or indeed identical with the "mediated" object.

Everything becomes clear when one sees that the loathed rival is actually a mediator. Max Scheler himself is not far from the truth when he states in *Ressentiment* that "the fact of choosing a model for oneself" is the result of a certain tendency, common to all men, to compare oneself with others, and he goes on to say, "all jealousy, all ambition, and even an ideal like the 'imitation of Christ' is based on such comparisons." But this intuition remains isolated. Only the great artists attribute to the mediator the position usurped by the object; only they reverse the commonly accepted hierarchy of desire.

In *The Memoirs of a Tourist,* Stendhal warns his readers against what he calls the *modern* emotions, the fruits of universal vanity: "envy, jealousy, and impotent hatred." Stendhal's formula gathers together the three triangular emotions; it considers them apart from any particular object; it associates them with that imperative need to imitate by which, according to the novelist, the nineteenth century is completely possessed. For his part, Scheler asserts, following Nietzsche—who acknowledged a large debt to Stendhal—that the romantic state of mind is pervaded by *"ressentiment."* Stendhal says precisely this, but he looks for the source of this spiritual poison in the passionate imitation of individuals who are fundamentally our equals and whom we endow with an arbitrary prestige. If the *modern* emotions flourish, it is not because "envious natures" and "jealous temperaments" have unfortunately and mysteriously increased in number, but because *internal* mediation triumphs in a universe where the differences between men are gradually erased.

The great novelists reveal the imitative nature of desire.

In our days its nature is hard to perceive because the most
fervent imitation is the most vigorously denied. Don
Quixote proclaimed himself the disciple of Amadis and
the writers of his time proclaimed themselves the disciples of the Ancients. The romantic *vaniteux* does not want
to be anyone's disciple. He convinces himself that he is
thoroughly *original*. In the nineteenth century spontaneity becomes a universal dogma, succeeding imitation.
Stendhal warns us at every step that we must not be
fooled by these individualisms professed with fanfare, for
they merely hide a new form of imitation. Romantic revulsion, hatred of society, nostalgia for the desert, just as
gregariousness, usually conceal a morbid concern for the
Other.

In order to camouflage the essential role which the
Other plays in his desires, Stendhal's *vaniteux* frequently
appeals to the clichés of the reigning ideology. Behind
the devotion, the mawkish altruism, the hypocritical *engagement* of the *grandes dames* of 1830, Stendhal finds
not the generous impulse of a being truly prepared to give
itself but rather the tormented recourse of vanity at bay,
the centrifugal movement of an ego powerless to desire by
itself. The novelist lets his characters act and speak; then,
in the twinkling of an eye, he reveals to us the mediator.
He re-establishes covertly the true hierarchy of desire
while pretending to believe in the weak reasoning advanced by his character in support of the contrary hierarchy. This is one of the perpetual methods of Stendhal's
irony.

The romantic *vaniteux* always wants to convince himself that his desire is written into the nature of things, or,
which amounts to the same thing, that it is the emanation
of a serene subjectivity, the creation *ex nihilo* of a quasi-
divine ego. Desire is no longer rooted in the object perhaps, but it is rooted in the subject; it is certainly not

rooted in the Other. The objective and subjective fallacies are one and the same; both originate in the image which we all have of our own desires. Subjectivisms and objectivisms, romanticisms and realisms, individualisms and scientisms, idealisms and positivisms appear to be in opposition but are secretly in agreement to conceal the presence of the mediator. All these dogmas are the aesthetic or philosophic translation of world views peculiar to internal mediation. They all depend directly or indirectly on the lie of spontaneous desire. They all defend the same illusion of autonomy to which modern man is passionately devoted.

It is this same illusion which the great novel does not succeed in shattering although it never ceases to denounce it. Unlike the romantics and neoromantics, a Cervantes, a Flaubert, and a Stendhal reveal the truth of desire in their great novels. But this truth remains hidden even at the heart of its revelation. The reader, who is usually convinced of his own spontaneity, applies to the work the meanings he already applies to the world. The nineteenth century, which failed completely to understand Cervantes, continually praised the "originality" of his hero. The romantic reader, by a marvelous misinterpretation which fundamentally is only a superior truth, identifies himself with Don Quixote, the supreme imitator, and makes of him the *model individual*.

Thus it should not surprise us that the term *romanesque* [2] still reflects, in its ambiguity, our unawareness of

[2] In the French original, constant association and opposition of "romantique" and "romanesque", with their same radical and different endings, tried to convey something of an essential, yet elusive, difference between the works which passively reflect and those which actively reveal "mediated" desire. The two words are not interchangeable, to be sure, but their opposition alone is fully significant. The essay must not be read as the indictment of a narrowly, or even broadly defined literary *school*. Neither is it an effort to circumscribe the *genre* of the novel. The author is aware that *Jean Santeuil is* a

all mediation. The term denotes the chivalric romances and it denotes *Don Quixote;* it can be synonymous with *romantic* and it can indicate the destruction of romantic pretentions. In the future we shall use the term *romantic* for the works which reflect the presence of a mediator without ever revealing it and the term *novelistic* for the works which reveal this presence. It is to the latter that this book is primarily devoted.

THE MEDIATOR'S prestige is imparted to the object of desire and confers upon it an illusory value. Triangular desire is the desire which transfigures its object. *Romantic* literature does not disregard this metamorphosis; on the contrary, it turns it to account and boasts of it, but never reveals its actual mechanism. The illusion is a living being whose conception demands a male and a female element. The poet's imagination is the female which remains sterile as long as it is not fertilized by the mediator. The novelist alone describes this actual genesis of the illusion for which romanticism always makes the poet alone responsible. The romantic insists on a "parthenogenesis" of the

---

novel and should be classified as such if classifications were the order of the day. *Jean Santeuil* can nevertheless be viewed as "romantic" within the context of the essay, in other words by contrast with the "romanesque"—novelistic—*Remembrance of Things Past.* Similarly, Chateaubriand's *Mémoires d'outre-Tombe* are not a novel but they partake somewhat of the "romanesque" by contrast with the romantic *René.* Unlike the categories of literary historians which are mechanistic and positivistic, the present categories, even though they are not Hegelian, are still dialectical. They are not independent labels stuck once and for all on a fixed amount of static and objective literary material. Neither are they literature-proof receptacles in which that same material would be contained. They have no value in themselves; no single category can be appraised separately. Oppositions are essential; their terms should not be dissociated. The whole *system* alone is truly significant and self-sufficient, in accordance with a *structural* hypothesis.

imagination. Forever in love with autonomy, he refuses to bow before his own gods. The series of solipsistic theories of poetry produced during the past century and a half are an expression of this refusal.

The romantics congratulate Don Quixote on mistaking an ordinary barber's basin for Mambrino's helmet, while they themselves secretly feel they refrain from such folly. They are mistaken. The Parisian world of "envy," "jealousy," and "impotent hatred" is no less illusory and no less desired than the helmet of Mambrino. All of its desires are based on abstractions; Stendhal tells us they are "cerebral desires." Joys and especially suffering are not rooted in things; they are "spiritual," but in an inferior sense which must be explained. From the mediator, a veritable artificial sun, descends a mysterious ray which makes the object shine with a false brilliance. There would be no illusion if Don Quixote were not imitating Amadis. Emma Bovary would not have taken Rudolph for a Prince Charming had she not been imitating romantic heroines. All of Stendhal's art is aimed at persuading us that the values of vanity, nobility, money, power, reputation only *seem* to be concrete . . .

It is this abstract character which allows the comparison of the desire stemming from vanity with Don Quixote's desire. The illusion is not the same but there is still an illusion. Desire projects a dream universe around the hero. In both cases the hero escapes from his fantasies only on his deathbed. If Julien seems more lucid than Don Quixote it is because the people who surround him, with the exception of Mme de Rênal, are even more bewitched than he.

The metamorphosis of the desired object occurred to Stendhal long before his novelistic period. In *De l'Amour* he gives a famous description of it based on the image of crystallization. The later novelistic developments appear faithful to the ideology of 1822. They diverge from it, however, on one essential point. According to the preceding analyses crystallization should be the result of vanity. But it is not under the heading of vanity that Stendhal presents this phenomenon to us in *De l'Amour*—it is under the heading of "passion."

Passion, in Stendhal, is the opposite of vanity. Fabrice del Dongo is the perfect example of the passionate person; he is distinguished by his emotional autonomy, by the spontaneity of his desires, by his absolute indifference to the opinion of Others. The passionate person draws the strength of his desire from within himself and not from others.

Can it be that we are mistaken? Could it be authentic passion, in the novels, which is accompanied by crystallization? All Stendhal's great pairs of lovers contradict this point of view. True love, such as that of Fabrice for Clélia and that which Julien finally knows with Mme de Rênal, does not transfigure. The qualities which this love discovers in its object, the happiness it expects from it, are not illusory. Love-passion is always accompanied by esteem, in Corneille's sense of the word. It is based on a perfect agreement among reason, will, and sensibility. The real Mme de Rênal is the one desired by Julien. The real Mathilde is the one he does not desire. In the first case it is a question of passion, in the second of vanity. It is indeed, therefore, vanity which transforms its object.

There is a radical difference between the essay of 1822 and the novelistic masterpieces which is not always easy to perceive because in both cases a distinction is made between passion and vanity. In *De l'Amour* Stendhal describes for us the subjective effects of triangular desire but he attributes them to spontaneous desire. The real criterion of spontaneous desire is the intensity of that desire. The strongest desires are the passionate desires. The desires of vanity are tarnished reflections of authentic desires. Thus it is always Others' desires which derive from vanity, for we are all under the impression that we desire more intensely than Others. The distinction between passion and vanity serves to vindicate Stendhal— and his reader—of the charge of vanity. The mediator remains hidden precisely where his revelation is of the utmost significance, in the existence of the author himself, and so the point of view of 1822 must be characterized as romantic. The passion-vanity dialectic remains "individualistic." It reminds one a little of Gide's dialectic of the natural Self and the social Self in *The Immoralist*.

The Stendhal of whom the critics speak, especially Paul Valéry in his preface to *Lucien Leuwen,* is almost always this "Gide-like" Stendhal of the youthful period. It is obvious that the youthful Stendhal would have been in vogue during the heyday of the ethics of desire of which he himself was the precursor. This first Stendhal, who triumphed at the end of the nineteenth century and the beginning of the twentieth century, offers us a contrast between the spontaneous being who desires intensely and the gregarious man who desires feebly by copying Others.

One might maintain, basing one's view on *The Italian Chronicles* and a few sentences taken from the *écrits intimes,* that the vanity-passion opposition has kept its original meaning in the mature Stendhal. But neither *The Italian Chronicles* nor the *écrits intimes* belong to the pattern of the great novelistic works. A close look at the structure of the latter will readily show that in them vanity becomes at once the transfiguring desire and the most intense desire.

Even in the texts of his youth the vanity-passion opposition never coincided with Gide's opposition of the social and the natural Self such as it is shown, for example, in the contrast between Fleurissoire and Lafcadio in *Lafcadio's Adventures*. Already in *De l'Amour* Stendhal asserts that "vanity gives birth to rapture." He does not therefore totally conceal from himself the prodigious strength of imitated desire. And he is only at the beginning of an evolution which will end in the pure and simple overturning of the initial hierarchy. The further one goes in his work, the more the strength of desire is associated with vanity. It is vanity which causes Julien's suffering when Mathilde turns away from him and this suffering is the most violent the hero has ever known. All the intense desires of Julien are imitated desires. His ambition is a triangular sentiment nourished by hatred for the members of the "establishment." As he places his feet on the ladder, the lover's ultimate thoughts go to the husbands, fathers, and fiancés, i.e., the rivals—never to the woman who is waiting for him on the balcony. The evolution which makes of vanity the stronger desire is completed in the prodigious Sansfin of *Lamiel*, in whom vanity is a veritable frenzy.

As for passion, in these great novels it begins only with that *silence* which Jean Prévost discusses so ably in his *La Création Chez Stendhal*. This passion which keeps silent is hardly desire. As soon as there is really desire, even in the passionate characters, we find the mediator. And so we shall find the triangle of desire even in heroes less impure and less complex than Julien. In Lucien Leuwen the thought of the mythical Colonel Busant de Sicile stirs a vague desire for Mme de Chasteller, a vague desire of desiring which could just as well have settled on another young lady of the Nancy aristocracy. Mme de Rênal herself is jealous of Elisa, jealous too of the unknown person whose portrait she thinks Julien is hiding in his mattress. In the birth of desire, the third person is always present.

We must yield to the evidence. In the later Stendhal

there is no longer spontaneous desire. Every "psychological" analysis is an analysis of vanity, in other words, a revelation of triangular desire. True passion eventually supplants this madness in the best of Stendhal's heroes. It comes to them with the calm of the summits which these heroes attain in their supreme moments. In *The Red and the Black* the peace before Julien's execution is in marked contrast with the morbid agitation of the preceding period. Fabrice and Clélia enjoy peace and tranquility in the Tour Farnèse, above desires and vanity which always threaten them but never harm them.

Why does Stendhal still speak of passion when desire has disappeared? Perhaps because these moments of ecstasy are always the result of a feminine mediation. For Stendhal woman can be the mediatrix of peace and serenity after mediating desire, anguish, and vanity. As in Nerval, it is not so much a question of opposition between two types of women as two antinomic functions exercised by the feminine element in the existence and the creation of the novelist.

In the great works, the transition from vanity to passion is inseparable from aesthetic happiness. It is the delight of creation which wins out over desire and anguish. The transition always takes place under the sign of the deceased Mathilde, the woman who had rejected him in Milan, and, as it were, as a result of her intercession. Stendhalian passion cannot be understood without taking into account the problems of aesthetic creation. It is to the full and complete revelation of triangular desire, in other words, to his own liberation, that the novelist owes these moments of happiness. Even though it is the novelist's supreme reward, passion is scarcely present in the novel itself. Freed, it rises out of a novelistic world totally given over to vanity and desire.

IT IS THE transfiguration of the desired object which constitutes the unity of external and internal mediation. The hero's imagination is the mother of the illusion but the child must still have a father: the mediator. Proust's work also bears witness to this marriage and this birth. The concepts so far developed should enable us to perceive the unity of certain works of genius, which Proust himself did not fear to assert. The idea of mediation encourages literary comparisons at a level which is no longer that of *genre* criticism or thematic criticism. It may illuminate the works through each other; it may unite them without destroying their irreducible singularity.

The analogies between Stendhalian vanity and Proustian desire strike the least critical reader. But they strike only him, for it seems that critical reflection never begins from such elementary intuitions. The resemblance is taken for granted by those interpreters who are fond of "realism": the novel is a photograph of a reality external to the novelist; observation bears on a substratum of psychological truth which has neither time nor place. For existentialist or aesthetic criticism, however, the "autonomy" of the novelistic world is an untouchable dogma; it is dishonorable to suggest the slightest connection between one's own novelist and that of one's neighbor.

It is clear nevertheless that features of Stendhalian vanity reappear, emphasized and intensified, in Proustian desire. The metamorphosis of the desired object is more radical now than before, jealousy and envy are even more frequent and intense. It is not an exaggeration to say that, in all of the characters of *Remembrance of Things Past,* love is strictly subordinated to jealousy, to the presence of the rival. The privileged role of the mediator in the genesis of desire is therefore more obvious than ever. Again and again the Proustian narrator defines clearly a triangular structure which remains more or less implicit in *The Red and the Black:*

> In love, our successful rival, that is our enemy, is our benefactor. To a person who aroused in us only an insignificant physical desire, he adds an immense prestige and value, which we immediately recognize in him. If we had no rivals, if we were to believe there were none. . . . For it is not necessary for them really to exist.

The triangular structure is no less obvious in social snobbism than it is in love-jealousy. The snob is also an imitator. He slavishly copies the person whose birth, fortune, or stylishness he envies. Proustian snobbism could be defined as a caricature of Stendhalian vanity; it could also be defined as an exaggeration of Flaubertian bovarysm. Jules de Gaultier terms this shortcoming "bovarysm triumphant" and quite rightly dedicates a passage in his book to it. The snob does not dare trust his own judgment, he desires only objects desired by others. That is why he is the slave of the fashionable.

For the first time, moreover, we come across a term in current usage, "snobbism," which does not conceal the truth of triangular desire. Just to call a desire snobbish is enough to underscore its imitative character. The mediator is no longer hidden; the object is relegated to the background for the very reason that snobbism, unlike jealousy for example, is not limited to a particular category of desires. One can be a snob in aesthetic pleasure, in intellectual life, in clothes, food, etc. To be a snob in love is to doom oneself to jealousy. Proustian love therefore is synonomous with snobbism and we have only to give a slightly broader meaning to the term than is normally done in order to discern in it the unity of Proustian desire. The mimetic nature of desire in *Remembrance of Things Past* is such that the characters can be called jealous or snobbish depending on whether their mediator is a lover or a member of high society. The triangular conception of desire gives us access to what is most central in Proust, to the conjunction of love-jealousy and snobbism. Proust continually asserts that these two "vices" are identical. "Society," he writes, "is only a reflection of what happens in love." This is an example of those "psychological laws" to which the novelist refers constantly but which he did not always manage to formulate with sufficient clarity. Most critics do not bother with these laws. They attribute them to out-of-date psychological theories which are supposed to have influenced Proust. They think that the essence of novelistic genius is foreign to any *law* because inevitably it is on the side of *beauty*, or *liberty*. We believe that the critics are mistaken. Proust's laws are identical with the laws of triangular desire. They define a new type of internal mediation which occurs when the distance between mediator and desiring subject is even less than in Stendhal.

One might object that Stendhal celebrates passion while Proust denounces it. This is true, but the opposition is purely verbal. What Proust denounces under the name of passion, Stendhal denounces under the name of vanity. And what Proust praises under the name of *The Past Recaptured* is not always so far from what Stendhal's heroes celebrate in the solitude of their prisons.

Differences of novelistic tonality frequently hide from us the close relationship of structure between Stendhalian vanity and Proustian desire. Stendhal is almost always external to the desire which he describes; he throws an ironic light on phenomena which in Proust are bathed in a light of anguish. And even this difference of perspective is not constant. Proustian tragedy does not exclude humor, especially in the case of secondary characters. Stendhalian comedy, on the other hand, sometimes borders on tragedy. Julien suffered more, the author tells us, during his brief and vain passion for Mathilde than during the darkest hours of his childhood.

Nevertheless it must be recognized that psychological conflicts are more aggravated in Proust's work than in Stendhal's. The differences of perspective reflect essential oppositions. We do not wish to minimize these in order to guarantee a mechanical unity of the writers we consider. On the contrary, we want to emphasize contrasts which will bring out one of our fundamental data: the distance between mediator and subject, whose variations shed light on the most diverse aspects of novelistic works.

The closer the mediator gets to the desiring subject, the more the possibilities of the two rivals merge and the more insuperable becomes the obstacle they set in each other's way. Thus we should not be surprised that human experience in Proust is even more "negative" and painful than the experience of Stendhal's *vaniteux*.

BUT, one might ask, what is the significance of these similarities between vanity in Stendhal's works and snobbism in Proust's? Would it not be better to turn our attention immediately from these minor aspects and concentrate on the shining summits of the great masterpieces? Would it not be better to skip over the parts of the work which are perhaps the least worthy of the great writer? Is it not all the more imperative to do so, since we have at our disposal another Proust, completely admirable, "original," and reassuring, the Proust of the *"mémoire affective"* and the *"intermittences du coeur,"* a Proust who seems as naturally solitary and profound as the other seems frivolous and gregarious?

There is a strong temptation to separate the wheat from the tares and to reserve for the second Proust the attention which the first does not always seem to deserve. But the full implication of such a temptation should be examined. One would be inserting into the work itself the distinction which Proust made between the two individuals he was *successively:* first the snob, then the great writer. The author would be divided into two simultaneous and contradictory writers: a snob whose concern would be snobbism, and a "great writer" to whom would be reserved the subjects deemed worthy of him. Nothing is further from the idea that Proust had of his own work. Proust maintained that there was unity in *Remembrance of Things Past.* But Proust may have been mistaken. The truth of what he says therefore must be verified.

Since the desires of the narrator, or rather the memories of those desires, comprise almost the whole subject matter of the novel, the problem of the novel's unity is identical with the problem of the unity of Proustian desire. There would be two simultaneous Prousts, if there were two perfectly distinct and even opposed types of desires. Side by side with the impure, novelistic desire whose history we are writing, side by side with this triangular desire which breeds jealousy and snobbism, must exist a linear desire, poetic and spontaneous. To separate once and for all the good Proust from the bad, Proust the solitary poet from Proust the gregarious novelist, one would have to prove that, in *Remembrance of Things Past,* there is at least some desire without a mediator.

This, we will be told, has already been demonstrated. A great deal has been said about a Proustian desire which has nothing to do with the desire we have been discussing. This desire offers no threat to the autonomy of the individual; it has little direct connection with an object, let alone with a mediator. The descriptions given of it are not original; they are borrowed from certain theoreticians of symbolism.

The proud symbolist subjectivity casts an uninterested glance on the world. It never discovers there anything as precious as itself. And so it prefers itself to the world and turns away from it, but never turns away so quickly that it does not see some object. This object slips into the consciousness like a grain of sand into the shell of an oyster; a pearl of imagination forms around this one small atom of reality. It is from the Self and from the Self alone that the imagination draws its strength. It is for the Self that it builds its splendid palaces. And in them the Self entertains itself, indescribably contented, until the day when the treacherous magician—reality—brushes against the fragile dream buildings and reduces them to dust.

Is this description truly Proustian? Several passages seem to corroborate it strikingly. Proust asserts that everything is in the subject, and nothing in the object. He speaks of the "golden door of imagination" and of the "low door of experience" as if there could be absolute subjective data, independent of all dialectic between the Self and the Other. The tradition of "symbolist" desire seems therefore to be supported by solid evidence.

Fortunately we still have the novel itself. No one dreams of searching there for answers. The critics faithfully hand on the subjectivist dogma to each other without putting it to the test. It is true that they have the novelist's own guarantee. This guarantee, to which they paid little heed in the case of "psychological laws," now seems to them worthy of trust. Proust's opinions are respected so long as they can be linked with one of the modern individualisms: romanticism, symbolism, Nietzscheanism, Valéryism, etc. We have chosen a contrary criterion. We believe that "novelistic" genius is won by a great struggle against these attitudes we have lumped together under the name "romantic" because they all appear to us intended to maintain the illusion of spontaneous desire and of a subjectivity almost divine in its autonomy. Only slowly and with difficulty does the novelist go beyond the romantic he was at first and who refuses to die. He finally achieves this in the "novelistic" work and in that work alone. And so it is quite possible that the novelist's abstract vocabulary and even his "ideas" do not always reflect him accurately.

We have already seen that Stendhal continually uses certain key-words which reveal many of the driving forces in his novels: vanity, copy, imitation. Some of these keys, however, are not in the right lock; some substitutions are necessary. In the case of Proust, who borrows his theoretic vocabulary from the literary milieux of his time—perhaps because he never frequented them—mistakes are also possible.

We must once more compare the writer's theory with his practice. We have already established that vanity—triangular vanity—permits us to delve deep into the substance of *The Red and the Black*. We shall see that in Proust, "symbolist" desire—linear desire—only skims over the same substance. For the evidence to be convincing it should deal with a desire which is as different as possible from those worldly or amorous desires which we have already found to be triangular. Which of the Proustian desires seem to offer the best guarantee of spontaneity? Undoubtedly the answer is the desire of the child and that of the artist. Let us therefore choose a desire which is at once artistic and childlike, so that no one will accuse us of tipping the scales in our favor.

The narrator experiences an intense desire to see Berma, the famous actress, perform. The spiritual benefits he hopes to gain from the performance are of a truly sacramental type. The imagination has done its work. The object is transfigured. But where is this object? What is the grain of sand which has violated the solitude of the oyster-consciousness? It is not the great Berma, for the narrator has never seen her. Nor is it the memory of previous performances; the child has had no direct contact with the dramatic art; he even conjures up a fantastic idea of the physical nature of a theater. We will find no object here because there is none.

Can it be that the symbolists are still too timid? Should we completely deny the role of object and proclaim the perfect autonomy of desire? Such a conclusion would please solipsistic critics. Unfortunately, the narrator has not *invented* the great Berma. The actress is quite real; she exists outside of the Self who desires her. It is therefore impossible to dispense with a point of contact with the outside world. But it is not an object which assures this contact; it is another consciousness. A third person indicates to the narrator the object he will begin desiring passionately. Marcel knows that Bergotte admires the great actress. In his eyes Bergotte enjoys an immense prestige. The slightest word of the master becomes a law for him. The Swanns are the priests of a religion of which Bergotte is the god. They receive Bergotte in their house and through their mediation the Word is revealed to the narrator.

We see repeated in the Proustian novel the strange process described by the preceding novelists. We witness the spiritual wedding without which the virgin imagination could not give birth to fantasies. As in Cervantes, the oral suggestion is reinforced by a written suggestion. Gilberte Swann has Marcel read a booklet of Bergotte's on the *Phèdre* of Racine, one of Berma's great rôles:". . . plastic nobility, Christian hair-shirt, Jansenist pallor, Princesse de Trézene and de Clèves . . ."; these mysterious words, poetic and incomprehensible, have a powerful effect on the mind of Marcel.

The printed word has a magical power of suggestion,

and the author never tires of giving us examples of it. When his mother sends him to the Champs-Elysées, the narrator finds his walks at first very boring. No mediator has *designated* the Champs-Elysées: "If only Bergotte had described the place in one of his books, I should, no doubt, have longed to see and to know it, like so many things else of which a simulacrum first found its way into my imagination." At the end of the novel a reading of the Goncourts' *Journal* transfigures in retrospect the Verdurin salon which had never had any prestige in the mind of the narrator because no artist had as yet described it:

> But I was incapable of seeing a thing unless a desire to do so had been aroused in me by reading. . . . Even had that page of the Goncourts not enlightened me, I knew how often I had been unable to give my attention to things or to people, whom afterwards, once their image had been presented to me in solitude by an artist, I would have gone leagues and risked death to rediscover.

We must also include under the rubric of literary suggestion those theatrical posters the narrator reads so eagerly during his walks along the Champs-Elysées. The highest forms of suggestion are not separated from the lowest. The distance between Don Quixote and the petty bourgeois victim of advertising is not so great as romanticism would have us believe.

The attitude of the narrator toward his mediator, Bergotte, recalls that of Don Quixote toward Amadis:

> upon almost everything in the world his opinion was unknown to me. I had no doubt that it would differ entirely from my own, since his came down from an unknown sphere towards which I was striving to raise myself; convinced that my thoughts would have seemed pure foolishness to that perfected spirit, I

had so completely obliterated them all that, if I happened to find in one of his books something which
had already occurred to my own mind, my heart
would swell with gratitude and pride as though some
deity had, in his infinite bounty, restored it to me,
had pronounced it to be beautiful and right. . . .
And so too, in later years, when I began to compose a
book of my own, and the quality of some of my sentences seemed so inadequate that I could not make
up my mind to go on with the undertaking, I would
find the equivalent of my sentences in Bergotte's. But
it was only then, when I read them in his pages, that
I could enjoy them.

Don Quixote becomes a knight-errant to imitate Amadis; similarly, Marcel wants to be a writer in order to imitate Bergotte. The imitation of the contemporary hero is
more humble, more submissive and, as it were, paralyzed
by a religious terror. The power of the Other over the Self
is greater than ever and we shall see that it is not limited
to a *single* mediator as in the case of previous heroes.

The narrator finally goes to a performance of Berma's.
On his return to the family's apartment he makes the acquaintance of M. de Norpois, who has been invited to din-
ner that evening. Urged to give his impressions of the
theater, Marcel naïvely admits his disappointment. His father is very embarrassed and M. de Norpois feels obliged
to pay homage to the great actress with a few pompous
clichés. The results of this banal exchange are typically,
essentially Proustian. The words of the elderly diplomat
fill the gap created in the mind and sensibility of Marcel
by the disappointing performance. Faith in Berma is renewed. The next day a dull review given in a fashionable
paper completes the work of M. de Norpois. As in the previous novelists, oral and literary suggestion lend each
other mutual support. Marcel henceforth has no hesita-

tions about the beauty of the performance or about the intensity of his own enjoyment. Not only does the Other and only the Other set desire in motion, but his testimony easily overcomes actual experience when the latter contradicts it.

One can choose other examples but the result will always be the same. Each and every time Proustian desire is the triumph of suggestion over impression. At its birth, in other words at the very source of the subjectivity, one always finds a victorious Other. It is true that the source of the "transfiguration" is within us, but the spring gushes forth only when the mediator strikes the rock with his magic wand. Never does the narrator simply wish to play, to read a book, to contemplate a work of art; it is always the pleasure he reads on the faces of the players, a conversation, or a first reading which releases the work of the imagination and provokes desire:

> what was from the first the most permanent and the most intimate part of me, the lever whose incessant movements controlled all the rest, was my belief in the philosophic richness and beauty of the book I was reading, and my desire to appropriate these to myself, whatever the book might be. For even if I had purchased it at Combray . . . I should have noticed and bought it there simply because I had recognized it as a book which had been well spoken of, in my hearing, by the school-master or the school-friend who, at that particular time, seemed to me to be entrusted with the secret of Truth and Beauty, things half-felt by me, half-incomprehensible, the full understanding of which was the vague but permanent object of my thoughts.

The interior garden so often praised by the critics is therefore never a solitary garden. In the light of all these childhood desires which are already "triangular," the

meaning of jealousy and snobbism becomes more evident
than ever. Proustian desire is *always* a borrowed desire.
There is nothing in *Remembrance of Things Past* which
corresponds to the symbolist and solipsistic theory which
we outlined above. One may object that the theory is that
of Proust himself. That is possible, but Proust too can be
mistaken. The theory is false and we reject it.

The exceptions to the rule of desire are never more than
apparent. There is no mediator in the case of the "madeleine" or the steeples of Martinville; however, the steeples
do not evoke a desire of possession but a desire of expression. The aesthetic emotion is not desire but the ending of
all desire, a return to calm and joy. Like Stendhal's "passion," these privileged moments are already outside of the
novelistic world. They prepare the way for *The Past Recaptured;* they are in a sense its *annunciation.*

Desire is *one:* there is no break in continuity between
the child and the snob, between "Combray" and *Cities of
the Plain.* We often wonder a little uneasily about the age
of the narrator, for childhood does not exist in Proust. Autonomous childhood, indifferent to the world of adults, is
a myth for grown-ups. The romantic art of recovering
childhood is no more serious than Hugo's *art d'être grand-
père.* Those who flaunt a childish "spontaneity" wish
above all to distinguish themselves from Others, the
adults, their fellow men, and nothing is less childish than
that. True childhood does not desire more spontaneously
than the snob; the snob desires no less intensely than the
child. Those who see an abyss between the snob and the
child should take another look at the episode of the actress Berma. Is it the snob or the child in whom the writings of a Bergotte or the words of a Norpois stir up an emotion that is forever foreign to the work of art, which serves
merely as a pretext for that emotion? The genius of Proust
wipes out frontiers which to us seem carved into human

nature. We may choose to re-establish them; we can draw an arbitrary line in the novelistic universe; we can bless Combray and curse the Faubourg Saint-Germain. We can read Proust as we read the world around us, always finding the child in ourselves and the snob in others. But we shall never see the meeting of Swann's way and the Guermantes' way. We shall always remain ignorant of the essential truth of *Remembrance of Things Past.*

Desire is triangular in the child just as it is in the snob. This does not mean that it is impossible to make any distinction between the happiness of the one and the sufferings of the other. But this true distinction no longer has its source in the excommunication of the snob. It does not concern the *essence* of desire but rather the *distance* between mediator and desiring subject. The mediators of Proustian childhood are the parents and the great writer Bergotte—people whom Marcel admires and imitates openly without any fear of rivalry on their part. The child's mediation therefore constitutes a new kind of *external mediation.*

The child enjoys, in his universe, both happiness and peace. But this universe is already threatened. When the mother refuses her son a kiss she is already playing the double role characteristic of internal mediation: she is both the instigator of desire and a relentless guardian forbidding its fulfillment. The god of the family brutally changes face. The nightly agonies of Combray foreshadow the agonies of the snob and of the lover.

Proust is not the only one who sees a close relationship, paradoxical to us, between snob and child. Together with that "bovarysm triumphant" which is snobbism, Jules de Gaultier discovers "puerile bovarysm," and he describes the two in very similar terms. Snobbism is "all the means used by a person to prevent the appearance of his true self in the field of his consciousness, in order to project continuously into it a finer character in which he recognizes himself." As for the child, "in order to see himself differently, he attributes to himself the qualities and aptitudes of the model who has fascinated him." Puerile bovarysm reproduces exactly the mechanism of Proustian desire as revealed in the episode of the actress Berma:

> childhood is the natural state in which the ability to *imagine oneself otherwise* is most evident . . . the child exhibits an extraordinary sensitivity to all impulses coming from outside, and at the same time a surprising eagerness for all the learning acquired by human knowledge and enclosed in ideas which enable it to be communicated. . . . By referring to our memories each can see how slight a power reality has over the mind at this age, and how great, on the other hand, was the mind's ability to distort reality. . . . [The child's] eagerness has . . . on the contrary a boundless faith in what is taught. The printed word bears even more certainty than what his eye can see. For a long time an idea, because of its universal character, holds more authority for him than his individual experiences.

One would think this a commentary on the passages just quoted from Proust. But Gaultier was writing before Proust and it was Flaubert he had in mind. Strong in his fundamental intuition and confident of adhering to the heart of Flaubert's inspiration, Gaultier radiates freely from that center, applying the idea to areas which Flaubert had not noticed and drawing conclusions which he might have repudiated. It is a fact that for Flaubert suggestion plays a more limited role than Gaultier claims for it—suggestion never goes so far as to triumph over an experience which it would formally contradict; it limits itself to enlarging an incomplete experience in order to distort its meaning or, at most, filling the void left by the lack of experience. The most suggestive passages of the essay are sometimes the most debatable from a strictly Flaubertian point of view. But Gaultier, for all that, does not fall into the purely imaginary. He has only to give himself up to his "bovaryque" inspiration, he has only to push to their ultimate conclusions the principles he has extracted from the works of Flaubert in order to sketch the great "laws" of Proustian "psychology." Would this be the case if the works of the two novelists were not rooted in the same intersubjective and metaphysical substratum?

TWENTY-FOUR hours after her performance Marcel is convinced that Berma has given him all the pleasure he had expected from her. The agonizing conflict between personal experience and the testimony of others is resolved in favor of the others. But choosing the Other in such cases is only a particular way of choosing oneself. It is to choose again the old self whose competence and taste will not be questioned, thanks to M. de Norpois and the journalist in *Le Figaro*. It is to believe in oneself thanks to the Other. The operation would not be possible without an almost instantaneous forgetting of the genuine impression. This self-interested forgetfulness lasts until *The Past Recaptured*, a veritable river of *living memory*, a veritable resurrection of truth, which makes it possible to write the episode about Berma.

Before this rediscovery of "time," the Berma episode would have been confined, had Proust written it then, to the opinion of M. de Norpois and that of *Le Figaro*. Proust would have presented this as his own authentic opinion and the reader of 1905 would have been in ecstasies over the precociousness of the young artist and the subtlety of his judgment. *Jean Santeuil* is full of scenes of this kind. The hero of this first novel is always seen in a romantic and favorable light. *Jean Santeuil* is a book which lacks genius. It precedes the experience of *The Past Recaptured*—novelistic genius springs from the latter. Proust always maintained that the aesthetic revolution of *The Past Recaptured* was in the first place a spiritual revolution; now we see how right Proust was. Recapturing the past is recapturing the original impression beneath the opinion of others which hides it; it is to recognize that this opinion is not one's own. It is to understand that the process of mediation creates a very vivid impression of autonomy and spontaneity precisely when we are no longer autonomous and spontaneous. Recapturing the past is to welcome a truth which most men spend their lives trying to escape, to recognize that one has always copied Others in order to seem original in their eyes and in one's own. Recapturing the past is to destroy a little of one's pride.

Novelistic genius begins with the collapse of the "autonomous" self. Bergotte, Norpois, the article in *Le Figaro* —the second-rate writer would represent all these as deriving from himself—but the genius shows them to us as the opinion of the Other, thereby achieving a real *intimacy* of consciousness.

All this of course is very banal, very common—this holds true of everyone—except *us*. Romantic pride willingly denounces the presence of the mediator in Others in order to found its own autonomy on the ruins of rival pretensions. There is novelistic genius when what is true about Others becomes true about the hero, in fact true about the novelist himself. After cursing Others the Oedipus-novelist realizes he himself is guilty. Pride can never reach its own mediator; but the experience of *The Past Recaptured* is the death of pride, the birth of humility and thus of truth. When Dostoyevsky praises the *terri-*

ble strength of humility he is speaking of novelistic creation.

The "symbolist" theory of desire is therefore as anti-novelistic as Stendhalian crystallization in its original form. These theories describe a desire without a mediator. They express the point of view of the desiring subject who is determined to forget the role of the Other in his vision of the world.

If Proust resorts to symbolist vocabulary it is because the omission of the mediator never occurs to him when he is no longer dealing with a concrete novelistic description. He is not considering what the theory suppresses but what it expresses: the vanity of desire, the insignificance of the object, the subjective transfiguration, and that disappointment which is called possession. Everything in this description is true; it is false only when one claims it is complete. Proust writes thousands of pages to complete it. The critics write none. They isolate a few rather banal sentences in the whole of *The Past Recaptured* and say: "This is Proustian desire." These sentences seem precious to them because, unwittingly, they encourage the very illusion which the novel crushes, that illusion of autonomy to which modern man clings more tenaciously as it becomes increasingly false. The critics tear up the seamless tunic which the novelist has struggled to weave. They come back down to the level of common experience. They mutilate the work of art just as Proust at first mutilated his own experience by *forgetting* Bergotte and Norpois in the Berma episode. The "symbolist" critics thus fail to grasp the significance of *The Past Recaptured*. They reduce the novelistic work to the level of the romantic work.

Romantics and symbolists want a transfiguring desire which is completely spontaneous; they do not want to hear any talk about the Other. They turn away from the dark side of desire, claiming it is unrelated to their lovely poetic dream and denying that it is its price. At the end of his dream the novelist shows us the sinister retinue of internal mediation: "envy, jealousy, and impotent hatred." Stendhal's formula remains strikingly true when it is applied to Proust's universe. Once childhood is left behind, every transfiguration is accompanied by intense suffering. *Rêverie* and rivalry overlap so perfectly that novelistic truth separates like curdled milk when one isolates the elements of Proustian desire. Only two wretched lies are left, the "interior" Proust and the "psychologist" Proust. We are left an unanswerable question: how did these two contradictory abstractions ever create *Remembrance of Things Past?*

As WE have seen, the approach of the mediator tends to bring together the two spheres of *possibilities,* of which the rivals occupy the respective centers. The resentment they feel for each other is therefore always increasing. In Proust the birth of passion coincides with the birth of hate. This "ambivalence" of desire is already very clear in the case of Gilberte. When the narrator sees the girl for the first time, he expresses his desire by making ugly faces at her. From that moment on, outside the immediate family circle there is room for only one emotion, that provoked by the mediator when he relentlessly refuses access to the "higher kingdom" to which he holds the key.

Proust still speaks of desire, hate, love, and jealousy but he repeatedly asserts their equivalence. As early as *Jean Santeuil* he gives an excellent triangular definition of hate, which is also a definition of desire:

> Of such a nature is hatred which compounds from the lives of our enemies a fiction which is wholly false. Instead of thinking of them as ordinary human

beings knowing ordinary human happiness and occasionally exposed to the sorrows which afflict all mankind and ought to arouse in us a feeling of kindly sympathy, we attribute to them an attitude of arrogant self-satisfaction which pours oil upon the flames of our anger. For hatred transfigures individuals no less than does desire and like desire sets us thirsting for human blood. On the other hand since it can find satisfaction only in the destruction of the supposed self-satisfaction which so irritates us, we imagine that self-satisfaction, see it, believe it to be in a perpetual process of disintegration. No more than love does hatred follow the dictates of reason, but goes through life with eyes fixed on an unconquerable hope.

In *De l'Amour* Stendhal had already noticed that there is a crystallization of hatred. One step further and the two crystallizations become one. Proust constantly reveals hatred in desire, desire in hatred. But he remains faithful to the traditional language; he never eliminates the "like"s and the "as much as"s which are strewn through the preceding quotation. He will never reach the highest level of internal mediation. This last stage was reserved for another novelist, the Russian, Dostoyevsky, who precedes Proust chronologically but succeeds him in the history of triangular desire.

Except for a few characters who entirely escape imitated desire, in Dostoyevsky there is no longer any love without jealousy, any friendship without envy, any attraction without repulsion. The characters insult each other, spit in each other's faces, and minutes later they fall at the enemy's feet, they abjectly beg mercy. This fascination coupled with hatred is no different in principle from Proustian snobbism and Stendhalian vanity. The inevitable consequences of desire copied from another desire are "envy, jealousy, and impotent hatred." As one moves from Stendhal to Proust and from Proust to Dostoyevsky, and the closer the mediator comes, the more bitter are the fruits of triangular desire.

In Dostoyevsky hatred is so intense it finally "explodes," revealing its double nature, or rather the double role of model and obstacle played by the mediator. This adoring hatred, this admiration that insults and even kills its object, are the paroxysms of the conflict caused by internal mediation. In his words and gestures, Dostoyevsky's hero constantly reveals a truth which remains a secret in the consciousness of previous heroes. The "contradictory" feelings are so violent that the hero can no longer control them.

Western readers sometimes feel a little lost in Dostoyevsky's universe. Internal mediation exerts its dissolving power at the very heart of the family itself. It affects a dimension of existence which remains more or less inviolable in the French novelists. The three great novelists of internal mediation each have their own privileged territory. In Stendhal public and political life are threatened by borrowed desire. In Proust the evil spreads to private life but usually excludes the family circle. In Dostoyevsky this intimate circle itself is contaminated. Thus we find within internal mediation one can distinguish *exogamic* mediation in Stendhal and Proust from *endogamic* mediation in Dostoyevsky.

This is not, however, a strict division. Stendhal encroaches on Proustian territory when he describes the extreme forms of cerebral love and even on Dostoyevskian territory when he shows us the hatred of son for father. Similarly Marcel's relations with his parents are sometimes "pre-Dostoyevskian." The novelists often venture out of their own domain, but the further they wander, the more hurried, schematic, and uncertain they are.

This rough division of the existential domain among our

novelists represents an invasion of the vital centers of the individual by triangular desire, a desecration which gradually infects the most intimate parts of being. This desire is a corrosive disease which first attacks the periphery and then spreads toward the center; it is an *alienation* which grows more complete as the distance between model and disciple diminishes. This distance is smallest in familial mediation of father to son, brother to brother, husband to wife, or mother to son, as in Dostoyevsky and many contemporary novelists.

In terms of mediation, the Dostoyevskian universe is "this side of"—one might also say "beyond"—that of Proust, just as Proust is "this side of" or "beyond" Stendhal. The Dostoyevskian universe differs from those of his predecessors in the same way that they differ from each other. This difference does not imply an absence of relationships and points of contact. If Dostoyevsky were as "autonomous" as is sometimes claimed, we would never be able to understand his works. They would be as meaningless to us as the words of a foreign language: we could spell them out but we would be unable to grasp their significance.

Dostoyevsky's "admirable monsters" should not be considered as so many meteorites with unpredictable trajectories. In the time of the Marquis de Vogüé people often said that Dostoyevsky's characters were too "Russian" to be completely accessible to the French Cartesian mind. His mysterious work would by definition elude our rational, Western criteria. Today it is no longer Dostoyevsky the Russian who seems most important to us, but rather the apostle of "liberty," the brilliant innovator, the iconoclast who smashed the molds in which novels had previously been cast. The Dostoyevskian man and his free existence are constantly opposed to the simplistic analyses of our own novelists who are seen as old fashioned, bourgeois, and psychologizing. This fanatic cult, as much as the mistrust of times past, prevents us from seeing in Dostoyevsky the final and supreme stage of the development of the modern novel.

The relative esoterism of Dostoyevsky makes him neither superior nor inferior to our own novelists. It is not the writer but the reader who creates the obscurity here. Our hesitations would not surprise Dostoyevsky, convinced as he was that Russian forms of experience were in advance of those in the West. Russia has passed, without any transitional period, from traditional and feudal structures to the most *modern* society. She has not known any bourgeois interregnum. Stendhal and Proust are the novelists of this interregnum. They occupy the upper regions of internal mediation, while Dostoyevsky occupies its lowest.

A Raw Youth gives a very good illustration of the characteristics peculiar to Dostoyevskian desire. The relations between Dolgorouki and Versilov can be interpreted only in terms of mediation. Son and father love the same woman. Dolgorouki's passion for Akhmakova, the general's wife, is copied from that of his father. This mediation of father for son is not the *external* mediation of Proustian childhood, which we defined in talking of Combray, but an *internal* mediation, which turns the mediator into a loathed rival. The unfortunate bastard is both the equal of a father who does not fulfill his obligations and the fascinated victim of this being who has rejected him for some unknown reason. To understand Dolgorouki one should not therefore compare him with the children and parents of previous novels, but rather with the Proustian snob obsessed by the person who *refuses to accept him*. Nevertheless this comparison is not entirely exact, for the distance between father and son is less than the distance between the two snobs. Dolgorouki's ordeal therefore is even more painful than that of the Proustian snob or lover.

THE CLOSER the mediator comes, the greater his role becomes and the smaller that of the object. Dostoyevsky by a stroke of genius places the mediator in the foreground and relegates the object to the background. At last novelistic composition reflects the real hierarchy of desire. Had Stendhal or Proust written *A Raw Youth*, everything would be centered on the principal hero, or on Akhmakova, the general's wife. Dostoyevsky puts the mediator, Versilov, at the center of his novel. But, from our point of view, *A Raw Youth* is not the most daring of Dostoyevsky's works. It is a compromise between several solutions. The transfer of the novelistic center of gravity is best and most spectacularly illustrated by *The Eternal Husband*. Veltchaninov, a rich bachelor, is a middle-aged Don Juan who is beginning to give in to weariness and boredom. For several days he has been obsessed by the fleeting apparitions of a man, at once mysterious and familiar, disturbing and odd. The character's identity is soon revealed. It seems he is a certain Pavel Pavlovitch Troussotzki, whose wife, a former mistress of Veltchaninov's, has just died. Pavel Pavlovitch has left his province in order to find in St. Petersburg the lovers of his dead wife. One of the lovers also dies, and Pavel Pavlovitch, in deep mourning, follows the funeral procession. There remains Veltchaninov on whom he heaps the most grotesque attentions and whom he wears out by his constant presence. The deceived husband makes very strange statements concerning the past. He pays his rival a visit in the middle of the night, drinks to his health, kisses him on the lips, and very cleverly tortures him, using an unfortunate little girl whose father remains unknown.

The woman is dead and the lover remains. There is no longer an object but the mediator, Veltchaninov, still exerts an irresistible attraction. This mediator makes an ideal narrator since he is the center of the action and yet scarcely participates in it. He describes events all the more carefully since he does not always succeed in interpreting them and is afraid of neglecting some important detail.

Pavel Pavlovitch considers a second marriage. Fascinated, he goes again to his first wife's lover; he asks him to help him choose a present for his latest choice; he begs him to go with him to her house. Veltchaninov demurs but Pavel Pavlovitch insists, begs, and ends by getting his way.

The two "friends" are given a warm reception at the young lady's house. Veltchaninov's conversation is entertaining and he plays the piano. His social ability arouses admiration: the whole family crowds around him, including the young lady whom Pavel Pavlovitch already looks on as his fiancée. The scorned suitor tries to be seductive without success. No one takes him seriously. He reflects on this new disaster, trembling with anguish and desire. Some years later Veltchaninov meets Pavel Pavlovitch again in a railroad station. The eternal husband is not alone; a charming lady, his wife, accompanies him, along with a dashing young soldier . . .

The Eternal Husband reveals the essence of internal mediation in the simplest and purest form possible. No digression distracts or misleads the reader. The text seems enigmatic only because it is too clear. It throws on the novelistic triangle a light so brilliant it dazzles us.

Confronted with Pavel Pavlovitch we can have no more doubts about the priority of the Other in desire, a principle first laid down by Stendhal. The hero is always trying to convince us that his relationship to the object of desire is independent of the rival. Here we clearly see that the hero is deceiving us. The mediator is immobile and the hero turns around him like a planet around the sun. The behavior of Pavel Pavlovitch seems strange to us but it is completely consistent with the logic of triangular desire. Pavel Pavlovitch can desire only through the mediation of Veltchaninov, *in* Veltchaninov as the mystics would say. He drags Veltchaninov along to the house of the lady he has chosen, so that he might desire her and thus guarantee her erotic value.

Some critics would like to see in Pavel Pavlovitch a "latent homosexual." But the homosexuality, whether it is latent or not does not explain the structure of desire. It puts a distance between Pavel Pavlovitch and the so-called normal man. Nothing is gained by reducing triangular desire to a homosexuality which is necessarily opaque to the heterosexual. If one turned the explanation around, the results would be much more interesting. An attempt should be made to *understand* at least some forms of homosexuality from the standpoint of triangular desire. Proustian homosexuality, for example, can be defined as a gradual transferring to the mediator of an erotic value which in "normal" Don Juanism remains attached to the object itself. This gradual transfer is not, a priori, impossible; it is even likely, in the acute stages of internal mediation, characterized by a noticeably increased preponderance of the mediator and a gradual obliteration of the object. Certain passages in *The Eternal Husband* clearly show the beginning of an erotic deviation toward the fascinating rival.

The novels considered here illuminate each other and the critic should borrow from the novels themselves his methods, concepts, and even the direction of his efforts. We must turn to the Proust of *The Captive,* who is close enough to Dostoyevsky to let us understand what it is that Pavel Pavlovitch desires:

> It would fall to our lot, were we better able to analyse our loves, to see that often women rise in our estimation only because of the dead weight of men

with whom we have to compete for them, although
we can hardly bear the thought of that competition;
the counterpoise removed, the charm of the woman
declines. We have a painful and salutary example of
this . . . in the man who, conscious of a decline in
his affection for the woman whom he loves, spontaneously applies the rules that he has deduced, and, to
make sure of his not ceasing to love the woman,
places her in a dangerous environment from which he
is obliged to protect her daily.

Beneath the casual tone is the fundamental Proustian anguish which is also the anguish of Pavel Pavlovitch. Dostoyevsky's hero, too, applies "spontaneously," if not se-
renely, rules which he has not really "analyzed" but
which only control his miserable existence all the more.

Triangular desire is *one*. We can start with Don Quixote and end with Pavel Pavlovitch, or we can begin with
Tristan and Isolde as Denis de Rougemont does in *Love in
the Western World* and quickly reach that "psychology of
jealousy" which pervades our analyses. When he defines
this psychology as a "profanation of the myth" embodied
in the poem of Tristan, De Rougemont explicitly acknowledges the bond uniting the most "noble" forms of passion
with morbid jealousy, such as Proust or Dostoyevsky describe for us: "Jealousy, desired, provoked, and cunningly
encouraged." De Rougemont correctly observes: "One
reaches the point of wanting the beloved to be unfaithful
so that one can court her again."

Such is—or very close to it—the desire of Pavel Pavlovitch. The eternal husband cannot do without jealousy.
Trusting our analyses and the testimony of De Rougemont, we shall now see behind all forms of triangular desire the same diabolic trap into which the hero slowly
sinks. Triangular desire is *one* and we think we are able to

furnish a striking proof of its unity precisely where skepticism seems most justified. The two "extremes" of desire, one illustrated by Cervantes, the other by Dostoyevsky, seem the hardest to incorporate in the same structure. We can accept that Pavel Pavlovitch is a brother to Proust's snob and even to Stendhal's *vaniteux*, but who would recognize in him a distant cousin of the famous Don Quixote? The impassioned eulogists of that hero cannot help but consider our comparison sacrilegious. For them Don Quixote lives only on the summits. How could the creator of this sublime being have an inkling of the swamps in which the eternal husband wallows?

The answer is to be found in one of the short stories with which Cervantes padded *Don Quixote*. Although they were all cast in a pastoral or chivalric mold these texts do not all fall back into the "romantic," nonnovelistic pattern. One of them, "The Curious Impertinent," portrays a triangular desire exactly like that of Pavel Pavlovitch.

Anselmo has just married the pretty young Camilla. The marriage was arranged with the help of Lothario, a very dear friend of the happy husband. Some time after the wedding Anselmo makes a curious request to Lothario. He begs him to pay court to Camilla, claiming that he wishes "to test" her faithfulness. Lothario refuses indignantly but Anselmo does not give up. He entreats his friend in a thousand different ways and in all his suggestions reveals the obsessive nature of his request. For a long time Lothario manages to put him off and finally pretends to accept in order to put him at ease. Anselmo arranges for the two young people to be alone together. He leaves on a journey, returns without warning, bitterly reproaches Lothario for not taking his role seriously. In short his behavior is so mad that he finally drives

Lothario and Camilla into each other's arms. Learning that he has been betrayed, Anselmo kills himself in despair.

When one rereads the story in the light of *The Eternal Husband* and *The Captive* it is no longer possible to consider it artificial and lacking in interest. Dostoyevsky and Proust enable us to dig down to its true meaning. "The Curious Impertinent" is Cervantes' *Eternal Husband;* the only difference between the two stories is in technique and the details of the intrigue.

Pavel Pavlovitch entices Veltchaninov to his fiancée's house; Anselmo asks Lothario to pay court to his wife. In both cases only the prestige of the mediator can certify the excellence of a sexual choice. Cervantes, at the beginning of his story, describes at length the friendship between the two protagonists, Anselmo's high opinion of Lothario, and the role of go-between which Lothario played with the two families on the occasion of the marriage.

It is clear that their ardent friendship is accompanied by a sharp feeling of rivalry. But this rivalry remains in the shadows. In *The Eternal Husband* the other side of the "triangular" feeling remains hidden. The hatred of the betrayed husband is obvious; we gradually guess at the admiration which this hatred hides. Pavel Pavlovitch asks Veltchaninov to choose the jewel he will give to his fiancée because to him Veltchaninov enjoys immense sexual prestige.

In both stories the hero seems to offer the beloved wife freely to the mediator, as a believer would offer a sacrifice to his god. But the believer offers the object in order that the god might enjoy it, whereas the hero of internal mediation offers his sacrifice to the god in order that he might not enjoy it. He pushes the loved woman into the mediator's arms in order to arouse his desire and then triumph over the rival desire. He does not desire *in* his mediator but rather *against* him. The hero only desires the object which will frustrate his mediator. Ultimately all that interests him is a decisive victory over his insolent mediator. Anselmo and Pavel Pavlovitch are driven by sexual pride, and it is this pride which plunges them into the most humiliating defeats.

"The Curious Impertinent" and *The Eternal Husband* suggest a nonromantic interpretation of Don Juan. Anselmo and Pavel Pavlovitch are the very opposite of the prattling, conceited, "Promethean" fops with which our century abounds. Pride creates Don Juan and it is pride which sooner or later makes us a slave to someone else. The real Don Juan is not autonomous; on the contrary, he is incapable of doing without Others. This truth is not apparent today. But it can be seen in some of Shakespeare's seducers and in Molière's *Don Juan:*

> By chance I saw this pair of lovers three or four days before their journey. I have never seen two people more happy with one another or who shone so with their love. The obvious tenderness of their passion for one another moved me; I was struck to the heart and my love began through jealousy. Yes, I could not bear to see them so happy together; resentment aroused my desires, and I foresaw great pleasure in being able to upset their understanding and break this engagement which offended my delicate feelings.

No LITERARY influence can explain the points of contact between "The Curious Impertinent" and *The Eternal Husband*. The differences are all differences of form, while the resemblances are resemblances of essence. No doubt Dostoyevsky never realized these similarities. Like so many nineteenth-century readers he saw the Spanish masterpiece only through romantic exegeses and probably had a most inaccurate picture of Cervantes. All his remarks on *Don Quixote* betray a romantic influence.

The existence of "The Curious Impertinent" next to *Don Quixote* has always intrigued critics. The question arises of whether the short story is compatible with the novel; the unity of the masterpiece seems somewhat compromised. It is this unity which is revealed by our journey through novelistic literature. Having begun with Cervantes, we return to Cervantes and ascertain that this novelist's genius has grasped the extreme forms of imitated desire. No small distance separates the Cervantes of Don Quixote and the Cervantes of Anselmo since it encompasses all the novels we have considered in this chapter. Yet the distance is not insuperable since all the novelists are linked to each other; Flaubert, Stendhal, Proust, and Dostoyevsky form an unbroken chain from one Cervantes to the other.

The simultaneous presence of external and internal mediation in the same work seems to us to confirm the unity of novelistic literature. And in turn, the unity of this literature confirms that of *Don Quixote*. One is proved by the other, just as one proves that the earth is round by going around it. The creative force of Cervantes is so great that it is exerted effortlessly throughout the whole novelistic "space." All the ideas of the Western novel are present in germ in *Don Quixote*. And the idea of these ideas, the idea whose central role is constantly being confirmed, the basic idea from which one can rediscover everything is triangular desire. And triangular desire is the basis of the theory of the *novelistic* novel for which this first chapter serves as an introduction.

CHAPTER II

MEN BECOME GODS IN
THE EYES OF EACH OTHER

EVERY HERO of a novel expects his being to be radically changed by the act of possession. In *Remembrance of Things Past* Marcel's parents are reluctant to let him go to the theater because of his poor health. The child cannot understand their hesitations; anxiety over his health seems ridiculous in comparison with the enormous benefits to be gained from the performance.

The object is only a means of reaching the mediator. The desire is aimed at the mediator's *being*. Proust compares this terrible desire to be the Other with thirst: "Thirst—like that which burns a parched land—for a life which would be a more perfect drink for my soul to absorb in long gulps, all the more greedily because it has never tasted a single drop."

The desire to absorb the being of the mediator in Proust often takes the form of a desire to be initiated into a new life: an "athletic" life, or a country life, or a life "without routine." The sudden prestige which the narrator gives to an unfamiliar way of life always coincides with his meeting a being who awakens this desire.

The meaning of mediation is particularly clear at the two "extremes" of desire. Don Quixote shouts the truth of his passion to us and Pavel Pavlovitch can no longer hide it from us. The intermediate stages are harder to detect but the desiring subject wants to become his mediator; he wants to steal from the mediator his very being of "perfect knight" or "irresistible seducer."

In love and in hate this purpose does not change. The hero of *Notes from the Underground* is jostled in a billiard-saloon by an unknown officer and is immediately tormented by a terrible thirst for vengeance. We could consider this hate "legitimate" and "rational" were it not for the revelation of its metaphysical significance in a letter written by the underground man to overwhelm and beguile his offender:

> I composed a splendid, charming letter to him, imploring him to apologize to me, and hinting rather plainly at a duel in case of refusal. The letter was so composed that if the officer had had the least understanding of the good and the beautiful he would certainly have flung himself on my neck and have offered me his friendship. And how fine that would have been! How we should have got on together! "He could have shielded me with his higher rank, while I could have improved his mind with my culture, and, well . . . my ideas, and all sorts of things might have happened."

Like Proust's, Dostoyevsky's hero dreams of absorbing and assimilating the mediator's being. He imagines a perfect synthesis of his mediator's strength with his own "intelligence." He wants to become the Other and still be himself. But why does he have this desire and why does he prefer this particular mediator when he could choose another? Why does he choose this model, idolized and spurned so hastily and so uncritically?

The wish to be absorbed into the substance of the Other implies an insuperable revulsion for one's own substance. The underground man is in fact puny and sickly.

Mme Bovary belongs to the provincial middle class. One can see why these heroes would wish to change their being. If we consider all the heroes individually we shall be tempted to take seriously the excuses they give for their desires. We run the risk of missing the metaphysical meaning of that desire.

To grasp this metaphysical meaning we must look beyond the individual cases and see the totality. All the heroes surrender their most fundamental individual prerogative, that of choosing their own desire; we cannot attribute this unanimous abandonment to the always different qualities of the heroes. For a single phenomenon a single cause must be found. All heroes of novels hate themselves on a more essential level than that of "qualities." It is exactly as the narrator says at the beginning of *Swann's Way:* "Everything which was not myself, the earth and the creatures upon it, seemed to me more precious and more important, endowed with a more real existence." The curse with which the hero is burdened is indistinguishable from his subjectivity. Even Myshkin, the purest of Dostoyevsky's heroes, suffers the anguish of one who is set apart, the individual being:

> He saw before him a dazzling sky, at his feet a lake, and all around a luminous horizon, so huge it seemed boundless. He gazed at the sight a long time, his heart torn with anguish. He remembered now having stretched out his arms to that ocean of light and blue and wept. He was tormented by the idea that he was separated from all that. What was this feast, this endless festival, to which he had so long felt himself drawn, ever since his childhood, without ever being able to participate in it? . . . Every being has a path and knows it; he comes and goes singing; but he, he alone knows nothing and understands nothing, neither men nor the voices of nature, for he is everywhere a stranger and an outcast.

The curse on the hero is so terrible and total that it extends to the people and things which come under his influence. Like a Hindu untouchable the hero contaminates everyone and everything with which he is in contact.

The closer things were the more his thought turned aside from them. Everything immediately surrounding him—boring countryside, bourgeois idiots, mediocre existence—seemed to him an exception in the world, trapped by some accident, while beyond stretched as far as the eye could see an immense land of happiness and passion.

Society does not make the hero an untouchable; he condemns himself. Why is subjectivity so charged with self-hatred? The underground man remarks that "a cultivated and decent man cannot be vain without setting a fearfully high standard for himself, and without despising and almost hating himself at certain moments." But what is the source of these demands which the self cannot satisfy? They cannot originate in the self. An exigency arising from the self and bearing on the self must be capable of being satisfied by the self. The subject must have placed his faith in a false promise from the outside.

In Dostoyevsky's eyes the false promise is essentially a promise of metaphysical autonomy. For two or three centuries this has been the underlying principle of every "new" Western doctrine: God is dead, man must take his place. Pride has always been a temptation but in modern times it has become irresistible because it is organized and amplified in an unheard-of way. The modern "glad tidings" are heard by everyone. The more deeply it is engraved in our hearts the more violent is the contrast between this marvelous promise and the brutal disappointment inflicted by experience.

As the voice of pride swells, the consciousness of existence becomes more bitter and solitary. Yet it is common to all men. Why is there this illusion of solitude which doubles the agony? Why can men no longer alleviate their suffering by sharing it? Why is the truth about all men locked up in the deepest recesses of each individual consciousness?

Each individual discovers in the solitude of his consciousness that the promise is false but no one is able to universalize his experience. The promise remains true for Others. Each one believes that he alone is excluded from the divine inheritance and takes pains to hide this misfortune. Original sin is no longer the truth about all men as in a religious universe but rather each individual's secret, the unique possession of that subjectivity which broadcasts its omnipotence and its dazzling supremacy: "I did not believe," remarks the underground man, "it was the same with other people, and all my life I hid this fact about myself as a secret."

The bastard, Dolgorouki, offers a perfect example of this dialectic of the broken promise. He bears the name of a very well-known princely family. This identity of name subjects him to endless humiliating mistakes, a second bastardy which is added to the first. What modern man is not Dolgorouki, the prince, to the Others, and Dolgorouki, the bastard, to himself? The hero of a novel is always the child who was forgotten by the good fairies at his baptism.

Everyone thinks that he alone is condemned to hell, and that is what makes it hell. The more general the illusion the more glaring it becomes. The farcical side of underground life is revealed in this exclamation of Dostoyevsky's "anti-hero": "*I* am alone, and *they* are together." So grotesque is the illusion that a crack appears in nearly every existence created by Dostoyevsky. In a brief moment of insight the subject perceives the universal deception and can no longer believe in its continuance; it seems to him

that men will throw their arms around each other in sorrow. But this is an empty hope, and even the man whom it
arouses soon becomes afraid that he has given away his
horrible secret to the Others. He is even more afraid of
having betrayed it to himself. The humility of a Myshkin
at first seems able to penetrate the armor of pride; the in-
terlocutor opens his heart but is soon overcome with
shame. He loudly proclaims that he does not wish to
change his being and that he is self-sufficient; thus the victims of the modern gospel become its best allies. The more
one becomes a slave the more ardently one defends slavery.
Pride can survive only with the help of the lie, and the lie
is sustained by triangular desire. The hero turns passionately toward the Other, who seems to enjoy the divine inheritance. So great is the disciple's faith that he perpetually thinks he is about to steal the marvelous secret from
the mediator. He begins to enjoy his inheritance in advance. He shuns the present and lives in the brilliant future. Nothing separates him from divinity, nothing but
the mediator himself, whose rival desire is the obstacle to
his own desire.

Dostoyevsky's consciousness, like Kierkegaard's Self,
cannot exist without an external prop. It renounces the
divine mediator only to fall back on the human mediator.
Just as three-dimensional perspective directs all the lines
of a picture toward a fixed point, either beyond or in front
of the canvas, Christianity directs existence toward a van-
ishing point, either toward God or toward the Other.
Choice always involves choosing a model, and true freedom lies in the basic choice between a human or a divine
model.

The impulse of the soul toward God is inseparable from
a retreat into the Self. Inversely the turning in on itself of
pride is inseparable from a movement of panic toward the
Other. To refashion St. Augustine's formula, pride is more

exterior to us than the external world. This externality of pride is magnificently illustrated by all Christian and non-Christian novelists. In *The Past Recaptured* Proust states that vanity makes us live a life turned away from ourselves, and several times he links this vanity with the *spirit of imitation.*

In his later years Dostoyevsky's vision reveals even more clearly the profound significance of novelistic works. It provides a coherent interpretation of the very strict analogies and of the radical difference between Christianity and imitative desire. To express this supreme truth which is illustrated implicitly or explicitly by all novelistic works of genius, we will borrow an abstract formula from Louis Ferrero's *Désespoirs:* "Passion is the change of address of a force awakened by Christianity and oriented toward God."

Denial of God does not eliminate transcendency but diverts it from the *au-delà* to the *en-deçà.* The imitation of Christ becomes the imitation of one's neighbor. The surge of pride breaks against the humanity of the mediator, and the result of this conflict is hatred. Max Scheler did not understand the imitative nature of desire and for this reason never succeeded in distinguishing *ressentiment* from Christian religious feeling. He did not dare to put the two phenomena side by side in order to distinguish them more clearly and thus remained within the Nietzschean confusion which he was trying to dispel.

THE DOSTOYEVSKIAN insight into internal mediation is best seen in the crucial character of Stavrogin, who is the mediator of all the characters in *The Possessed.* We should not hesitate to recognize in him an image of Antichrist.

To understand Stavrogin we must look on him as a

model and consider his relations with his "disciples." If we are to grasp his importance we must not isolate him from his fictional context, and above all we must not allow ourselves, like the possessed, to become fascinated with his "satanic grandeur."

The possessed get their ideas and desires from Stavrogin; he becomes, as it were, their idol. Each feels for him the mixture of reverence and hatred which characterizes internal mediation. Each is shattered against the icy wall of his indifference. The unfortunate Gaganov fights a duel with Stavrogin; neither insults nor bullets can touch the demigod. The universe of the possessed is the reverse image of the Christian universe. The positive mediation of the saint is replaced by the negative mediation of anguish and hate. Shatov reminds Stavrogin that "there was a master who announced great things and a disciple who was raised from the dead." Kirillov, Shatov, Lebiadkine, and all the women in *The Possessed* succumb to Stavrogin's strange power and reveal to him in almost identical terms the part he plays in their existence. Stavrogin is their "light," they wait for him as for the "sun"; before him they feel they are "before the Almighty"; they speak to him as "to God himself"; Shatov says to him, "You know I shall kiss your foot-prints when you leave. I cannot tear you from my heart, Nicolai Stavrogin."

Stavrogin is astonished that Shatov looks on him as "a kind of star" beside which he himself would be "only an insect." Everyone wants to place a banner in the hands of Stavrogin. Finally Verhovenski himself, the coldest character of *The Possessed*, the most secretive, and, one would think, the most "autonomous," throws himself at the feet of his idol, kisses his hand, babbles deliriously, and finally suggests he is "the Tsarevitch Ivan," the savior of revolutionary Russia, who will rise from the chaos and as an all-powerful dictator will re-establish order.

Stavrogin, you are beautiful! exclaims Piotr Stepano-
vitch as if in ecstasy. . . . You are my idol! You
offend no one yet everyone hates you; you treat people as though they were your equals, but they are
nevertheless afraid of you. . . . You are the leader,
you are the sun, and I am only a worm.

The lame Maria Timofeievna feels frenzied fear and
rapture in Stavrogin's presence: "May I kneel before
you?" she humbly asks him. But the spell is soon broken;
only Maria is able to unmask the impostor, for she alone is
free from pride. Stavrogin provides a veritable allegory of
internal mediation.

Hate is the reverse image of divine love. We have already seen the eternal husband and the curious impertinent offer the beloved as a sacrifice to the monstrous divinity. The characters in *The Possessed* offer themselves
as sacrifice and offer to Stavrogin everything that is most
precious to them. Deviated transcendency is a caricature
of vertical transcendency. There is not one element of this
distorted mysticism which does not have its luminous
counterpart in Christian truth.

The false prophets proclaim that in tomorrow's world
men will be gods for each other. This ambiguous message
is always carried by the most blind of Dostoyevsky's characters. The wretched creatures rejoice in the thought of a
great fraternity. They do not perceive the irony of their
own formula; they think they are heralding paradise but
they are talking about hell, a hell into which they themselves are already sinking.

To praise or to deplore the progress of "materialism" is
equally foreign to Dostoyevskian thought. There is nothing less "materialistic" than triangular desire. The passion
that drives men to seize or gain more possessions is not
materialistic; it is the triumph of the mediator, the god
with the human face. In this world of demoniacal spiritu-

ality only a Myshkin has the right to call himself a "materialist." Men boast of having discarded their old superstitions but they are gradually sinking into an underworld ruled by illusions which become increasingly obvious. But as the gods are pulled down from heaven the sacred flows over the earth; it separates the individual from all earthly goods; it creates a gulf between him and the world of *icibas* far greater than that which used to separate him from the *au-delà*. The earth's surface where Others live becomes an inaccessible paradise.

The problem of divinity no longer occurs at this low level. The need for transcendency is "satisfied" by mediation. Religious debates remain academic, especially perhaps when they separate the debaters into two rival camps, each of which passionately defends its position and condemns the other. It matters little whether the underground man believes in or denies the existence of God; however violently he argues for or against God, it is only his lips which speak. For the sacred to have concrete significance, the underground man must first return to the earth's surface. Thus, in Dostoyevsky, the return to mother earth is the first and necessary stage on the road to salvation. When the hero emerges victorious from the underground he embraces the earth from which he sprang.

THE OPPOSITION and the analogies between the two transcendencies are found in all novelists of imitative desire, Christian and non-Christian alike. Knight errantry is the mysticism of Don Quixote. In a curious chapter of that novel Sancho asks his master why he did not choose saintliness rather than knighthood—Flaubert similarly looked on bovarysm as a deviation of the need for transcendency. The adolescent Emma has a crisis of pseudo-mysticism before she slips into bovarysm proper.

Jules de Gaultier's well-known analysis of bovarysm coincides at many points with the Dostoyevskian scheme
which we have just traced. According to Gaultier, Flaubert's characters are marked by "an essential lack of a
fixed character and originality of their own . . . so that
being *nothing* by themselves, they become *something*, one
thing or another, through the suggestion which they
obey." These characters "cannot equal the model they
have chosen. Yet their vanity prevents them from admit-
ting their failure. Blinding their judgment, it puts them in
a position to deceive themselves and to identify themselves in their own eyes, with the image which they have
substituted for their own personality." This description is
correct, but we must add that contempt and hatred of the
self underlie the vanity and control it. The *objective* mediocrity of Flaubert's heroes together with their ridiculous
pretentions blinds the critic and prevents him from seeing
that it is the heroes themselves—or at least the more
metaphysical of them, like Mme Bovary—who see their
own insufficiency and plunge into bovarysm in order to
escape the condemnation which, deep in their consciousness, they are the first and possibly the only ones to make.
Therefore at the origin of bovarysm, as of Dostoyevskian
madness, is the failure of a more or less conscious attempt
at an apotheosis of the self. Admittedly Flaubert does not
reveal as clearly as Dostoyevsky the metaphysical roots of
desire. Nevertheless numerous passages of *Madame Bovary* portray just as precisely the "transcendent" character
of passion.

Emma Bovary writes love-letters to Rudolph:

But as she wrote she saw in her mind's eye another
man, a phantom composed of her most passionate
memories, her most enjoyable books and her strongest desires; at last he became so real and so tangible
that she was thrilled and amazed, yet he was so hid-

den under the abundance of his virtues that she was unable to imagine him clearly.

The metaphysical sense of desire is a little harder to see in the higher, bourgeois regions of internal mediation. Yet Stendhalian vanity is sister to Flaubertian bovarysm; it is merely a less deep underground in which the characters struggle in vain. The *vaniteux* wants to draw everything to himself, gather everything into his own Self but he never succeeds. He always suffers from a "flight" toward the Other through which the substance of his being flows away.

Like Dostoyevsky, Stendhal realized that a *broken promise* must have been at the origin of this misfortune. This is why the education of his characters is so important for him. *Vaniteux* are very often spoiled children, who have been flattered by unscrupulous sycophants. They are miserable because "every day for ten years they had been told that they should be happier than others."

The broken promise appears in another form in Stendhal's work, a more general form which is more appropriate to the grandeur of the theme. As in Dostoyevsky, modern historical development and especially the irresistible appeal of political freedom give rise to or heighten vanity. Critics are sometimes unable to reconcile this fundamental principle with Stendhal's "advanced" ideas. Any such difficulty disappears on reading a thinker such as Tocqueville, who has almost the same conception of liberty as Stendhal. The modern promise is not intrinsically false and diabolic as in Dostoyevsky, but one must be very strong indeed to accept its responsibility like a man. All of Stendhal's social and political thought is imbued with the ancient idea that it is harder to live life as a free man than as a slave. At the end of *Memoirs of a Tourist* Stendhal writes that only those who can conquer freedom deserve it. Only a strong man can live without vanity. In a universe of peers the feeble are prey to metaphysical desire and we see the triumph of modern feelings: "envy, jealousy, and impotent hatred."

Men who cannot look freedom in the face are exposed to anguish. They look for a banner on which they can fix their eyes. There is no longer God, king, or lord to link them to the universal. To escape the feeling of particularity they imitate *another's* desires; they choose substitute gods because they are not able to give up infinity.

Stendhal's *egotist,* unlike the romantic, is not trying to inflate his ego to universal proportions. Such an attempt is always based on some hidden mediation. The egotist recognizes his limits and gives up any idea of exceeding them. He says "I" from modesty and prudence. He is not thrown back on *nothing* because he has given up desiring *everything.* Thus egotism in Stendhal represents an attempt to sketch the outlines of a modern humanism.

Interesting as this attempt is, it has hardly any repercussions on the business of writing the novels. In the latter there is no middle term between vanity and passion, between immediate existence characterized by ignorance, superstition, action, happiness, and mediate reflection characterized by fear of truth, indecision, weakness, and vanity. In the early Stendhal and in some of his essays we find an opposition, inherited from the eighteenth century, between the lucid skepticism of honest people and the hypocritical religion of everyone else. In his great works this opposition has disappeared. It has been replaced by a contrast between the hypocritical religion of the vain and the "true" religion of the passionate. All the passionate characters, Mme de Rênal, Mme de Chasteller, Fabrice, Clélia, and the heroes of the *Italian Chronicles,* are religious.

Stendhal never succeeded in creating a passionate hero who was not a believer, but it was not for want of trying. The results are disappointing. Lucien Leuwen vacillates between vanity and naïveté; Lamiel is a puppet and Stendhal abandons her in favor of the vain Sansfin. Julien Sorel must also have been, at a certain stage in the creative process, the hero at once passionate and apostate, whom Stendhal was trying to create. But Julien is merely clearer-minded and more energetic than the other hypocrites. He will know true passion only at his death, when he has renounced himself, and at that point we are no longer sure that he is still a skeptic.

Stendhal's inability to create such a hero is revealing. The being of passion is a creature of the past, narrowly, superstitiously religious. The *vaniteux* is the man of the present; he is a Christian only by an opportunism of which he himself is not always aware. The triumph of vanity coincides with the crumbling of the traditional universe. Men of triangular desire no longer believe but are unable to get along without transcendency. Stendhal wants to convince himself that one can escape vanity without having to give up modern self-awareness but this ideal was never incarnated in the novels.

We need not, therefore, make Stendhal a Christian or Dostoyevsky an atheist in order to compare their novels. The truth suffices. Stendhalian vanity is the cousin of all the metaphysical desires met with in the other novelists. If we are to grasp the concept in all its profundity we must always bear in mind its double sense, metaphysical and worldly, biblical and everyday. It is because the *vaniteux* feels the emptiness mentioned in Ecclesiastes growing inside him that he takes refuge in shallow behavior and imitation. Because he cannot face his nothingness he throws himself on Another who seems to be spared by the curse.

THIS STERILE oscillation between pride and shame is also found in Proustian snobbism. We shall never despise the snob as much as he despises himself. The snob is not essentially despicable; he tries to escape his own subjective feeling of contemptibility by assuming the new being which he supposedly procures through snobbism. The snob thinks he is always on the point of securing this being and behaves as if he has already done so. Thus he acts with intolerable arrogance. Snobbism is an inextricable mixture of pride and meanness, and it is this very mixture which defines metaphysical desire.

It is to be expected that some of us may have misgivings about this comparison of the snob with other novelistic heroes. Snobbism excites tremendous indignation. This is the one offense which our *avant-garde,* despite its passion for justice, has not thought to "rehabilitate." Moralists of old and new schools alike compete in raising their eyebrows at *The Guermantes Way.* It is considered a little embarrassing that Stendhal and Proust, as well as Balzac, devoted such a large part of their work to snobbism. Benevolent exegetes try to minimize the importance of these ugly flaws in France's most illustrious novelists.

We do not despise Dostoyevsky's heroes, but we despise the snob because snobbism is felt to belong to our "normal" everyday world. We like to think of snobbism as a vice we ourselves have fortunately been spared, but whose deplorable results we see all around us. Snobbism thus becomes the object of a *moral* judgment. The underground man's obsession, on the other hand, seems pathological or metaphysical to us. It belongs to the world of the psychiatrist or philosopher. We have not the heart to condemn one who is possessed.

Is Proust's snob really so different from Dostoyevsky's hero, as is often thought? *Notes from the Underground* suggests the contrary. Let us observe the underground man with his old schoolfellows. These dull men organize a banquet for a certain Zverkov, who is leaving for the Caucasus where he has been stationed. The underground man is present during the preparations for the party but no one thinks of inviting him. This unexpected snub—or perhaps only too expected—unleashes in him a morbid passion, a frantic desire "to crush, conquer and charm" these people whom he does not need and for whom, moreover, he feels genuine contempt.

After abject grovelling he finally gets the coveted invitation. He goes to the banquet and behaves ridiculously, while remaining all the time perfectly aware of his own shameful conduct.

We should read *The Guermantes Way* in the light of this episode, and not be distracted by the difference in surroundings. The structure is identical. The emptiness of a Babal de Bréauté and many another Proustian character is certainly the equal of Zverkov and his buddies. Proust's snob is as shrewd a psychologist as the man from the underground and he sees through his mediator's emptiness. As in Dostoyevsky, nevertheless, this lucidity is impotent. It does not succeed in rescuing from his fascination the person who is so perspicacious.

At this point the Proustian hero's truth merges with his creator's truth. As a wealthy and brilliant young man of middle-class family, Marcel Proust was irresistibly drawn to the only Parisian milieu where his wealth, charm, and ability were of no assistance to him. The only company he sought, like Jean Santeuil in school, was that of people *who wanted to have nothing to do with him.*

In Proust, as in Dostoyevsky, a negative criterion determines the choice of mediator. The snob, like the lover, pursues the "person who flees him" and there is pursuit only when there is flight. In Proust, as in Dostoyevsky, obsessive desire is unleashed by the refusal of an invitation, the Other's brutal rejection. *Notes from the Underground* throws as harsh a light on Proust's experience of fashionable society as *The Eternal Husband* does on his sexual life.

Proust's snob finds himself faced with the same temptations as the underground man—the *letter* to the mediator is a good example. This letter is meant to be insulting but in reality it is an anguished appeal. Gilberte Swann, driven to despair by her failure to be invited to the Guermantes', sends the Duchess a letter rather similar to that composed by the underground man in the episode of the insolent officer. In *Jean Santeuil* the hero writes to his schoolmates who are persecuting him and begs for their friendship. The raving messages of flattery sent by Nastasya Filippovna to Aglaia in *The Idiot* fit into the same structure as the Proustian letters.

There is no gulf between the great novelists. The analogies between them are inexhaustible. For example, the Dostoyevskian man, like Stendhal's *vaniteux* and Proust's snob, is haunted by the fear of ridicule. Like Proust's narrator invited by the Princess of Guermantes for the first time, he thinks he is the victim of a hoax and that the real guests, who have a divine right to life's banquet, will poke fun at him. The same fears are found in Proust but here they are expressed with an unparalleled violence. In the preceding chapter we saw in Proust a caricature of Stendhalian vanity. Now we find in Dostoyevsky a caricature of Proustian snobbism.

Why under these circumstances does the snob particularly arouse our disdain? If pressed, our answer would be that we are irritated by the arbitrariness of his imitation. A child's imitation is excusable because it is rooted in an actual inferiority. Childhood has neither the physical strength, nor the experience, nor the resources of adulthood. But in the snob we can find no sign of any definite inferiority. The snob is not base yet he debases himself. In a society where individuals are "free and equal by law" there *should* be no snobs. But there *can* be snobs only in this sort of society. In fact snobbism requires concrete equality. When individuals are inferior or superior to each other, we find servility and tyranny, flattery and arrogance, but never snobbism in the proper sense of the word. The snob will fawn and cringe in order to be accepted by people whom he has endowed with an arbitrary prestige. Proust insists a great deal on this point. The snobs of *Remembrance of Things Past* are nearly always superior to their models; they excel in wealth, charm, and ability. The essence of snobbism lies, therefore, in the absurd.

Snobbism begins with equality. This certainly does not mean that Proust lived in a classless society. But the actual concrete differences between these classes have nothing to do with the abstract distinctions of snobbism. In the eyes of sociologists the Verdurins belong to the same class as the Guermantes.

The snob bows before a noble title which has lost all real value, before a social prestige so esoteric that it is really appreciated by only a few elderly ladies. The more arbitrary the imitation the more contemptible it seems. The "nearness" of the mediator makes this imitation arbitrary and that nearness leads us back to Dostoyevsky's hero. All concrete difference has disappeared between the underground man and his old schoolmates; all are bureaucrats in that "artificial and studied" town of St. Petersburg: there is now complete equality and the imitation is even more absurd than in Proust.

Underground heroes should disgust us even more than Proust's snobs. But we do not feel this disgust. We condemn one and forgive the other on the same moral grounds. Our attempt at isolating a specific and evil es-

sence in snobbism has failed completely; we always discover Stendhalian vanity on the one hand and Dostoyevskian madness on the other. In all the novelists the pen-
dulum oscillates between pride and shame, only the
length of the arc varies.

Why do we frown upon the snob so much more than on
other victims of imitative desire? If the novel provides no
explanation, we must look to the reader. The areas of desire which seem to us praiseworthy or picturesque are
always the most remote from our own world. It is rather
the intermediate and bourgeois regions of desire which
arouse our indignation. Perhaps this historical and social
distribution is not fortuitous.

Since it is once again a question of imitative desire our
investigations should be guided by the novelists themselves. Proust is no stranger to anything even remotely
connected with snobbism—he must certainly have something to say of the disapproval this "vice" provokes in us.

In a remarkable episode in *Swann's Way* we witness the
discovery of Legrandin's snobbism by Marcel's family.
Legrandin flutters around the local nobility after Mass.
Instead of his usual friendly greetings to Marcel's parents,
he merely nods his head and turns sharply away. This in-
cident is repeated on the following two Sundays. The parents need no further enlightenment. Legrandin is a snob.

Only the grandmother is not convinced by the evidence; she remembers that Legrandin is the enemy of
snobs. In fact she thinks he is even a little too hard on
them. How could Legrandin be guilty of the sin he criti-
cizes so fiercely in *others*? But the parents are not taken in
by this "bad faith." In their eyes it only makes him more
of a scoundrel. It is the father who throughout the affair
shows the greatest severity—and the greatest perspicacity.

There is just one scene but three spectators and three

different interpretations. There are three ways of looking
at the event but they are not autonomous and thus of
equal standing as the subjectivists would have it. They
can be classified and given a hierarchy from two different
points of view. The first is the comprehension of the
scene. As one goes from grandmother to mother, and from
mother to father, Legrandin's snobbism is more and more
clearly *understood*. The different degrees of understanding form a sort of ladder on which the three characters are
spaced. Behind this first ladder we see another, more
faintly sketched, representing moral purity. The grandmother is at the top of this ladder since she is completely
innocent of snobbism. The mother stands a little lower;
she is no longer completely untarnished. Although she is
always afraid of "hurting people" and although she is especially fond of Swann, yet she still refuses to receive his
wife, that former "cocotte." The father stands still lower
on the ladder. In his own way he is the biggest snob of the
family. He experiences the joys and pangs of vanity from
the capricious attention and flattery of his colleague
Norpois, the elderly diplomat. Taboos flourish in all
milieux, not just in the Faubourg Saint-Germain, and excommunication is felt everywhere. The professions are
particularly susceptible to the development of what
Proust calls snobbism.

We merely have to reverse the ladder of comprehension
to obtain the ladder of moral purity. The degree of our
own indignation at the snob therefore is the measure of
our own snobbism. And Legrandin is no exception to this
rule. He holds the lowest position on the ladder of purity
and therefore the highest on that of comprehension. Legrandin is painfully aware of the slightest manifestations
of snobbism. The hatred inspired in him by the "sin
against the spirit" is not feigned. The doors of the salons
where he wishes to be received are closed to him by the

snobs. One must be a snob oneself in order to suffer from the snobbism of Others.

It is no unfortunate coincidence that the desiring subject chooses to be indignant at the evil by which he himself is consumed. There is a necessary link between indignation and culpability, and this indignation is fed by the most penetrating insight. Only a snob can really know another snob since he *copies* the latter's desire, that is, the very essence of his being. There is no question here of looking for the usual difference between copy and original for the very good reason that there is no original. The mediator of a snob is himself a snob—a first copy.

There is a close and direct connection between comprehension and participation in metaphysical desire. Snobs understand each other at first glance and hate each other almost as quickly, for nothing is worse for the desiring subject than to see his own imitation brought into the open.

As the distance between mediator and subject decreases, the difference diminishes, the comprehension becomes more acute and the hatred more intense. It is always his own desire that the subject condemns in the Other without knowing it. Hatred is individualistic. It nourishes fiercely the illusion of an absolute difference between the Self and that Other from which nothing separates it. Indignant comprehension is therefore an imperfect comprehension—not nonexistent as some moralists claim, but imperfect, for the subject does not recognize in the Other the void gnawing at himself. He makes of him a monstrous divinity. The subject's indignant knowledge of the Other returns in a circle to strike him when he is least expecting it. This psychological circle is inscribed in the triangle of desire. Most of our ethical judgments are rooted in hatred of a mediator, a rival whom we copy.

While the mediator is still remote the circle is vast. It is very easy to confuse the trajectory of ethical judgment with a straight line, and the desiring subject always makes this confusion. The space of desire is "Euclidian." We always think we move in a straight line toward the object of our desires and hates. Novelistic space is "Einsteinian." The novelist shows us that the straight line is in reality a circle which inevitably turns us back on ourselves

When the mediator is very close, observers can see the hero's psychological circle and speak of *obsession*. The man obsessed is like a fortress surrounded by the enemy. He is forced back on his own resources. Legrandin eloquently stigmatizes snobbism, Bloch rages against social climbing, and Charlus against homosexuality. Each one speaks only of his own vice. The obsessed man astounds us with his clear understanding of those like himself—in other words, his rivals—and his complete inability to see himself. This lucidity and blindness both increase as the mediator becomes nearer.

The law of the psychological circle is basic. It is found in all the novelists of imitative desire. Among the brothers Karamazov, Ivan is most like his father and Alyosha least. It is Ivan who hates most and Alyosha who hates least. We have no difficulty in discovering the two Proustian ladders in these relationships.

The psychological circle can be found in Cervantes as well. It is those who are most inclined to the ontological sin who attempt to cure Don Quixote. The sickest persons are always the most worried by the sickness of Others. After cursing Others, Oedipus finds he himself is guilty. Novelistic psychology is even more banal than French avant-garde critics deem it. In its best moments, it returns to the psychology of the great religions: "Therefore thou art inexcusable, O man, whosoever thou art that judgest: for wherein thou judgest another, thou condemnest thyself; for thou that judgest doest the same things" (Saint Paul's Epistle to the Romans).

THE "springtime of society" which awakens in the heart of a young snob is no more despicable in itself than other desires. But our psychological circle creates the illusion of a fundamental difference. We do not all secretly dream of the Faubourg Saint-Germain, but we are particularly hard on snobs because they inhabit the same historical world as we do. We are hostile to the bourgeois forms of metaphysical desire because we see in them the desires of our neighbors and the grinning caricature of our own temptations.

Not to understand the snob and not to understand a Dostoyevskian character are two quite different things. In the first case it is a lack of sympathy, in the second a lack of comprehension. We do not understand what drives the underground man to worship, to hate, to collapse sobbing at the feet of his mediator, to send him incoherent messages full of insults mixed with endearments. On the other hand we understand very clearly the temptation to which Gilberte yields when she writes to the Duchess of Guermantes. However unjustifiable the snob's imitation seems to us, it is nevertheless much more justifiable than that of the Dostoyevskian hero. The snob's values may perhaps not be ours but they are not so unfamiliar that they elude our grasp completely. The proof of this is that we think ourselves always capable of smelling out a snob. We see through his affectation of spontaneity and eccentricity. We can guess at the phenomena of literary and social disease that have infected him. We perceive the inadequate props he seeks in history, aesthetics, and poetry; we are not fooled by his excuses, his irresistible sympathy, or, on the other hand, by the cynical ambition with which he tries to conceal the ineffable, irrational, and yet familiar essence of snobbism.

It is always the most familiar forms of imitative desire which excite indignation. Don Quixote's neighbors are no less brutal and unjust in their narrow-minded justice than

Marcel's father when he condemns Legrandin. In the eyes of his peers, the petty squires, Don Quixote is merely a snob. He is reproached for having assumed the title of *Don* to which he "has no right." Sancho too acts like a snob when he tries to persuade his wife that she should be a duchess!

The great novelists share neither our indignation nor our enthusiasm for their creations. They seem to us either too indulgent or too cruel because of our own passion. Cervantes looks on Don Quixote in the same way that Proust regards Baron de Charlus. If we cannot recognize the analogies between all these heroes it is because we are sometimes in the shoes of Marcel's severe parents and sometimes in those of the indulgent grandmother, depending on the proximity or remoteness of the heroes.

We must overcome the irritation which snobbism causes in us. We cannot reach the standpoint of novelistic unity until we have traveled the road taken by the novelists. After condemning Others the Oedipus-novelist finds that he himself is guilty. Thus he arrives at a position of justice beyond pessimistic psychology and romantic idolatry. This novelistic justice is distinct from moralizing hypocrisy and false detachment; it is something concrete, verifiable from the novel itself. And it is this which permits a synthesis of introspection and observation from which spring existence and truth. This synthesis, by destroying the barriers between the Self and the Other, creates the Don Quixotes and the Charlus.

IT IS NOT enough to show the relationship between the snob and other novelistic heroes in order to make Proust the equal of Cervantes and Dostoyevsky. We still have to prove that the metaphysical significance of desire has not eluded him. This significance is very clearly stated in a passage of *The Past Recaptured:*

Every person who makes us suffer we can associate with a divinity, of which that person is only a fragmentary reflexion—the lowest step of the approach to the temple, as it were—and the contemplation of this divinity as a pure idea gives us instant joy in place of the sorrow we were suffering.

Such passages are not lacking and we could simply go on quoting them. But compared with the metaphysical vision of Dostoyevsky they are so many meager and isolated sentences. Proust never emphasizes deviated transcendency to the degree that Dostoyevsky, or even Stendhal, does, for he does not probe so deeply into the question of freedom as does the latter. As we have seen above, Proust frequently adopts or seems to adopt a solipsistic theory of desire which completely falsifies the experience of his characters.

The mediator's divinity is central to novelistic genius; thus it should be expressed at that precise point where the art of an individual novel triumphs. Where is this point in Proust? If we should ask the author himself he would reply that novelistic art—and it is understood Proustian art—reaches its culmination in the creation of *metaphors*. The metaphor, therefore, should reveal the metaphysical significance of desire. And this is precisely what it does. In Proust's masterpiece the sacred is not merely another metaphoric domain: it is present whenever the author deals with the relationship between the subject and his mediator. The whole gamut of feelings experienced by the narrator before his successive idols corresponds to the various aspects of a religious experience in which terror, anathema, and taboos play an increasing role. The images and metaphors portray the mediator as the relentless guardian of a closed garden where only the elect may enjoy eternal beatitude.[1]

[1] See, for example, the passage on Bergotte quoted above.

The narrator always approaches his god in fear and trembling. Thanks to the images, the most insignificant gestures take on a ritual value. Accompanied by his nurse-maid, Françoise, Marcel makes a "pilgrimage" to the Swann residence. This bourgeois apartment is in turn compared to a temple, a sanctuary, a church, a cathedral, an oratory—there is scarcely a cult from which Proust has not borrowed sacred terms. Magic, occultism, the primitive world, and Christian mysticism are never absent. The vocabulary of transcendency is extraordinarily rich in this author who never, or almost never, speaks of metaphysics and religion.

Even classical mythology has a part in the deification of the mediator. Toward the beginning of *Within a Budding Grove* the narrator goes to the opera and from his seat in the orchestra gazes at the Guermantes and their friends who sit, majestic and indifferent, enthroned above the ordinary spectators. Their closed boxes, separated from the rest of the theater, seem another world, inaccessible to simple mortals. The word *baignoire* [2] and the bluish lighting call to the narrator's mind a whole mythology of the liquid element. The social elite are transformed into nymphs, nereids, and tritons. This passage is an example of the somewhat excessive virtuosity and of the "gay nineties" ornateness which make purists feel a little uneasy when they come upon them in the work of Proust.

On a lower level of literary creation the image is simply a decoration which the writer can include or leave out at will. Proust does not permit himself this liberty. The novelist is not "realistic" in portraying the object but he is "realistic" in his treatment of the desire. The images are supposed to "transfigure" the object. The type of poetic distortion undergone by this object is very specific: it is

[2] This word in French has two meanings, a box in a theater and a bath. (*Translator's note.*)

that of a young middle-class man who sees the world through the lenses of his scholarly and bookish training. The growing desire of the student who dreams of the world of high society around 1890, the sickly and sheltered childhood of the narrator, and even the interior decoration of the theater blend wonderfully and find expression in the images of mythology. The purists do not understand within what narrow limits the author's choice is made.

Proust's demands on the old mythological apparatus for services it is notoriously unable to render are somewhat ironic. In the mind of the cultivated reader, these classical allusions do not evoke the sacred but rather an atmosphere where everything sacred wilts and finally dies, the profane world of Greco-Roman culture. Thus Proust chooses the images which are least well suited to the role he wants them to play. And yet he succeeds in fitting them into his aesthetic system. He succeeds because at this point in the novelistic development the mediator's divinity is firmly established. Marcel has only to let his "fixed and agonized" gaze rest on someone and we see the abyss of transcendency open between this person and himself. The metaphor is no longer needed to give the flavor of the sacred; the effect is so well achieved that the perception itself sanctifies the metaphor. Thus Proust rejuvenates worn-out metaphors, making them reflect the transcendency emanating from the mediator. The metaphor reflects the transcendent as an echo sends back the sound to its point of origin. This is not a pointless game. It does not destroy the realism of desire, but rather consummates it perfectly. Everything, in fact, is false, theatrical, and artificial in desire except the immense hunger for the sacred. It is this hunger which transforms the elements of a poor and positive existence from the moment when the child discovers his god, from the moment when he manages to throw off onto Another—his mediator—the burden of divine omnipotence which is crushing him.

A childhood deprived of the sacred succeeds in resurrecting myths which have been dead for centuries; it revivifies the most lifeless symbols. Against his middle-class background, which we find hard to forgive him, Proust pursues the same ends as Nerval, one of his favorite writers. The Nerval of *Sylvie* makes the Goddess of Reason sacred and transforms the architectural fantasies of skeptical eighteenth-century noblemen into veritable sanctuaries. Metaphysical life is so vigorous in certain beings that it reappears under the most unfavorable conditions. It can finally end, however, by assuming quite monstrous shapes.

THE IDEA of a transcendency deviated in the direction of the human throws light on Proust's poetics; it enables us to clear up the persistent confusion concerning *The Past Recaptured*. It is the transcendent quality of a former desire which is relived on contact with a relic of the past. The memory is no longer poisoned, as was the desire, by the rival desire. "Every person who makes us suffer we can associate with a divinity, of which that person is only a fragmentary reflexion . . . and the contemplation of this divinity as a pure idea gives us instant joy in place of the sorrow we were suffering."

The affective memory experiences again the impulse toward the transcendent and this impulse is pure joy because it is no longer interrupted by the mediator. The *petite madeleine* is a veritable *communion;* it has all the virtues of a sacrament. The memory disassociates the contradictory elements of desire. The transcendent releases its perfume while the attentive and detached intelligence can now recognize the obstacle on which it stumbled. It understands the role of mediator and reveals to us the infernal mechanism of desire.

Thus the affective memory carries with it condemnation of the original desire. Critics speak here of a "contradiction." The experience which, in the last analysis, procures happiness is repudiated. This is true. But the contradiction is not Proust's; it is that of metaphysical desire. To see the truth of desire is to see the double role, evil and sacred, of the mediator. The ecstasy of the memory and the condemnation of desire imply each other in the same way as length implies breadth, or heads implies tails. Proustian "psychology" is inseparable from mystic revelation. It is its other side. It is not, as is claimed these days, a second literary undertaking of rather mediocre interest.

The affective memory is the Last Judgment of Proustian existence. It separates the wheat from the tares, but the tares must appear in the novel since the novel is the past. The affective memory is the nucleus of all Proust's work. It is the source of the true and the sacred; from it spring the religious metaphors, and through it is revealed the divine and diabolical function of the mediator. We must not confine its effects to the oldest and happiest recollections. Vivid remembrance is never more necessary than in periods of suffering, for it dispels the fog of hatred. The affective memory is active through the whole temporal series. It lights up the hell of *Cities of the Plain* as well as the paradise of "Combray."

The memory is the salvation of the writer and of the man Marcel Proust. We shrink from the transparent message of *The Past Recaptured*. Our romanticism will tolerate only an imaginary salvation, it will tolerate only a truth that brings despair. The affective memory is ecstasy but it is also comprehension. If it transfigured the object, as has so often been said, the novel would not describe for us the illusion experienced at the moment of desire, but a new illusion, the result of this new transfiguration. There would be no realism of desire.

CHAPTER III

THE METAMORPHOSIS
OF DESIRE

IMITATIVE desire is always a desire to be Another. There is only one metaphysical desire but the particular desires which instantiate this primordial desire are of infinite variety. From what we can observe directly, nothing is constant in the desire of a hero of a novel. Even its intensity is variable. It depends on the degree of "metaphysical virtue" possessed by the object. And this virtue, in turn, depends on the distance between object and mediator.

The object is to the mediator what the relic is to a saint. The rosary used by a saint or his vestments are more sought after than a medal which has simply been touched or blessed by him. The value of a relic depends on its closeness to the saint. It is the same with the object in metaphysical desire.

We must, therefore, look at that other side of the novelistic triangle which connects the mediator with the object of desire. Hitherto we have confined our attention to the first side which joins mediator and desiring subject. Fortunately the two sides vary in much the same way. The triangle of desire is an isosceles triangle. Thus desire always increases in intensity as the mediator approaches the desiring subject.

The mediator is most remote in the case of Don Quixote, and the particular desires of that hero are therefore less tortured. Stubbornness is unknown to so sensible a hero. Faced with failure he philosophically leaves the completion of his task to another knight and goes off to seek his fortune elsewhere.

Don Quixote's activity remains fairly close to the level of play. A child's play is already triangular: an imitation of adults. But the distance between object and mediator —i.e., between toy and the adult activity which endows it with meaning—is always sufficient to prevent the player from completely losing sight of the illusory character of the importance conferred on the toy. Don Quixote has gone beyond the game, but not very far as yet. For this reason he is the most serene of the novelistic heroes.

His distant mediator sheds a diffused light over a vast surface. Amadis does not indicate precisely any particular object of desire, but on the other hand he designates vaguely almost everything. Adventures follow one another in rapid succession, but not one of them alone could make of Don Quixote a second Amadis. This explains why he does not think it necessary to persist in the face of bad luck.

As the mediator grows nearer, the directions become more precise; "metaphyscal virtue" increases and the object becomes "irreplaceable." Emma Bovary's desires are more violent than Don Quixote's and Julien's desires are more violent than those of Emma. The projector gradually comes nearer and its light is slowly concentrated on a smaller and yet smaller surface.

Emma's adventures have become more "serious" than Don Quixote's, but the truly desirable objects, which would make of Emma the woman she wants to be, are not to be found in the provinces. Rudolph and Léon are still only metaphysical makeshifts. They are more or less interchangeable and the mediator's light shines dimly on them.

The behavior of the heroes reflects the changing conditions of mediation. Don Quixote is excited and exerts himself a great deal but is a little like a child at play. Emma Bovary is more anguished. The mediator is still inaccessible but no longer so remote that the desiring subject can resign himself to the impossibility of reaching him, and the reflection playing over reality no longer suffices. It is this which gives bovarysm its special tonality. Essentially it is contemplative. Emma dreams a great deal and desires little, whereas the heroes of Stendhal, Proust, and Dostoyevsky dream little and desire a great deal. Action reappears with internal mediation but that action no longer has any resemblance to play. The revered object has come close; it seems within reach of the hand; only one obstacle remains between subject and object—the mediator himself. The closer the mediator comes, the more feverish the action becomes. In Dostoyevsky, thwarted desire is so violent that it can lead to murder.

As THE role of the *metaphysical* grows greater in desire, that of the *physical* diminishes in importance. As the mediator draws nearer, passion becomes more intense and the object is emptied of its concrete value.

If we are to believe the romantics and neoromantics, the results of an ever greater triumph of the imagination can only be good. But as reality diminishes, the rivalry which engenders desire is inevitably aggravated. This law, which holds good in every case, gives a perfect definition of the differences and analogies between Stendhal's and Proust's universes. Stendhal's *vaniteux* and Proust's snobs seem to covet the same object—the Faubourg Saint-Germain. But Proust's Faubourg Saint-Germain is no longer the same as Stendhal's. During the nineteenth century the aristocracy lost the last of its concrete privileges. In Proust's day, keeping company with the old nobility carried with it no tangible advantage. If the strength of desire were in direct proportion to the concrete value of the object then Proustian snobbism would be less intense than Stendhalian vanity; but the truth is exactly the reverse. The snobs of *Remembrance of Things Past* suffer much more than the *vaniteux* of *The Red and the Black*. Thus the transition from one novelist to the other might well be defined as the advance of the metaphysical at the expense of the physical. Stendhal, of course, was aware of the inverse relationship between the strength of desire and the importance of the object. He writes: "The pettier the social difference, the more affectation it produces." This law does not govern merely Stendhalian vanity; the whole of novelistic literature offers proof of it and it enables us to situate the novels in relation to one another. Proustian snobbism, and *a fortiori*, Dostoyevsky's underground, are only following out the implications of this Stendhalian law to their logical conclusions. The most extreme forms of internal mediation should therefore be defined as *a minimum difference producing a maximum affectation*. This is, moreover, approximately the same as Proust's own definition of snobbism: "High society being the kingdom of futility, there are merely insignificant degrees between the merits of the different fashionable ladies which alone can inflate out of all proportion on M. de Charlus' grudges or imagination."

In Stendhal's *Lucien Leuwen* the rivalry between the hero and the young aristocrats of Nancy finally settles on a very real object, the lovely Mme de Chasteller, who combines the graces of the nobility with the very real advantages of wealth. The social context is the same in Proust; the chief concern is still laying siege to the aristocratic salons but there is no longer any Mme de Chasteller.

There are the Guermantes to be sure, but it is not their beauty nor even their money which interests the snobs. The dinners given by the Duchess are no more elegant than many others, her receptions no more brilliant. The difference between the people who are received and those who are not is purely metaphysical. What Proust calls "a fine social position" is something ephemeral, elusive, and almost imperceptible unless one is a snob oneself. Initiation into society has no more "objective" value than Don Quixote's dubbing at the hands of a country innkeeper.

The underground man represents the final stage in this evolution toward abstract desire. The object has disappeared completely. A passionate desire to be invited to the banquet in honor of Zverkov cannot be understood even in terms of material gain or social advantage.

Romantic and symbolist theories of desire reflect in their own way this progressive elimination of reality. The actual prop for the desire is already very minor in Stendhal's concept of "crystallization." The twig dipped in the Salzburg fountain [1] is reduced to a "grain of sand" in the allegory of the oyster and the pearl. These descriptions are correct, except that they completely overlook the mediator—it is the mediator who makes the imagination fertile. The romantic is always falling on his knees before the wrong altar; he thinks he is sacrificing the world on the altar of his Self whereas the real object of his worship is the Other.

The "physical" and "metaphysical" in desire always fluctuate at the expense of each other. This law has myriad aspects. It explains for example the progressive disappearance of sexual pleasure in the most advanced stages of ontological sickness. The mediator's "virtue" acts on the senses like a poison which constantly spreads and slowly paralyzes the hero.

[1] See Stendhal, *De l'Amour*, Chapter VI.

Emma Bovary still knows sensual pleasure, for her desire is not very metaphysical. But in the case of Stendhal's *vaniteux*, there has been a significant reduction in the pleasure derived from sexual activity. Almost nonexistent at the moment of conquest, it frequently reappears when the metaphysical virtue has evaporated. In Proust, pleasure has almost entirely disappeared, and in Dostoyevsky there is not even any question of it.

EVEN in the most favorable cases, the physical qualities of the object play only a subordinate role. They can neither rouse metaphysical desire nor prolong it; moreover, the absence of physical enjoyment does not cause the disappointment in Stendhal's or Proust's hero when he finally possesses the object of his desire. The disappointment is entirely metaphysical. The subject discovers that possession of the object has not changed his being—the expected metamorphosis has not taken place. The greater the apparent "virtue" of the object the more terrible is the disappointment, thus disappointment deepens as the mediator draws closer to the hero.

Don Quixote and Mme Bovary as yet experience no metaphysical disappointment in the proper sense of the term. The phenomenon appears with Stendhal. The moment the hero takes hold of the desired object its "virtue" disappears like gas from a burst balloon. The object has been suddenly desecrated by possession and reduced to its objective qualities, thus provoking the famous Stendhalian exclamation: "Is that all it is?!" Yet Julien's shrug reflects a lack of concern which no longer exists in the crushing Proustian disillusionment. So profound is the confusion caused by metaphysical failure in Dostoyevsky's hero it may even lead to suicide.

The disappointment is irrefutable proof of the absurdity of triangular desire. It would seem that the hero must now submit to the evidence. No person or object now separates him from the abject and humiliated Self which desire had somehow hidden from him with the mask of the future. Deprived of desire the hero is in danger of falling into the abyss of the present like a well-digger whose rope breaks. How can he escape this terrible destiny?

He cannot deny the failure of his desire but he can confine its results to the object which he now possesses and possibly to the mediator who directed him to it. The disappointment does not prove the absurdity of *all* metaphysical desires but only that of this particular desire which has just led to disillusionment. The hero realizes that he was mistaken. The object never did have the power of "initiation" which he had attributed to it. But this power he confers elsewhere, on a second object, on a new desire. The hero goes through his existence, from desire to desire, as one crosses a stream, jumping from one slippery stone to another.

Two possibilities present themselves. The disillusioned hero can let his former mediator point out another object for him, or he can change mediators. The decision does not depend on "psychology" nor on "freedom," but, like so many other aspects of metaphysical desire, on the distance separating hero and mediator.

When this distance is great, we know that the object has little metaphysical value. The prestige of the mediator is not involved in particular desires. The god is above the vicissitudes of existence. He is unique and eternal. Don Quixote has many adventures but there is only one Amadis; Mme Bovary could go on changing lovers endlessly without ever changing her dream. As the mediator draws near, the object is very closely linked with him and the god's divine image is at stake, so to speak. The failure of desire can now have repercussions beyond the object and provoke doubts concerning the mediator himself. At first the idol trembles on its pedestal; it may even collapse if the disillusionment is great enough. Proust described the fall of the mediator with an extraordinary wealth of detail. The event is truly a revolution in the existence of the subject. All the elements of this existence seem drawn to the mediator as if to a magnet; he determines their hierarchy and even their meaning. Thus we can readily understand why the hero does all he can to put off an experience which is bound to be very disruptive.

When the narrator is finally invited by the Guermantes, after longing in vain for the invitation for several years, he experiences the inevitable disappointment. He finds the same mediocrity, the same clichés as in other salons. Can it be that the Guermantes and their guests, these superhuman beings, get together to talk about the Dreyfus affair or the latest novel, and moreover to talk of them in the same terms and the same tone as other people? Marcel searches for an answer which would reconcile the sacred prestige of the mediator and the negative experience of possession. He almost manages to convince himself, that first evening, that it is his presence which has profaned and interrupted the aristocratic mysteries whose celebration cannot be resumed until he leaves. The will to believe is so strong in this upside-down St. Thomas that it even survives a while after the concrete proof of the idol's emptiness.

Every mediation projects its mirage; the mirages follow one another like so many "truths" which take the place of former truths by a veritable murdering of the living memory and which protect themselves from future truths by an implacable censure of daily experience. Proust calls "Selves" the "worlds" projected by successive mediations. The Selves are completely isolated from each other and

are incapable of recalling the former Selves or antici-
pating future Selves.

The first signs of the hero's fragmentation into monadic
Selves can be seen in Stendhal. The Stendhalian hero's
sensibility is subjected to abrupt changes which foreshadow the successive personalities of *Remembrance of
Things Past*. The personality of Julien Sorel remains an
unbroken unity but this unity is threatened at the time of
that temporary aberration which is his love for Mathilde.

In Proust, life loses definitively the stability and unity
which was insured by the permanence of the divinity in
previous novels. This "decomposition of the personality,"
which worried and annoyed Proust's early readers, comes
about as a result of the multiplication of mediators. The
cries of alarm were, perhaps, only partly justified. As long
as the mediator is remote, and therefore unique, the hero
maintains his unity, but this unity is composed of lies and
illusions. A single lie encompassing the whole of existence
is not preferable morally to a series of temporary lies.
Proust's hero may be more seriously ill than the others
but he suffers from the same disease, and if he is more
culpable, it is of the same fault. We should not therefore
heap abuse upon him, but we should definitely pity him,
for he is more unfortunate than his predecessors.

The briefer the reign of the mediator, the more tyranni-
cal it becomes. The greatest suffering is reserved for Dostoyevsky's hero. The underground man's mediators succeed one another so rapidly we can no longer even speak
of distinct Selves. The periods of relative stability, separated by violent crises or intervals of spiritual emptiness,
which we have seen in Proust, are supplanted in Dostoyevsky by a perpetual crisis. The elements which in the
other novelists are ranged in a permanent or temporary
hierarchy are now in a state of chaos. In fact the man

from the underground is often torn between several simultaneous mediations. He is a different person every moment of his existence and for everyone he is with—this is
the *polymorphosis* of the Dostoyevskian being which has
been pointed out by all the critics.

As the mediator draws nearer, unity is broken up into
multiplicity. We move in stages from the solitary mediator of Don Quixote, atemporal and legendary, to the multitude in Dostoyevsky's throng. The "five or six models"
among whom, according to Stendhal, the fine society of
his time was divided, and the multiple Selves of Proust
are the stages of this downward march. The demon of the
possessed is called legion and he takes refuge in a *herd* of
swine. He is both one and many. This atomization of the
personality is the final stage of internal mediation.

Many writers have taken note of this multiplication of
mediators. In his last novel, *Der Komet,* Jean Paul takes
his inspiration from *Don Quixote*. His hero, Nicolaus
Markgraf, "like an actor, exchanges his soul for another's."
But he is incapable of sticking with the chosen role and
every time he reads a new book he changes his mediator.
Jean Paul's novel, however, explores only certain aspects
of imitative desire in the nineteenth century. The mediators remain distant. In Stendhal, Proust, and Dostoyevsky
it is on the level of *internal* mediation that the number of
models increases. And it is in internal mediation that the
profoundest meaning of the *modern* is found.

Beginning with Proust, the mediator may be literally
anyone at all and he may pop up *anywhere*. Mystical revelation presents a constant danger. A chance encounter
along the promenade at Balbec decides Marcel's fate. One
glance at "the little band" is enough to cast a spell on him.

> if by chance, I did catch sight of no matter which of
> the girls, since they all partook of the same special
> essence, it was as if I had seen projected before my

face in a shifting, diabolical hallucination, a little of the unfriendly and yet passionately coveted dream which, but a moment ago, had existed only—where it lay stagnant for all time—in my brain.

Proust's "no matter which" becomes so automatic in Dostoyevsky that it provokes a farcical horror. In this case as in others, Dostoyevsky presents us with the truth of the Proustian experience in an exaggerated form. The underground man, like Marcel, succumbs to the Other's prestige and suffers an attack of ontological fever in public. In both cases the hero finds he is in the presence of a "dream which is hostile yet passionately desired." If we read carefully we find that the two novelists reveal identical structures. The unknown officer, finding the underground man in his way, simply takes him by the shoulders and "removes" him. Proust's narrator is not himself the object of the little band's mistreatment, but he watches Albertine jump over the head of a terrified old man and he identifies with the victim. Proust and Dostoyevsky describe in the same way the mediator's arrogant bearing as he forces his way through the crowd, his disdainful indifference to the insects swarming at his feet, the impression of irresistible strength which he makes on the fascinated spectator. Everything in this mediator reveals a calm and serene superiority of *essence* which the miserable victim, crushed and trembling with hatred and adoration, tries in vain to steal.[2]

As the mediation becomes more unstable the yoke grows heavier. Don Quixote's mediation is a feudal monarchy which is sometimes more symbolic than real. But the underground man's mediation is a series of dictatorships as savage as they are temporary. The results of this convulsive state are not limited to any particular area of existence; on the contrary, they are *totalitarian*.

[2] See Chapter VIII for a treatment of this "masochism."

The empty eclecticism, the passing infatuations, the increasingly transitory fashions, the ever more rapid successions of theories, systems, and schools, and this "acceleration of history" which excites us these days, are, in Dostoyevsky's eyes, just so many converging aspects of the evolution we have just traced. The underground is a disintegration of individual and collective being. Dostoyevsky alone describes for us a phenomenon which must, however, be considered in the framework of history. We must not see in it, as some of the Russian novelist's admirers do, the sudden revelation of an eternal truth which previous writers and thinkers had all missed. Dostoyevsky himself envisaged the polymorphosis of his characters historically. The temporal advent of the underground mode of existence is stressed by Prince Myshkin in a passage of *The Idiot* tinged with excruciating irony:

> People of long ago (and I swear I have always been struck by this) were very different from people of our time: they were like another kind of human species. . . . In those days man had, as it were, one idea only; our own contemporaries are more nervous, further developed, more sensitive, capable of following two or three ideas at the same time. Modern man is broader and it is this, I would say, which prevents him from being a single, unified being as in past centuries.

Dostoyevsky summarizes in one sentence the whole road we have traveled. Starting with Cervantes' hero, who is steadfast in his loyalty and always identical with himself, we gradually come down to the underground man, a human rag soaked in shame and servitude, a ridiculous weather-vane placed atop the ruins of "Western humanism."

Thus the most diverse forms of triangular desire are organized into a universal structure. There is no aspect of desire, in any novelist, which cannot be linked with other aspects of his own novel and with all other novels. Desire thus appears as a dynamic structure extending from one end of novelistic literature to the other. This structure can be compared to an object falling in space, whose shape is always changing because of the increasing speed given it by the fall. Novelists, situated at different levels, describe this object as it appears to them. Usually they have only a suspicion of the various changes it has undergone and will yet undergo. They do not always see the connection between their own observations and those of their predecessors. The task of revealing that connection is incumbent upon a "phenomenology" of the novelistic work. This phenomenology does not have to observe the divisions between the various novels—moving freely from one to another it attempts to espouse the very movement of the metaphysical structure: it seeks to establish a "topology" of imitative desire.

CHAPTER IV

MASTER AND SLAVE

METAPHYSICAL desire is eminently contagious. Sometimes it is very hard to detect this quality, for desire follows the most unexpected paths in order to spread from
one person to another; it gains support from the obstacles
we set in its way, from the indignation it arouses, from the
ridicule we try to heap on it.

On several occasions we see the friends of Don Quixote
imitate his madness in order to cure him; they rush after
him, put on disguises, invent a thousand different distractions, and gradually reach the same heights of extravagance as the hero. This, for Cervantes, is the moment of
reckoning. He pauses a moment and pretends to be astonished at the sight of these doctors who are just as rabid as
their patient.

We must not conclude, like the romantics and like all
redressers of literary wrongs, that Cervantes has finally
decided to confound the "enemies of the ideal" and avenge
all the insults which he continuously heaps on Don Quixote. One of the arguments supporting the romantic interpretation is the obvious lack of sympathy Cervantes feels
for all who try to cure his hero. Since Cervantes is *against*
Don Quixote's sermonizers, he must be *for* his hero. This
is the way our romantic logic operates. Cervantes is much
simpler and at the same time much subtler. Nothing is
further from him than the "right and wrong," Manichean

concept of the novel. Cervantes quite simply wants to show us that Don Quixote spreads the ontological sickness to those around him. The contagion, which is obvious in the case of Sancho, affects everyone in contact with the hero and *especially those who are shocked or roused to indignation by his madness.*

The university graduate Samson Carrasco takes up arms as a knight only in order to restore the unfortunate gentleman to his lost health, but he begins to take the game seriously even before Don Quixote unseats him. "I don't think there is anyone more insane than my master," Samson's squire remarks, "for in order to restore another knight to his lost senses he has become insane himself, and is off in search of something which, when he finds it, might clout him one on the snout."

The squire proves a good prophet. Carrasco resents the humiliation suffered at the hands of Don Quixote. Now he cannot lay down his weapons until he has made his triumphant rival bite the dust. This psychological mechanism obviously fascinates Cervantes and we find more and more examples of it as we read on in the book. Altisidora, the Duchess' young companion, pretends she is in love with Don Quixote but her anger is real when she finds herself rejected. What can this anger mean but the beginning of desire?

The truly diabolical subtlety of the ontological sickness provides the clue to numerous episodes. We can particularly understand why the clumsy imitation of Avellaneda and the success of the first part become a capital theme in the second part of *Don Quixote*. The ambiguous nature of this success is marvelously typical of Don Quixote. The book's popularity spreads the knight's name and the account of his exploits to the farthest boundaries of the Christian world. The possibilities of contagion multiply. The supreme imitator is imitated; the work denouncing metaphysical desire is enlisted under its banner and becomes its best ally. What would Cervantes say if he could read the delirious interpretations which have appeared one after another since the end of the eighteenth century; what would we have said about Chamisso, Unamuno, or André Suarès? And the novelist suggests ironically that when he thinks he is denouncing the ontological sickness perhaps he too bears some resemblance to all the good Samaritans who rush at Don Quixote's heels along the road of folly.

The contagious nature of metaphysical desire is one of the most important points of novelistic revelation. Cervantes brings this out again and again. During his stay in Barcelona Don Quixote is addressed by an unknown man in these words:

> Go to the devil, Don Quixote de la Mancha! . . . You are a madman, and if you were that way for your self alone and behind the closed doors of your madness, there wouldn't be so much harm; but you have this talent for making anyone who has anything to do with you mad and senseless. And, for proof of what I say, you have only to look at the gentlemen who accompany you.

Don Quixote is not the only character of Cervantes' whose desire is contagious. Anselmo and Lothario provide another example of this strange phenomenon. Lothario's refusal to comply with the crazy demands of his friend is less emphatic and above all less insistent than the character attributed to him and the nature of his relationship with Anselmo would seem to require. Lothario succumbs to a sort of giddiness.

This same giddiness leads Veltchaninov to the house of Pavel Pavlovitch's fiancée. Here too we expect a firmer refusal, but Veltchaninov accepts the invitation. Like Lothario he enters into the game of his partner in mediation;

Dostoyevsky tells us he is the victim "of a strange seduction." There is no end to the similarities between *The Eternal Husband* and "The Curious Impertinent"!

Metaphysical desire is always contagious. It becomes even more so as the mediator draws nearer to the hero. Contagion and proximity are, after all, one and the same phenomenon. Internal mediation is present when one "catches" a nearby desire just as one would catch the plague or cholera, simply by contact with an infected person.

Vanity and snobbism obviously can flourish only in well-prepared ground, at the heart of a previously established vanity or snobbism. The nearer the mediator comes the more extensive are the ravages of mediation. Collective manifestations outweigh individual manifestations. The results of this evolution are infinite and appear only gradually.

In the world of internal mediation, the contagion is so widespread that everyone can become his neighbor's mediator without ever understanding the role he is playing. This person who is a mediator without realizing it may himself be incapable of spontaneous desire. Thus he will be tempted to copy the copy of his own desire. What was for him in the beginning only a whim is now transformed into a violent passion. We all know that every desire redoubles when it is seen to be shared. Two identical but opposite triangles are thus superimposed on each other. Desire circulates between the two rivals more and more quickly, and with every cycle it increases in intensity like the electric current in a battery which is being charged.

We now have a subject-mediator and a mediator-subject, a model-disciple and a disciple-model. Each imitates the other while claiming that his own desire is prior and previous. Each looks on the other as an atrociously cruel persecutor. All the relationships are symmetrical;

the two partners believe themselves separated by a bottomless abyss but there is nothing we can say of one which is not equally true of the other. There is a sterile opposition of contraries, which becomes more and more atrocious and empty as the two subjects approach each other and as their desire intensifies.

The more intense the hatred the nearer it brings us to the loathed rival. Everything it suggests to one, it suggests equally to the other, including the desire to *distinguish oneself* at all costs. The brother-enemies therefore always follow the same paths, which only increases their fury. They remind us of the two aldermen in *Don Quixote* who run over the mountains, braying, in search of a lost donkey. Their *imitation* is so good that the two companions constantly rush up to one another, believing that they have found the lost beast. But the beast is no longer alive; the wolves have devoured it.

Cervantes' allegory transposes the sufferings and vanity of double mediation into an ambiguous comic key. Novelists see little value in romantic individualism which, despite vain efforts to hide it, is always a product of opposition. Modern society is no longer anything but a *negative imitation* and the effort to leave the beaten paths forces everyone inevitably into the same ditch. Each novelist has described this failure, the mechanism of which is repeated in the smallest details of daily existence. Take for example the walk along the "front" taken by the ladies and gentlemen on holiday at Balbec:

> All these people . . . pretending not to see so as to let it be thought that they were not interested, but covertly watching, for fear of running against the people who were walking beside or coming towards them, did, in fact, butt into them, became entangled with them, because each was mutually the object of the same secret attention veiled beneath the same apparent disdain.

DOUBLE, or reciprocal, mediation enables us to complete certain descriptions sketched in the first chapter. We observed M. de Rênal copying his desire for a tutor on an *imaginary* desire of Valenod's. This imagination is the result of a completely subjective anguish. Valenod never considered making Julien his children's tutor. It was just a stroke of genius that made the old rogue of a father say: "We have a better offer." No one had made any such offer. He is the first to be surprised when he learns that the Mayor is interested in his good-for-nothing son.

Yet a little later we find Valenod suggesting to Julien that he enter his employ. Is Stendhal confusing the Valenod of M. de Rênal's imagination with the real Valenod who hasn't given a thought to Julien? Stendhal is not confusing anything: like Cervantes he wants to show the contagious nature of metaphysical desire. Rênal thought he was imitating Valenod's desire and now Valenod is imitating Rênal's desire.

The situation is now inextricable. Even if the whole world were to band together in order to convince M. de Rênal of the truth he would still refuse to accept it. The business man in him has always been suspicious of Valenod's intentions with regard to Julien; he is not likely to doubt them now when events have confirmed his false intuition. Reality springs from the illusion and provides it with a misleading guarantee. It is by an analogous process that peoples and politicians blame each other, with the greatest possible sincerity, for the conflicts between them.

In double mediation the metamorphosis of the object is common to both partners. We can see in it the fruit of a strange negative collaboration. Bourgeois thus do not need to "go over their proofs," as Rimbaud would say. They gaze at them every day in the scornful or envious eyes of their fellows. The opinion of a friendly neighbor can be overlooked, but the involuntary confession of a rival permits no doubt.

Whatever Julien was worth had nothing to do with his early successes. Those who made his career for him had neither real interest in him nor sincere affection for him. They cannot even appreciate what the young man can do for them. It is their rivalry which provides Julien with increases in salary and future prospects, and it is this rivalry which gains him admittance to the Hôtel de la Mole. There is as much difference between the real Julien and the Julien over whom the two worthies of Verrières argue as there is between the barber's basin and the helmet of Mambrino, but the nature of the difference has changed. The illusion is no longer humorous as in *Don Quixote*, and strangely enough, for that very reason, it is taken more seriously. The true bourgeois believes only in disagreeable platitudes. He even makes the disagreeable platitude the criterion of all truth. In double mediation it is not that one wants the object but that one does not want to see it in someone else's hands. Like all other elements of a universe that the bourgeois would like to be completely "positive," the transfiguration of the desired object itself has become negative.

The phenomenon of double mediation makes it possible to interpret a particularly puzzling passage in the second part of *Don Quixote*. Altisidora, the Duchess' maid who is able to mystify Don Quixote so easily, pretends to die and then to come to life again, and she describes to the onlookers her stay in the underworld:

> I arrived at the gate where I found a dozen devils playing ball, all wearing doublet and hose. They were wearing tabards with Flemish points and cuffs the same, leaving four finger-lengths of arm showing so that their hands would appear bigger. Their rackets were of fire. But what astonished me most was that they were using books instead of balls, and these books were filled with air and stuffing! a new and

original idea! But it wasn't that so much that made
me gape, as the fact that, although it would be natural for those who won to be happy and those who lost
to be sorry, everybody was grumbling and grousing
and cursing. . . . There was something else which
surprised me too . . . after the first volley the ball
was of no more use; so that with every strike the
number of old and new books grew astonishingly.

This devils' game of tennis symbolizes perfectly the reciprocal character which imitation assumes in double mediation. The players are opposed but alike, and even interchangeable, for they make exactly the same movements.
The ball they hit back and forth to one another represents
the oscillation of desire between the subject-mediator and
the mediator-subject. The players are *partners,* but they
agree only to disagree. No one wants to lose and yet,
strangely, there are only losers in that game: " . . .
everyone was grumbling and grousing and cursing." As
we know, each one holds the Other responsible for the
misfortune which falls upon him. This is truly double mediation, equal cause of suffering for all; it is a sterile conflict from which the players, who have come together of
their own accord, cannot withdraw. Altisidora's account is
a transparent allegory aimed at Don Quixote, for it is to
Don Quixote that the young girl is talking. It is this,
moreover, which gives the passage its enigmatic character: this story does not seem to belong in the novel of *Don
Quixote* any more than "The Curious Impertinent." It is
hard to see the connection between the sublime chivalric
folly and the sordid passion of the infernal players. But
the connection clarifies precisely the metaphysical theory
of desire and the inevitable transition from external to internal mediation. In this curious tale Cervantes ironically
affirms the unity of triangular desire. All imitated desire,
no matter how noble and inoffensive it appears at the be-

ginning, gradually drags its victims down into the infernal
regions. The solitary and distant mediation of Don Quixote is followed by double mediation. The partners in the
game of tennis are never less than two but their number
can increase indefinitely. Altisidora says vaguely that she
saw "a dozen" devils. From being double, reciprocal mediation could become triple, quadruple, multiple, until finally it affects the whole society. And the rapid play of
the rackets made of fire symbolizes the prodigious acceleration of the metaphysical process when one reaches the
"gates" of hell—the final stages of mediation.

The constraining force of the illusion grows as the contagion spreads and the number of its victims increases.
The initial madness grows, ripens, flowers, and is reflected
in the eyes of everyone. Everyone bears witness to it. Its
consequences are so spectacular that its imaginary germ is
buried for ever. All values are caught up in this whirlwind. Models and copies multiply more and more quickly
around the bourgeois who lives nonetheless in the eternal
—eternally ecstatic before the latest fashion, the latest
idol, the latest slogan. Ideas and men, systems and formulas follow one another in an ever more barren round. They
are the air and stuffing which Altisidora's diabolic players
hit back and forth to one another. As always in Cervantes,
the literary aspects of suggestion are particularly emphasized. At every strike of the racket "the number of old and
new books grew astonishingly." There is a gradual transition from chivalric novels to serial romances, to the modern
forms of collective suggestion which become increasingly abundant and obsessive. Thus the most skilful advertising does not try to convince that a product is superior but that it is desired by Others. Triangular structure
penetrates the most petty details of daily existence. As we
sink deeper into the hell of reciprocal mediation, the process described by Cervantes becomes more universal, more
ridiculous, and more catastrophic.

WE HAVE said that at the origin of a desire there is always the spectacle of another real or illusory desire. There would seem to be many exceptions to this law. It is Mathilde's sudden *indifference* which excites Julien's desire. A little later it is Julien's heroic pretense of indifference, even more than the rival desire of Mme de Fervacques, which reawakens Mathilde's desire. Indifference plays a role in the genesis of these desires which would seem to contradict the results of our analyses.

Before this objection is answered, something else must be said parenthetically. In sexual desire, the presence of a rival is not needed in order to term the desire triangular. The beloved is divided into both subject and object in the lover's eyes. Sartre perceived this phenomenon and based his analysis of love, sadism, and masochism on it in *Being and Nothingness*. This division produces a triangle whose three corners are occupied by the lover, the beloved, and the body of this beloved. Sexual desire, like other triangular desires, is always contagious. To speak of contagion is inevitably to speak of a second desire which is fixed on the same object as the original desire. To imitate one's lover's desire is to desire *oneself*, thanks to that lover's desire. This particular form of double mediation is called "coquetry."

The coquette does not wish to surrender her precious self to the desire which she arouses, but were she not to provoke it, she would not feel so precious. The favor she finds in her own eyes is based exclusively on the favor with which she is regarded by Others. For this reason the coquette is constantly looking for proofs of this favor; she encourages and stirs up her lover's desires, not in order to give herself to him but to enable her the better to refuse him.

The coquette's indifference toward her lover's sufferings is not feigned but it has nothing to do with ordinary indifference. It is not an absence of desire; it is the other side of a desire of oneself. The lover is fascinated by it. He even believes he sees in his mistress' indifference that divine autonomy of which he feels he has been deprived and which he burns to acquire. This is why desire is stimulated by coquetry, and in its turn desire feeds coquetry. Thus we have a vicious circle of double mediation.

The lover's "despair" and the loved one's coquetry increase step by step together for the two sentiments are copied from each other. It is the same desire, growing ever more intense, which circulates between the two partners. If the lovers are never in accord, it is not because they are too "different," as common sense and sentimental novels assert, but because they are too alike, because each is a copy of the other. But the more they grow alike the more different they imagine themselves. The *sameness* by which they are obsessed appears to them as an absolute *otherness*. Double mediation secures an opposition as radical as it is meaningless, a line by line and point by point opposition of two symmetrical and opposite figures.

In this case, as in others, it is nearness which brings about the conflict. A fundamental law is involved which has as much control over "cerebral" love as it has over social evolution. This proximity, never known but always felt, is the cause of the lover's despair; he cannot despise the loved one without despising himself; he cannot desire her without her desiring herself. Like Alceste, he sinks into *misanthropy.*[1]

We may now close the parenthesis and answer the objection we outlined before. In the universe of internal mediation indifference is never simply neutral; it is never pure absence of desire. To the observer it always appears as the exterior aspect of a desire of oneself. And it is this supposed desire which is imitated. Far from contradicting

[1] Moreover coquetry is a very unstable mediation, skin-deep, and constantly in need of being renewed by fresh desires. It belongs to

the laws of metaphysical desire, the dialectic of indifference confirms them.

The indifferent person always seems to possess that radiant self-mastery which we all seek. He seems to live in a
closed circuit, enjoying his own being, in a state of happiness which nothing can disturb. He is God. When he
feigns indifference to Mathilde and arouses Mme de Fervacques' desire, Julien is offering not one but two desires
for the girl to imitate. He is trying to multiply the chances
of contagion. This is the dandy Korassof's "Russian strategy." But it was no invention of Korassof's. M. Sorel, the
father, has already combined the two recipes in his negotiations with M. de Rênal. In the latter's presence, he pretends an indifference which accentuates his vague allusions to other more advantageous offers. There is no
difference of structure between the peasant's wiles and
the refinements of cerebral love.

In the world of internal mediation every desire can
produce other rival desires. If the desiring subject yields
to the impulse which draws him toward the object, if he
reveals his desire to others, then he creates new obstacles
at every step of the way and strengthens already existing
ones. The secret of success, in business as well as in love,
is dissimulation. One must hide the desire one feels and
pretend a desire one does not feel. One must lie. It is always by lying that Stendhal's characters achieve what

---

the upper regions of internal mediation. As the mediator approaches
the desiring subject, coquetry disappears. The loved woman does
not succumb to her lover's contagion. She devotes herself to a
secret disdain which is too intense for the lover's desire to be able
to counterbalance. Thus desire, instead of raising the woman in her
own eyes, lessens the lover in her opinion. The lover is relegated to
the realm of the banal, the insipid, and the sordid where dwell
objects who *let themselves be possessed.*

they want, at least as long as they are not dealing with a passionate being. But passionate beings are extremely rare in the post-revolutionary universe.

Stendhal remarks again and again that to show a vain woman that one desires her is to show oneself inferior. This means exposing oneself to endless desiring without ever arousing desire. When double mediation invades the domain of love, all hope of reciprocity vanishes. In his notes Flaubert formulates this absolute principle that "two beings never love each other at the same time." [2] All communion has disappeared from a sentiment which is defined by communion itself. The word outlives the thing and designates the *contrary* of what it originally designated. Deviated transcendency is always characterized by a slant in language which is both subtle and glaring. The love of Mathilde and of Mme de Rênal are as different as day and night yet the same word is used for both sentiments.

Romantic passion is thus exactly the reverse of what it pretends to be. It is not abandonment to the Other but an implacable war waged by two rival vanities. The egotistical love of Tristan and Isolde, the first of the romantic heroes, heralds a future of discord. Denis de Rougemont analyzes the myth with great precision and arrives at the truth hidden by the poet: the truth seen by the novelists. Tristan and Isolde "love each other, but each loves the other *from the standpoint of self and not from the other's standpoint.* Their unhappiness thus originates in a false reciprocity, which disguises a twin narcissism. So much is this so that at times there pierces through their excessive passion a kind of hatred of the beloved" [3] (italics added).

[2] Marie-Jeanne Durry, *Flaubert et Ses Projets Inédits* (Paris: Librairie Nizet [1950]), p. 25.

[3] *Love in the Western World,* trans. by Montgomery Belgion (New York: Doubleday, 1957), p. 44.

That which remains implicit in the lovers of Thomas and of Béroul is completely explicit in the Stendhalian novel. Like two dancers obeying the baton of an invisible conductor, the two partners observe a perfect symmetry: the mechanism of their desire is identical. By feigning indifference Julien is winding up a spring in Mathilde which is like his own spring to which the young girl holds the key. Double mediation transforms amorous relationships into a struggle which proceeds according to set rules. Victory belongs to the lover who can best maintain his lie. Revealing one's desire is an error which is only the more inexcusable for the fact that one is no longer tempted to make it once one's partner has revealed his own desire.

Julien made this mistake at the beginning of his relationship with Mathilde. He let down his guard for one moment. Mathilde was his; he did not know how to hide from her his happiness, rather mediocre, it is true, but sufficient to make the *vaniteuse* recoil from him. Julien succeeds in re-establishing the situation only by a truly heroic effort of hypocrisy. He must expiate one moment's frankness by a mountain of lies. He lies to Mathilde, he lies to Mme de Fervacques, he lies to the whole De la Mole family. The accumulated weight of these lies finally tips the scales in his favor; the current of the imitation is reversed and Mathilde throws herself into his arms.

Mathilde admits that she is a *slave*. The word is not too strong and it reveals the nature of the struggle. In double mediation each one stakes his freedom against the other's. The struggle ends when one of the partners admits his desire and humbles his pride. Henceforth no reversal of imitation is possible, for the *slave's* admitted desire destroys that of the *master* and ensures his genuine indifference. This indifference in turn makes the slave desperate and increases his desire. The two sentiments are identical since they are copied from each other; they exert their force in the same direction and secure the stability of the structure.

This dialectic of "master and slave" presents curious analogies with the Hegelian dialectic, but there are also great differences. The Hegelian dialectic is situated in a violent past. It exhausts its last force with the appearance of the nineteenth century and of democracy. The novelistic dialectic on the contrary appears in the post-Napoleonic universe. For Stendhal as for Hegel the reign of individual violence is over; it must make way for something else. Hegel relied on logic and historical reflection to determine that something else. When violence and the arbitrary no longer control human relationships, then *Befriedigung*, reconciliation, must necessarily succeed them. The reign of spirit must begin. Contemporary Hegelians, especially the Marxists, still nourish this hope. They have simply postponed the coming of spirit. Hegel, they say, was a little mistaken about the date. He did not take certain economic factors into account in his calculations . . .

But the novelist mistrusts logical deductions. He looks around him and within him. He finds nothing to indicate that the famous reconciliation is just around the corner. Stendhalian vanity, Proustian snobbism, and the Dostoyevskian underground are the new forms assumed by the struggle of consciousnesses in a universe of physical non-violence. Force is only the crudest weapon available to consciousnesses drawn up against each other and consumed by their own nothingness. Deprive them of this weapon, Stendhal tells us, and they will make others such as past centuries were not able to foresee. They will choose new areas of combat, like impenitent gamblers whom paternal legislation cannot protect from themselves, for with every restriction they invent new ways of losing their money. Whatever political or social system is somehow imposed on them, men will never achieve the happiness and peace of which the revolutionaries dream, nor the bleating harmony which scares the reactionaries. They will always get on together just enough to enable them never to agree. They will adapt themselves to the circumstances which seem least propitious to discord and they will never tire of inventing new forms of conflict.

It is the "underground" forms of the struggle of consciousnesses which are studied by the modern novelists. If the novel is the source of the greatest existential and social truth in the nineteenth century, it is because only the novel has turned its attention to the regions of existence where spiritual energy has taken refuge. The triangle of desire has interested hardly anyone but vaudevillists and novelists of genius. Valéry was right in associating one with the other but he was wrong when he drew from this promiscuity, so scandalous in his eyes, an extremely bourgeois and academic argument against the novel. In the final analysis, Valéry's agility and the positivist clumsiness result in the same obtuseness when confronted with the novelists' truth. This need not surprise us since both sides are concerned with defending the myth of their own autonomy. Solipsistic idealism and positivism wish to recognize only the solitary individual and the collectivity; these two abstractions are no doubt flattering to the Self which wishes to view everything from on high, but one is just as hollow as the other. Only the novelist, precisely to the extent to which he is capable of recognizing his own servitude, gropes toward the concrete—toward that hostile dialogue between Self and Other which parodies the Hegelian struggle for recognition.

The two themes of *Phenomenology of the Mind* which particularly interest contemporary readers are the "unhappy consciousness" and the "dialectic of master and slave." We all have a vague feeling that only a synthesis of these two fascinating themes could throw light on our problems. That original synthesis, impossible in Hegel's system, is precisely what the novelistic dialectic permits us to glimpse. The hero of internal mediation is an unhappy consciousness who relives the primordial struggle beyond all physical threat and stakes his freedom on the least of his desires.

The Hegelian dialectic rested on physical courage. Whoever has no fear will be the master, whoever is afraid will be the slave. The novelistic dialectic rests on hypocrisy. Violence, far from serving the interests of whoever exerts it, reveals the intensity of his desire; thus it is a sign of slavery. Mathilde's eyes shine with joy when Julien seizes a rapier from the wall of the library. Julien notices her happiness and prudently puts down the weapon whose decorative role is symbolic.

In the universe of internal mediation—at least in the upper regions—force has lost its prestige. The elementary rights of individuals are respected but if one is not strong enough to live in freedom one succumbs to the evil spell of vain rivalry. The triumph of *Black* over *Red* symbolizes this defeat of force. The crumbling of Napoleon's Empire and the inauguration of a reactionary and clerical regime are the *signs* of a metaphysical and social revolution whose influence is incalculable. His contemporaries did not understand that, beginning with *The Red and the Black*, Stendhal rose above partisan quarrels. Have we understood it yet?

THE RED AND THE BLACK

ACCORDING to literary historians Stendhal inherited most of his ideas from the *philosophes* or the *idéologues.*

If this were true, this novelist whom we consider so great would not have a thought of his own; for his whole life he would remain faithful to the thought of others. It is a hard legend to kill. It is popular both with those who would deny intelligence in the novel and with those who are trying to find a complete Stendhalian system and think they have found it in his early writing, that is, in the only more or less didactic texts ever written by Stendhal.

Their thoughts dwell longingly on a huge key which would open all the gates of his work. A whole trousseau can be gathered effortlessly from the childish *Letters to Pauline,* from the *Journal,* and from his *New Philosophy.* There is a loud rattle in the lock but the gates remain closed. No page of *The Red and the Black* will ever be explained by means of Cabanis or Destutt de Tracy. Except for occasional borrowings from the system of temperaments there is no trace of the theories of his youth in the novels of his maturity. Stendhal is one of the few thinkers of his time who won his independence from the giants of the preceding epoch. For this reason he can render homage as an equal to the gods of his youth. Most of his romantic contemporaries are incapable of doing as much; they look on the rationalist Pantheon with great condescension, but should it enter their head to reason we find ourselves back in the century of the Enlightenment. Their opinions are different and even antithetical but the intellectual frameworks have not changed.

Stendhal does not give up thinking the day he stops copying the thought of others; he begins to think for himself. If the writer had never changed his opinion on the great political and social problems, why did he declare, at the beginning of the *Life of Henry Brulard,* that he had at last decided on his point of view regarding the nobility? Nothing in the Stendhalian vision is more important than the nobility, yet this definitive point of view is never systematically set down. The real Stendhal had an aversion to didacticism. His original thought *is* the novel and only the novel, for the moment Stendhal escapes from his characters the ghost of the Other begins to haunt him again. Therefore everything has to be gathered from his novels. The non-novelistic texts sometimes contribute details but they should be handled with care.

Far from blindly trusting the past, Stendhal, even as early as *De l'Amour,* considers the problem of the *error* in Montesquieu and other great minds of the eighteenth century. The alleged disciple wonders why such keen observers as the *philosophes* should have been so completely wrong in their visions of the future. At the end of *Memoirs of a Tourist* the theme of philosophical error is resumed and studied further. Stendhal finds nothing in Montesquieu to justify the condemnation of Louis-Philippe. The bourgeois king gave the French greater liberty and prosperity than ever before. The progress is real but it does not accord the people who benefit from it the increase of happiness foreseen by the theoreticians.

Stendhal's own duty is indicated to him by the mistakes of the *philosophes.* He must amend the conclusions of abstract intelligence by contact with experience. The intact Bastilles limited the vision of prerevolutionary thinkers.

The Bastilles have fallen and the world is changing at a dizzying pace. Stendhal finds he is straddling several universes. He is observing the constitutional monarchy but he has not forgotten the *ancien régime;* he has visited England; and he keeps up with the constant stream of books dealing with the United States.

All the nations Stendhal is concerned with have embarked on the same adventure but they are moving at different speeds. The novelist is living in a veritable laboratory of historical and sociological observation. His novels are, in a sense, merely this same laboratory carried to the second degree. In them Stendhal brings together various elements which would remain isolated from each other even in the modern world. He confronts the provinces and Paris, aristocrats and bourgeois, France and Italy, and even the present and the past. Various experiments are carried out and they all have the same aim— they are all meant to answer the same fundamental question: "Why are men not happy in the modern world?"

This question is not original. Everybody, or almost everybody, was asking it in Stendhal's day. But few ask it sincerely, without having already decided a priori that one more or one less revolution is required. In his non-novelistic writings Stendhal often seems to request both at the same time. But these secondary texts should not be allowed to worry us too much. Stendhal's real answer is blended into his novels, scattered through them; it is diffuse, full of hesitations and modifications. Stendhal is as prudent in the novels as he can be assertive, when he is expressing his own "personal" opinion in the face of the opinion of others.

WHY ARE men not happy in the modern world? Stendhal's answer cannot be expressed in the language of political parties or of the various "social sciences." It is nonsense to both bourgeois common sense and romantic "idealism." We are not happy, says Stendhal, because we are *vaniteux*.

Morality and psychology are not the only sources of this answer. Stendhalian vanity has a historical component which is essential and which we must now clarify. In order to do this, we must first set forth Stendhal's idea of nobility, which, he tells us in the *Life of Henry Brulard,* took a solid form rather late in his development.

In Stendhal's eyes, nobility belongs to the man whose desires come from within himself and who exerts every ounce of his energy to satisfy them. Nobility, in the spiritual sense of the term, is therefore exactly synonomous with passion. The noble being rises above others by the strength of his desire. There must originally be nobility in the spiritual sense for there to be nobility in the social sense. At a certain point in history both senses of the word "noble" coincided, at least theoretically. This coincidence is illustrated in *The Italian Chronicles.* In fourteenth- and fifteenth-century Italy the greatest passions were born and developed in the elite of society.

This relative accord between the social organization and natural hierarchy of men cannot last. The nobleman's becoming aware of it is, in a sense, sufficient to precipitate its dissolution. A comparison is necessary to discover that one is superior to others: comparison means bringing closer together, putting on the same level, and, to a certain extent, treating the things compared in the same way. The equality of man cannot be denied unless it is first posited, however briefly. The oscillation between pride and shame which defines metaphysical desire can already be found in this first comparison. The nobleman who makes the comparison becomes a little more noble in the social sense but a little less noble in the spiritual sense. He begins the reflection that will gradually cut him off from his own nobility and transform it into a mere possession mediated by the *look* of the commoner. The nobleman as an individual is thus the passionate being *par excellence,* but nobility as a class is devoted to vanity. The more nobility is transformed into a caste and becomes hereditary, the more it closes its ranks to the passionate being who might rise from the lower classes and the more serious the ontological sickness becomes. Henceforth the nobility will be leading constantly toward vanity the other classes dedicated to its imitation and will precede them along the fatal road of metaphysical desire.

Thus the nobility is the first class to become decadent, and the history of this decadence is identical with the inevitable evolution of metaphysical desire. The nobility is already eaten up with vanity when it rushes to Versailles, drawn by the lure of vain rewards. Louis XIV is not the demigod worshipped by the royalists, nor is he the oriental tyrant loathed by the Jacobins. He is a clever politician who distrusts the aristocracy and uses its vanity as a means of government, thereby hastening the decomposition of the noble soul. The aristocracy lets itself be drawn into sterile rivalries by the monarchy which reserves the right of arbitration. The Duc de Saint-Simon, perceptive but fascinated by the king, observes with quenchless rage this emasculation of the nobility. Saint-Simon, the historian of "impotent hatred," is one of Stendhal's and Proust's great teachers.

The absolute monarchy is one stage on the road to revolution and to the most modern forms of vanity. But it is only a stage. The vanity of the court presents a strong contrast with true nobility but it makes an equally strong contrast with the vanity of the bourgeois. At Versailles the slightest desires must be approved and permitted by a whim of the King. Existence at the court is a perpetual imitation of Louis XIV. The Sun King is the mediator for all who surround him, and this mediator remains separated from his faithful followers by an immense spiritual distance. The King cannot become the rival of his own subjects. M. de Montespan would suffer much more were his wife being unfaithful to him with an ordinary mortal. The theory of "divine right" provides a perfect definition of the particular type of *external mediation* which flourishes at Versailles and in the whole of France during the last two centuries of the monarchy.

What was the state of mind of a courtier of the *ancien régime,* or rather what was Stendhal's impression of it? Several secondary characters in his novels and the brief but suggestive remarks scattered through some twenty works provide us with a fairly precise answer to that question. The pain caused by vanity exists in the eighteenth century but it is not unbearable. It is still possible to enjoy oneself in the protective shade of the monarchy somewhat like children at the feet of their parents. Indeed a delicate pleasure is found in mocking the futile and rigorous rules of a perpetually idle existence. The great lord has a perfect ease and grace by knowing that he is nearer the sun than other human beings and thus a little less human than they, that he is illuminated by the divine rays. He always knows exactly what to say and what not to say, what to do and what not to do. He is not afraid of being ridiculed and he gladly laughs in ridicule of others. Anything which is the slightest bit different from the latest fashion at court is ridiculous in his eyes; thus everything outside Versailles and Paris is ridiculous. It is impossible to imagine a more favorable setting for the growth of a comic theater than this universe of courtiers. Not a single allusion is lost on this public which is not many but *one.* Diderot would have been astonished to discover that laughter in the theater disappears with the "tyrant!"

The revolution destroys only one thing—but that one thing is the most important of all though it seems trivial to barren minds—the divine right of kings. After the Restoration Louis, Charles, and Philippe ascend the throne; they cling to it and descend from it more or less precipitously; only fools pay any attention to these monotonous gymnastics. The monarchy no longer exists. Stendhal insists on this fact at some length in the last part of *Lucien Leuwen*. The ceremonies at Versailles cannot turn the head of a positive-minded banker. The real power is elsewhere. And this false king, Louis-Philippe, plays the stock exchange, making himself—the ultimate downfall!—the *rival* of his own subjects!

This last touch gives us the key to the situation. The courtier's external mediation is replaced by a system of internal mediation in which the pseudo-king himself takes part. The revolutionaries thought they would be destroying vanity when they destroyed the privileges of the noble. But vanity is like a virulent cancer that spreads in a more serious form throughout the body just when one thinks it has been removed. Who is there left to imitate after the "tyrant"? Henceforth men shall copy each other; idolatry of one person is replaced by hatred of a hundred thousand rivals. In Balzac's opinion, too, there is no other god but envy for the modern crowd whose greed is no longer stemmed and held within acceptable limits by the monarch. *Men will become gods for each other.* Young men of the nobility and of the middle class come to Paris to seek their fortune as courtiers once came to Versailles. They crowd into the garrets of the Latin Quarter as once they used to pile into the attics of Versailles. Democracy is one vast middle-class court where the courtiers are everywhere and the king is nowhere. Balzac, whose observations in all these matters frequently corroborate Stendhal's, has also described this phenomenon: "In the mon-

archy you have either courtiers or servants, whereas
under a Charter you are served, flattered and fawned on
by free men." When speaking of the United States,
Tocqueville too mentions the "esprit de cour" which
reigns in the democracies. The sociologist's reflection
throws a vivid light on the transition from external to internal mediation:

> When all the privileges of birth and fortune have
> been destroyed so that all professions are open to ev-
> eryone and it is possible to climb to the top by one-
> self, an immense and easy career seems available to
> men's ambitions, and they gladly imagine a great des-
> tiny for themselves. But they are mistaken, as daily
> experience proves to them. The very equality which
> enables each citizen to sustain great hopes makes all
> citizens equally weak. It limits their strength on all
> sides at the same time as it allows their desires to
> spread.
>
> . . . .
>
> They have destroyed the annoying privileges of
> some of their fellow-men; they encounter the compe-
> tition of everyone. The boundary has changed its
> shape rather than its position.
>
> . . . .
>
> The constant opposition on the one hand of in-
> stincts which give birth to equality and on the other
> of the means provided to satisfy them, torments and
> tires souls. . . . However democratic the social state
> and political constitution of a nation may be, yet in-
> evitably . . . each of its citizens will behold around
> him several aspects which dominate him, and it can
> be anticipated that he will obstinately fix his eyes in
> this one direction.

We find in Stendhal this "uneasiness" which Tocqueville
attributes to democratic regimes. The vanity of the *ancien
régime* was gay, unconcerned, and frivolous; the vanity of

the nineteenth century is sad and suspicious; it has a terrible fear of ridicule. "Envy, jealousy, and impotent hatred" are the accompaniment of internal mediation. Stendhal declares that everything has changed in a country when even fools—always the most stable element—have changed. The fool of 1780 wanted to be witty; to make people laugh was his only ambition. The fool of 1825 wants to be serious and formal. He is set on appearing profound and easily succeeds, the novelist adds, because he is truly unhappy. Stendhal never tires of describing the effects of *la vanité triste* on the customs and psychology of the French. The aristocrats are most hard hit.

When one stops considering the serious results of the revolution, one of the first sights that strikes one's imagination is the present state of French society. I spent my youth among great lords who were very pleasant; today they are old, disagreeable reactionaries. At first I thought their peevish humor was an unfortunate effect of age, so I made the acquaintance of their children who will inherit great wealth and noble titles, in fact most of the privileges that men drawn together in society can confer on some among them; I found them sunk even deeper in despondency than their parents.

The transition from external to internal mediation constitutes the supreme phase in the decline of the nobility. Revolution and emigration completed what reflection had begun; the nobleman, physically separated from his privileges, is henceforth forced to see them for what they really are—*arbitrary*. Stendhal clearly understood that the revolution could not destroy the nobility by taking away its privileges. But the nobility could destroy itself by desiring that of which it had been deprived by the bourgeoisie, and by devoting itself to the ignoble sentiments of internal mediation. To realize that the privilege is arbitrary and to still desire it is obviously the height of vanity. The noble thinks he is defending his nobility by fighting for its privileges against the other classes of a nation but he only succeeds in ruining it. He desires to recuperate his wealth as a bourgeois might and the envy of the bourgeoisie stimulates his desire and endows the pettiest of honorary trifles with immense value. Mediated by each other, henceforth the two classes will desire the same things in the same way. The Restoration duke who regains his titles and fortune, thanks to the millions granted to the *émigrés*, is little more than a bourgeois "who won in the lottery." The nobleman constantly grows nearer the bourgeois, even in the hatred he feels for him. They are all ignoble, Stendhal writes somewhat strongly in his letter to Balzac, *because they prize nobility...*

Only their elegant manners and politeness, the results of long training, give the nobles a little distinction over the bourgeoisie, and even this will soon disappear. Double mediation is a melting-pot in which differences among classes and individuals gradually dissolve. It functions all the more efficiently because it does not even appear to affect diversity. In fact, the latter is even given a fresh though deceptive brilliance: the opposition of the Same to the Same, which flourishes everywhere, will hide itself for a long time to come behind traditional diversity, sheltering new conflicts behind the shadow of old ones and nourishing belief in the integral survival of the past.

Under the Restoration the nobility seems more alive than ever. Never have its privileges been more desired, nor its ancient families so eager to emphasize the barriers between themselves and the common people. Superficial observers are not aware that internal mediation is at work; they can only conceive uniformity as that of marbles in a bag or sheep in a meadow. They do not recognize the modern tendency to identity in passionate divisions, their own divisions. But the clash of cymbals is loudest when they fit each other exactly.

Because it is no longer distinct the aristocracy tries to distinguish itself, and it succeeds marvelously—but that does not make it any more noble. It is a fact, for instance, that under the constitutional monarchy the aristocracy is the stuffiest and most virtuous class in the nation. The frivolous and seductive nobleman of the Louis XV era has been replaced by the scowling and morose gentleman of the Restoration. This depressing character lives on his property, he works hard, goes to bed early, and worst of all, even manages to economize. What is the significance of such austere morals? Is it really a return to the "ancestral virtues"? This is what we are told constantly in the *bien-pensant* journals but there is no need to believe it. This gloomy, sour-tempered, and totally negative kind of wisdom is typically bourgeois. The aristocracy is trying to prove to the Others that it has "earned" its privileges; that is why it borrows its code of ethics from the class which is competing for those same privileges. Mediated by its bourgeois audience, the nobility copies the bourgeoisie without even realizing it. In *Memoirs of a Tourist* Stendhal remarks sardonically that the revolution has bequeathed to the French aristocracy the customs of democratic, protestant Geneva.

Thus their very hatred of the bourgeoisie makes them middle-class. And, since mediation is reciprocal, we must expect to find a bourgeois-gentleman to match the gentleman-bourgeois, we must anticipate a bourgeois comedy which is symmetrical and inverse to the aristocratic comedy. The courtiers may copy Rousseau's *vicaire savoyard* in order to capture the good opinion of the bourgeois, but the bourgeois will also play at being great lords to impress the aristocrats. The type of the bourgeois imitator reaches the height of comic perfection in the character of Baron

Nerwinde in *Lamiel*. Nerwinde, the son of a general of the Empire, slavishly and laboriously copies a synthetic model, made up in equal parts of a *roué* of the *ancien régime* and a dandy from across the Channel. Nerwinde leads a tedious and boring existence, but its very disorder he has organized methodically. He goes bankrupt conscientiously while keeping very exact accounts. He does it all to make people forget—and to make himself forget—that he is the grandson of a hatter from Périgueux.

Double mediation flourishes everywhere; there is a "set to partners" in every figure of Stendhal's social ballet. Everything is reversed from its previous state. Stendhal's wit amuses us but it seems a little too geometric to be true. It is important to note that Tocqueville, who is a completely humorless observer, makes assertions parallel to Stendhal's. In *The Ancient Regime and the Revolution*, for instance, we find the paradox of an aristocracy that by its opposition to the middle class begins to resemble it, and that adopts all the virtues of which the middle class is trying to rid itself. He writes: "The most anti-democratic classes of the nation reveal most clearly to us the kind of morality it is reasonable to expect from a democracy."

When the aristocracy seems most alive is precisely when it is most dead. In an early edition of *Lamiel* Nerwinde is called D'Aubigné; this imitative dandy belonged to the aristocracy, not to the parvenu middle class: he was a descendant of Mme de Maintenon. Otherwise his conduct was exactly the same as in the last version of the novel. No doubt Stendhal chose the parvenu bourgeois—the commoner—to play the comedy of the nobility because he felt that the comic effect would be more apparent and reliable, but this does not mean he was mistaken in the first version; it illustrates an essential aspect of the Stendhalian truth. In that case it was a nobleman by blood who played the comedy of nobility. With or without a coat-of-arms, one can "desire" nobility, under Louis-Philippe, only in the manner of Molière's *bourgeois gentilhomme*. One can only mime it, as passionately as M. Jourdain but less naïvely. It is this kind of mimicry which Stendhal is trying to reveal to us. The complexity of the task and the fragmentation of the public—which are, ultimately, one and the same phenomenon—make the theater unsuited to carrying out this literary function. Comic theater died with the monarchy and "gay vanity." A more flexible genre is needed to describe the infinite metamorphoses of *vanité triste* and reveal how void are its oppositions. This genre is the novel. Stendhal finally understood this; after long years of effort and failure, which transformed his soul, he gave up the theater. But he never renounced his ambition of becoming a great comic writer. All novelistic works have a tendency to the comic and Stendhal's are no exception. Flaubert excels himself in *Bouvard et Pécuchet;* Proust reaches his peak in the comic figure of the Baron Charlus; Stendhal sums up and completes his work in the great comic scenes of *Lamiel.*

THE PARADOX of an aristocracy that becomes democratic through its very hatred of democracy is nowhere more striking than in political life. The tendency of the nobility to become bourgeois is clearly seen in its sympathy for the *ultra* party, a party devoted entirely to the defense of privilege; this party's conflict with Louis XVIII showed clearly that the monarchy was no longer the polar star of the nobility but a political instrument in the hands of the noble party. This noble party is oriented not toward the king but toward the rival bourgeoisie. The *ultra* ideology is merely the pure and simple reversal of revolutionary ideology. The theme throughout is *reaction* and reveals the negative slavery of internal mediation. Party rule is the

natural political expression of this mediation; party platforms do not bring about political opposition—opposition
brings about party platforms.

To understand how ignoble ultracism is, it must be
compared with a form of thought which was anterior to
the revolution and which, in its time, convinced a whole
section of the nobility: the philosophy of the Enlightenment. Stendhal believes that this philosophy is the only
one possible for nobility that intends to remain noble in
the exercise of its thought. When a genuine aristocrat—
and there were still a few during the last century of the
monarchy—enters the territory of thought, he does not
abandon his native virtues. He remains spontaneous even
in his reflection. Unlike the ultras he does not expect the
ideas he adopts to serve the interests of his class, any more
than he would ask a challenger, in a truly heroic era, to
present proof of nobility; the challenge alone would prove
the nobility of the challenger, in the eyes of someone with
self-respect. In the realm of thought rational evidence
takes the place of the challenge. The nobleman accepts
the challenge and judges everything in universal terms.
He goes straight to the most general truths and applies
them to all mankind. He does not acknowledge any exceptions, especially those from which he would profit. In
Montesquieu, and in the best of the enlightened nobles of
the eighteenth century, there is no distinction between
the aristocratic and the liberal mind. Eighteenth-century
rationalism is noble even in its illusions; it puts its trust in
"human nature." It does not allow for the irrational in
human relations, nor does it recognize metaphysical imitation, which frustrates the calculations of sound reflection. Montesquieu would have been less likeable had he
foreseen the *vanité triste* of the nineteenth century.

Moreover, we soon realize that rationalism means the
death of privilege. Truly noble reflection resigns itself to

that death, just as the truly noble warrior is prepared to die on the battlefield. The nobility cannot reflect on itself and remain noble without destroying itself as a caste; and since the revolution forced the nobility to think about itself, its own extinction is the only choice left to it. The nobility can die nobly by the one and only political gesture worthy of it, the destruction of its own privileged existence—the night of August 4, 1789.[1] It dies meanly, in a bourgeois fashion, on the benches of some House of Lords, confronted by Valenods whom it ends up resembling through fighting with them over the spoils. This was the solution of the ultras.

First came the nobility; then followed the noble class; finally only a noble party is left. After the period when the two coincided, spiritual and social nobility now tend to exclude each other; henceforth the incompatibilty of privilege with greatness of soul is so radical that it is patent even in the attempts to conceal it. Take for example the justification of privilege given by Dr. du Périer, the intellectual jack-of-all-trades of the Nancy nobility:

> A man is born a duke, a millionaire and a peer of France, it is not for him to consider whether his position conforms with virtue, or with the general good or with other fine ideas. His position is good; so he should do everything to maintain and improve it, or be despised generally as a coward and a fool.

Du Périer would like to convince us that the nineteenth-century nobleman is still living in a happy era, not yet affected by the "look" of the Other, still enjoying his privileges spontaneously. Yet the lie is so flagrant that Du Périer does not phrase it directly; he uses a negative periphrasis that suggests without affirming: "It is not for him to

[1] During the night the deputies of the aristocracy at the revolutionary *Assemblée constituante* voted the abolition of most feudal privileges.

consider," etc. Despite this oratorical precaution, the "look" of the Other is too obsessive and Du Périer is forced to acknowledge it in the following sentence. But then he imagines a cynical point of honor to which this "look" forces the aristocrat to submit. If the privileged person does not hang on to his privilege, "he will be despised as a coward or a fool." Du Périer is once again lying. Aristocrats are neither innocent nor cynical: they are merely *vaniteux;* they want privilege merely as parvenus. This is the horrible truth which must be hidden at all cost. They are ignoble *because they prize nobility.*

Since the Revolution no one can be privileged without knowing it. Stendhal's kind of hero is impossible in France. Stendhal likes to believe that he is still just possible in Italy. In that happy country, scarcely touched by the Revolution, reflection and concern with the Other have not yet completely poisoned enjoyment of the world and of oneself. A truly heroic soul is still compatible with the privileged circumstances which allow him free play. Fabrice del Dongo can be spontaneous and generous in the midst of an injustice from which he benefits.

First we see Fabrice flying to the aid of an emperor who embodies the spirit of the Revolution; a little later we find our hero, haughty, devout, and aristocratic, in the Italy of his childhood. Fabrice does not think for a minute he is "demeaning" himself when he challenges a simple soldier of the glorious imperial army to a duel. Yet he speaks harshly to the servant who risks his life for him. Still later, despite his devotion, he does not hesitate to join in the simoniac intrigues which will make him an archbishop of Parma. Fabrice is not a hypocrite, nor does he lack intelligence; he is merely lacking the historical foundations for the ability to reflect. The comparisons which a privileged young Frenchman would be forced to make never even enter his mind.

The French will never recover the innocence of a Fabrice for *it is not possible to move backward in the order of the passions.* Historic and psychic evolution are irreversible. Stendhal finds the Restoration revolting but not because he sees in it näively a "return to the *ancien régime.*" Such a return is unthinkable; moreover, Louis XVIII's Charter marks the first concrete step toward democracy " since 1792." The current interpretation of *The Red and the Black* therefore is inadmissible. The Jacobin novel described in the handbooks of literature does not exist. If Stendhal were writing for all those bourgeois who are temporarily cut off from lucrative careers by the temporary triumph of an absolutist and feudal party, his would be a very clumsy work. Traditional interpretations go counter to the most basic tenets of the author and disregard the *facts* of the novel, among which is the brilliant career of Julien. One might object that this career is broken by the reactionary and clerical *Congrégation.*[2] True, yet this same *Congrégation* a little later makes every effort to save the protégé of the Marquis de la Mole. Julien is not so much the victim of the ultras as of the wealthy and jealous bourgeois who will triumph in July, 1830. Moreover, we should not look for any partisan lesson in Stendhal's masterpieces—to understand this novelist who is always talking politics we must free ourselves of political ways of thinking.

Julien has a brilliant career which he owes to M. de la Mole. In his article on *The Red and the Black* Stendhal describes the latter in these words: "His character as nobleman was not formed by the revolution of 1794." In other words, M. de la Mole retains some genuine nobility; he has not become middle-class through hatred of the middle class. His freedom of thought has not made him a democrat but it prevents him from being a reactionary in

[2] A secret Catholic organization with great political influence.

the worst sense of the word. M. de la Mole does not depend exclusively on excommunications, negations, and re-
fusals; ultracism and the nobleman's reaction have not
smothered all other sentiments in him. His wife and his
friends judge men only by their birth, their fortune, and
their political orthodoxy, and so would a Valenod in their
place; but M. de la Mole is still capable of approving the
rise of a talented commoner. He proves it with Julien
Sorel. Only once does Stendhal find his character vulgar
—when he loses his temper at the thought that his daughter, by marrying Julien, will never be a duchess.

Julien owes his success to that element under the new
regime which has most truly survived from the *ancien régime*. This is a strange way for Stendhal to campaign
against a return to the past; even if the novelist had
shown the failure of the numerous young people who did
not have the good fortune to meet their Marquis de la
Mole, his novel would still not have proved anything
against the *ancien régime*. In fact it is the Revolution
which has increased the obstacles, since most people with
status owe "their character of nobleman"—i.e., their implacable ultracism—to the Revolution.

Must then the obstacle in the way of these young people be called democratic? Is not this an empty subtlety,
and even an untenable paradox? Surely it is only fair that
the bourgeoisie should take over the controls since it is
"the most energetic and active class in the nation." Is it
not true that a little more "democracy" would smooth the
way for the ambitious?

It is true; in any case, the stupidity of the ultras makes
their downfall inevitable. But Stendhal looks further. The
political elimination of the noble party cannot re-establish
harmony and satisfy the desires that have been awakened. The political conflict which rages under the constitutional monarchy is considered the sequel of a great

historic drama, the last thunderclaps of a storm that is moving away. The revolutionaries suppose they must clear the ground and make a fresh start; Stendhal is telling them that they have already started. Ancient historic appearances hide a new structure of human relations. The party struggle is rooted not in past inequality but in the present equality, no matter how imperfect it may be.

The historical justification of the internal struggles is scarcely more than a pretext now. Put aside the pretext and the true cause will appear. Ultracism will disappear like liberalism, but internal mediation remains; and internal mediation will never be lacking in excuses for maintaining the division into rival camps. Following religious society, civic society has become schismatic. To look forward optimistically to the democratic future under the pretext that the ultras, or their successors, are destined to disappear from the political scene is once again to put the object before the mediator and desire before envy. This error can be compared to that of the chronic sufferer from jealousy who always thinks his illness will be cured when the current rival is eliminated.

The last century of French history has proved Stendhal right. The party struggle is the only stable element in contemporary instability. Principles no longer cause rivalry; it is a metaphysical rivalry, which slips into contrary principles like mollusks that nature has not provided with shells and that install themselves in the first ones to come along, no matter what kind.

Proof of this can be furnished by the pair Rênal-Valenod. M. de Rênal abandons ultracism before the 1827 elections. He has himself entered as a candidate on the liberal ticket. Jean Prévost discovers in this sudden conversion proof that even Stendhal's secondary characters are capable of "surprising" the reader.[3] Prévost, usually

[3] *La Création Chez Stendhal.*

so perspicacious, in this point has fallen victim to the pernicious myths of the "true to life" and "spontaneity" which plague literary criticism.

Julien smiles when he learns of the political about-face of his former patron—he knows very well that nothing has changed. Once more it is a question of playing a role opposite Valenod. The latter has gotten in the good graces of the *Congrégation;* he will therefore be the ultras' candidate. For M. de Rênal there is nothing left to do but turn toward those liberals who seemed so formidable to him a few years before. We meet the mayor of Verrières again in the last pages of the novel. He introduces himself pompously as a "liberal of the defection," but from his second sentence on he merely echoes Valenod. Submission to the Other is no less absolute when it assumes negative forms—a puppet is no less a puppet when the strings are crossed. With regard to the virtues of opposition Stendhal does not share in the optimism of a Hegel or of our contemporary "rebels."

The figure cut by the two businessmen of Verrières was not perfect so long as they both belonged to the same political party. Double mediation demanded M. de Rênal's conversion to liberalism. There was a need for symmetry which had not yet been fulfilled. And that final *entrechat* was needed to bring to a proper end the ballet of Rênal-Valenod, which was being performed in a corner of the stage all through *The Red and the Black.*

Julien savors the "conversion" of M. de Rênal as a music lover who sees a melodic theme reappear under a new orchestral disguise. Most men are taken in by the disguises. Stendhal places a smile on Julien's lips so that his readers should not be deceived. He does not want us to be fooled: he wants to turn our attention away from the objects and fix it on the mediator; he wishes to reveal to us the genesis of desire, to teach us to distinguish true freedom from the negative slavery which caricatures it. If we take M. de Rênal's liberalism seriously we are destroying the very essence of *The Red and the Black* and reducing a work of genius to the proportions of a Victor Cousin or a Saint-Marc Girardin.

M. de Rênal's conversion is the first act of a political tragicomedy which excites the enthusiasm of naïve spectators throughout the nineteenth century. First the actors exchange threats, then they exchange roles. They leave the stage and return in a new costume. Behind this perpetually similar but different spectacle the same opposition continues to exist, becoming ever more empty and yet more ferocious. And internal mediation continues its underground work.

THE POLITICAL thinkers of our time are always seeking in Stendhal an echo of their own thoughts. They recreate a revolutionary Stendhal or a reactionary Stendhal according to their own passions. But the shroud is never large enough to cover the corpse. Aragon's Stendhal is no more satisfactory than that of Maurice Barrès or Charles Maurras. One line of the writer's own suffices to bring the weak ideological scaffoldings tumbling down into the void: "As regards extreme parties," we read in the preface to *Lucien Leuwen*, "it is always those we have seen most recently which seem the most ridiculous."

The youthful Stendhal most certainly leaned toward the republicans. The mature Stendhal is not lacking in sympathy for the incorruptible Catoes who, deaf to Louis-Philippe's objurgations, refuse to grow rich and are preparing in the shadows a new revolution. But we must not confuse with political affiliation this very particular feeling of sympathy. The problem is discussed at length in *Lucien Leuwen* and the position of the later Stendhal—

the Stendhal who carries most weight—is in no way ambiguous.

We must seek among the austere republicans whatever
is left of nobility in the political arena. Only these republicans still hope for the destruction of all forms of vanity.
They retain the eighteenth-century illusion concerning
the excellence of human nature. They have understood
neither the revolution nor *vanité triste*. They do not realize that the most beautiful fruits of ideological thought
will always be spoiled by the worm of irrationality. These
men of integrity do not have the *philosophes'* excuse of
living *before* the Revolution; thus they are much less intelligent than Montesquieu, and they are much less amus-
ing. If their hands were free, they would create a regime
identical with that which flourishes under republican,
protestant puritanism in the state of New York. Individual
rights would be respected; prosperity would be assured,
but the last refinements of aristocratic existence would
disappear; vanity would take an even baser form than under the constitutional monarchy. Stendhal concludes that
it is less distressing to flatter a Talleyrand or even a minis-
ter of Louis-Philippe's than to pay court "to one's shoe-
maker."

Stendhal is an atheist in politics, a fact hard to believe
either in his day or in ours. Despite the levity of its manifestations this atheism is not a frivolous skepticism but a
profound conviction. Stendhal does not evade problems;
his point of view is the outcome of a whole life of meditation. But it is a point of view which will never be understood by party-minded people nor by many other people
who unconsciously are influenced by the party spirit. An
ambiguous homage is paid to the novelist's thought,
which secretly denies its coherence. It is considered "im-
pulsive" and "disconcerting." It is full of "whims" and
"paradoxes." The unfortunate writer is lucky if "a double

heritage, both aristocratic and popular" is not invoked which would tear him apart. Let us leave to Mérimée the image of a Stendhal dominated by the spirit of contradiction and we shall understand perhaps that Stendhal is accusing *us* and our time of self-contradiction.

As usual, if we are to have a better understanding of the novelist's thought, we should compare it with a later work which will amply justify its perspectives and will make even its more daring aspects seem banal, merely by revealing a more advanced stage of metaphysical desire. In Stendhal's case, we must ask Flaubert to provide us with a key. Although Emma Bovary's desire still belongs to the area of external mediation, Flaubert's universe as a whole, and especially the urban life of *The Sentimental Education,* are the result of an internal mediation which is even more extreme than that of Stendhal. Flaubert's mediation exaggerates the characteristics of Stendhalian mediation and draws a caricature of it that is much easier for us to figure out than the original.

The environment of *The Sentimental Education* is the same as that of *The Red and the Black.* Again the provinces and Paris are opposed to one another, but it is clear that the center of gravity has moved toward Paris, the capital of desire, which increasingly polarizes the vital forces of the nation. Relationships between people remain the same and enable us to measure the progress of internal mediation. M. de la Mole has been replaced by M. Dambreuse, a "liberal" who owes his character of rapacious big banker as much to 1830 as to 1794. Mathilde is succeeded by the venal Mme Dambreuse. Julien Sorel is followed by a whole crowd of young men who come, like him, to "conquer" the capital. They are less talented but more greedy. Chances of success are not wanting but everybody wants the most "conspicuous" position, and the front row can never be stretched far since it owes its position purely to the inevitably limited attention of the crowd. The number of those who are called increases constantly but the number of the elect does not. Flaubert's ambitious man never attains the object of his desires. He knows neither the real misery nor the real despair caused by possession and disillusionment. His horizon never grows wider. He is doomed to bitterness, malice, and petty rivalries. Flaubert's novel confirms Stendhal's dire predictions on the future of the bourgeois.

The opposition between the ambitious younger men and those who are successful grows ever more bitter although there are no more ultras. The intellectual basis of the oppositions is even more ridiculous and unstable than in Stendhal. If there is a victor in this bourgeois *cursus honorum* described in *The Sentimental Education* then it is Martinon, the most insipid of the characters and the biggest schemer, who corresponds, though he is even duller witted, to little Tambeau of *The Red and the Black*. The democratic court which has replaced that of the monarchy grows larger, more anonymous, and more unjust. Unfit for true freedom, Flaubert's characters are always attracted by what attracts their fellow men. They can desire only what the Others desire. The priority of rivalry over desire inevitably increases the amount of suffering caused by vanity.

Flaubert too is an atheist in politics. If we make allowance for the differences of time and temperament, his attitude is amazingly similar to that of Stendhal. This spiritual relationship becomes more apparent on reading Tocqueville: the sociologist, too, is immunized against partisan positions, and the best of his work almost succeeds in providing the systematic expression of an historical and political truth which often remains implicit in the great works of the two novelists.

The increasing equality—the approach of the mediator

in our terms—does not give rise to harmony but to an even keener rivalry. Although this rivalry is the source of considerable material benefits, it also leads to even more considerable spiritual sufferings, for nothing material can appease it. Equality which alleviates poverty is in itself good but it cannot satisfy even those who are keenest in demanding it; it only exasperates their desire. When he emphasises the vicious circle in which the passion for equality is trapped, Tocqueville reveals an essential aspect of triangular desire. The ontological sickness, we know, always leads its victims toward the "solutions" that are most likely to aggravate it. The passion for equality is a madness unequalled except by the contrary and symmetrical passion for inequality, which is even more abstract and contributes even more directly to the unhappiness caused by freedom in those who are incapable of accepting it in a manly fashion. Rival ideologies merely reflect both the unhappiness and the incapability; thus they result from internal mediation—rival ideologies owe their power of persuasion only to the secret support the opposing factions lend each other. Fruits of the ontological scission, their duality reflects its unhuman geometry and in return they provide food for the devouring rivalry.

Stendhal, Flaubert, Tocqueville describe as "republican" or "democratic" an evolution which we today would call *totalitarian.* As the mediator comes nearer and the concrete differences between men grow smaller, abstract opposition plays an ever larger part in individual and collective existence. All the forces of being are gradually organized into twin structures whose opposition grows ever more exact. Thus every human force is braced in a struggle that is as relentless as it is senseless, since no concrete difference or positive value is involved. Totalitarianism is precisely this. The social and political aspects of this phenomenon cannot be distinguished from its personal and private aspects. Totalitarianism exists when all desires have been organized one by one into a general and permanent mobilization of being in the service of nothingness.

Balzac often treats very seriously the oppositions he sees around him; Stendhal and Flaubert, on the other hand, always point out their futility. In the work of these two authors, this double structure is embodied in "cerebral love," political struggles, petty rivalries among businessmen and the notables of the provinces. Starting from these particular areas, it is the truly schismatic tendency of romantic and modern society which in each case is demonstrated. But Stendhal and Flaubert did not foresee, and no doubt could not foresee, where this tendency would lead humanity. Double mediation has invaded the growing domain of collective existence and wormed its way into the more intimate depths of the individual soul, until finally it stretches beyond national boundaries and annexes countries, races, and continents, in the heart of a universe where technical progress is wiping away one by one the differences between men. Stendhal and Flaubert underestimated the extent to which triangular desire might expand, perhaps because they lived too early, or perhaps because they did not see clearly its metaphysical nature. Whatever the reason, they did not foresee the at once cataclysmic yet insignificant conflicts of the twentieth century. They perceived the grotesque element of the era which was about to begin but they did not suspect its tragedy.

CHAPTER VI

TECHNICAL PROBLEMS
IN STENDHAL, CERVANTES,
AND FLAUBERT

DOUBLE mediation gradually devours and digests ideas, beliefs, and values but it respects the outer shell: it leaves a semblance of life. This secret decomposition of values drags with it the language in which they are supposedly reflected. The novels of Stendhal, Flaubert, Proust, and Dostoyevsky are so many stages along the same road— they describe for us the successive states of a disorder that is constantly spreading and growing worse. But since these novelists have at their disposal only the one language which is already corrupted by metaphysical desire and, by definition, incapable of being used to reveal the truth, the revelation of this disorder presents complex problems.

The corruption of language is still in the first stage in the work of Stendhal; it is characterized by the pure and simple reversal of meaning. We have seen, for instance, that after that time in the distant past when the two coincided, the spiritual and the social sense of the word "noble" became contradictory. The *vaniteux* never recognizes this contradiction; he talks as if a perfect harmony still existed between things and their names. He talks as if the traditional hierarchies reflected in the language were still real. Thus he never realizes that there is more true nobility among commoners than among aristocrats and more high-mindedness in the philosophy of the Enlightenment than in ignoble ultracism. By remaining faithful to out-dated categories and to a fossilized vocabulary Stendhal's *vaniteux* can fail to perceive the real distinctions among men and multiply those which are unreal and abstract.

The passionate man is not even aware of crossing the walls of illusions built up by the world's vanity. He does not worry over the letter but goes straight to the spirit. He moves directly to the object of his desire without being concerned with Others. He is the only realist in a world of lies; for this reason he always seems a little mad. He chooses Mme de Rênal and renounces Mathilde; he chooses prison rather than Paris, Parma, or Verrières. If his name is M. de la Mole, he prefers Julien to his own son Norbert, the heir to his name and coat-of-arms. The passionate person baffles and bewilders the *vaniteux* because he goes straight to the truth. He is the involuntary negation of that negation which is Stendhalian vanity.

Novelistic affirmation always springs from that negation. Nobility, altruism, spontaneity, and originality are mentioned constantly. The passionate being appears and immediately we see that these words really meant slavery, copying, imitation of Others. Julien's inner smile reveals the artificiality of M. de Rênal's conversion to liberalism. Inversely the crude sarcasms of the citizens of Verrières bring into relief Mme de Rênal's solitary superiority. The passionate being is the arrow which points the direction in a topsy-turvy world. The passionate person is the *exception*, the creature of vanity the *rule*. In Stendhal, metaphysical desire is revealed through this perpetual contrast between what is normal and what is exceptional.

The method is not original. It is common to Cervantes and Stendhal. In *Don Quixote,* too, we find this contrast between normal and exceptional. But the roles are different. Don Quixote is the exception and the dumbfounded spectators are the rule. From one author to another the fundamental process is reversed. In Cervantes the exception desires metaphysically and the multitude desires spontaneously. In Stendhal, the exception desires spontaneously and the multitude desires metaphysically. Cervantes gives us an upside-down hero in a right-side up world; Stendhal gives us a right-side-up hero in an upside-down world.

We must not, however, credit these methods with an absolute value. The contrast between normal and exceptional does not create a gulf between the characters in *Don Quixote.* Let us say only that a triangular desire always appears in Cervantes against a background of ontologically healthy desire, but this background is never very distinct and its composition can vary. Don Quixote is usually the exception who stands out against a background of good sense, but the hero can very well become a spectator himself in the lucid interval between two bouts of chivalric madness. Then he is a part of the rational décor which Cervantes cannot do without but whose composition is of little importance to him. The only thing that counts is the revelation of metaphysical desire.

When he stands behind Don Quixote, Sancho provides, by himself, the indispensable rational décor—this is why the romantics so despise him—but as soon as he comes to the foreground the squire becomes the exception who again stands out against the collective good sense. Then it is Sancho's metaphysical desire which becomes the object of revelation. The novelist is a little like the hard-pressed director of a theatrical company who uses his actors as bit players in the intervals between their main roles. But above all he wants to show us that metaphysical desire is infinitely subtle: no one is beyond its reach, but at the same time no one is hopelessly condemned.

Beginning with *The Red and the Black,* Stendhal too applies this relativity in his novelistic contrasts. Although in principle the distinction between vanity and passion is radical, it does not allow a sharp division of people into clear-cut categories. As in Cervantes, one person can embody successively both ontological sickness and health, depending on whether he is faced with a vanity less or greater than his own. Thus Mathilde de la Mole in her mother's salon can embody passion; but, face to face with Julien, she changes roles: she becomes once more the rule and he the exception. As for Julien himself, not even he is an exception *en soi.* In his relations with Mme de Rênal —excluding of course the last scenes—he embodies the rule and she the exception.

Vanity and passion are the ideal extremes of a scale on which all Stendhal's characters are placed. The deeper one is immersed in vanity, the closer the mediator is to his subject. Mathilde de la Mole, dreaming of her ancestor Boniface, and Julien, dreaming of Napoleon, are further from their mediator than the characters surrounding them are from theirs. The slightest difference of "level" between two characters permits a revealing contrast to be brought out. Most of Stendhal's scenes are built on such contrasts. To create a better effect the novelist always underscores and emphasizes the oppositions; but, for all that, they do not acquire an absolute value—they are soon replaced by other oppositions which will bring into relief further aspects of Stendhalian mediation.

Romantic criticism isolates one contrast and from that point one sees only that one. It insists on a mechanical opposition which determines for the hero either unqualified admiration or hatred. It transforms Don Quixote and

Julien Sorel into absolute exceptions—champions of the "ideal" and martyred by those Others, who are all, we are to understand, equally intolerable.

Romantic criticism does not understand the novelistic dialectic of the rule and the exception, it thereby destroys the very essence of novelistic genius. It reinjects into the novel the Manichean division between Self and Others which that genius has overcome only with great difficulty.

This mistake in perspective does not surprise us. The absolute opposition many readers desire to find, at all costs, in the novelistic masterpiece are typically romantic. We can always find Manicheanism wherever internal mediation flourishes. The romantic exception embodies *Good* and the rule *Evil*. Thus the opposition is no longer functional but essential. Its content can change from one romantic to another without ever altering its fundamental significance. It is not for exactly the same reasons that Chatterton is superior to the English, Cinq-Mars to Richelieu, Meursault to his judges, and Roquentin to the bourgeois of Bouville, but these heroes are always superior and their superiority is always absolute. This is the only thing that really matters. This superiority expresses the very essence of romantic and individualist revelation.

The romantic work is a weapon aimed at Others. The roles of the English, Richelieu, the judges, and the bourgeois of Bouville are always played by the Others. The author feels such a pressing need for justification that he is perpetually on the lookout for the exception. He feels he must identify himself as closely as possible with that exception *against* all other men, in the same way as Don Quixote believes every woman he meets along the way is being persecuted and so attacks the brothers, lovers, husbands, or faithful servants escorting them. Many readers are no different. It is precisely this sort of "protection" that the romantic exegetes have been giving Don Quixote ever since the nineteenth century. Turnabout is fair play. The critics see in Don Quixote a superb exception and blindly embrace his cause; on his behalf they break lances with other characters in the novel and even with the author, if need be, without once asking themselves what might be the significance of the exceptional for Cervantes. Thus they do great wrong to a work whose champion they claim to be.

All this untimely rescuing ends by harming what it sets out to save. It is not surprising that every generous romantic gesture has such catastrophic consequences. What after all does Don Quixote care about the lovely ladies whose families he massacres! And what do the knights-errant of literature care about the novelistic work they praise to the skies! The "victim" to be rescued is never more than a pretext for asserting oneself gloriously against the whole universe. The romantics themselves, not we, say this more appropriately than they realize when they enroll under his banner. Nothing is more quixotic, certainly, than the romantic interpretation of Don Quixote. In fact we must give the prize to the modern imitators of knight-errantry; we have to admit that they surpass their model. Don Quixote was acting on a wrong assumption but he was fighting for real women, whereas romantic critics are championing a fictional character when they strike at the imaginary enemy—thus they increase exponentially Don Quixote's habitual extravagance. Fortunately Cervantes foresaw this peak of "idealism" and saw to it that his hero climbed it. We must not compare these noble defenders of a nonexistent literary cause to the Don Quixote we find slashing to right and left of him along the main roads of Castille, but to the Don Quixote who destroys Master Peter's puppets, who disrupts a performance he cannot watch with the proper aesthetic detachment. By raising the coefficient of illusion to the next power, Cervantes' inexhaustible genius provides us, just when it is required, with the metaphor we need.

In Stendhal's case the misinterpretation of the romantics is less spectacular but no less serious. This misinterpretation is all the more difficult to avoid since in Stendhal's works, as in those of the romantics, the exception is more admirable than the rule—but in a different sense, at least in his great novels. There is no identification in his work between the passionate hero, the creator, and the reader. Stendhal cannot be Fabrice because he understands Fabrice better than Fabrice understands himself. If the reader understands Stendhal, then he cannot identify with Fabrice either. If the reader understands Vigny then he identifies with Chatterton, if he understands Sartre he identifies with Roquentin. This is one of the main differences between the romantic view of exception and Stendhal's.

The romantic critic isolates those scenes in Stendhal's novel which delight contemporary sensibility. Julien was regarded as a scoundrel in the nineteenth century, only to become a hero and a saint in our day. A review of this whole series of revealing contrasts would only establish the inadequacy of the exaggerated interpretations offered by the romantic critics. We would discover again the ironic counterpoint for which we too often substitute the monotonous thunder of egotistical curses. If the oppositions are hardened and given only one interpretation then the novelist's supreme accomplishment is ruined. A Cervantes or a Stendhal manages a sublime equality of treatment of Self and Other which is not compromised but assured by the subtle dialectic of the rule and the exception.

The differences supposedly are moral and metaphysical. No doubt this is true, but in the great novels aesthetics is not a separate area—it combines with ethics and metaphysics. The novelist multiplies the contrasts; like a sculptor he achieves relief by multiplying surfaces on different planes. The romantic is a prisoner of the Manichean opposition between Self and Others and thus always works on one plane only. Opposite the empty and faceless hero who says "I" is the grinning mask of the Other. Absolute exteriority is opposed to absolute interiority.

The romantic, like the modern painter, paints in two dimensions. He cannot achieve novelistic depth because he is unable to reach the Other. The novelist goes beyond romantic justification. More or less surreptitiously, more or less openly, he crosses the barrier between Self and Other. This memorable crossing, as we shall see in the last chapter, is recorded in the novel itself in the form of a reconciliation between hero and the world at the moment of death. It is at the conclusion, and only then, that the hero speaks in the name of the author. And the dying hero always renounces his past existence.

Novelistic reconciliation has both an aesthetic and an ethical sense. The hero-novelist achieves the third novelistic dimension because he goes beyond metaphysical desire and because he discovers a *man like himself* in the mediator who fascinates him. Novelistic reconciliation allows a synthesis of Other and Self, of observation and introspection, which is impossible in the romantic revolt. It enables the novelist to *view his characters from different perspectives* and, with the third dimension, give them true freedom and motion.

THE STENDHALIAN exception always flourishes in ground which would appear most unfavorable to his development: in the provinces rather than in Paris, among women rather than men, among common people, not the nobility. There is more true nobility, Stendhal tells us, in his grandfather than in the whole of M. de Polignac's ministry. Thus the social hierarchy in the universe of the novel is not without significance. Instead of directly reflecting the Stendhalian virtues of energy and spontaneity, it reflects them indirectly; like a diabolical mirror it returns an inverted image.

Stendhal's last heroine, Lamiel, "la fille du diable" combines in her charming person all the signs of the elect which the *vaniteux* mistake for curses: she is a woman, an orphan, poor, ignorant, provincial, and of the common people, but Lamiel has more energy than the men, more distinction than the aristocrats, more refinement than Parisians, and more spontaneity than would-be wits.

The disorder of the novelistic universe nevertheless still reflects the traditional order of society. We have not yet reached the point of complete absence of order, of absolute disorder; Stendhal's universe is a pyramid balanced on its point. This almost miraculous balance cannot last, for it belongs to the period immediately following the revolutionary era. The pyramid of the former society will soon crumble and break into a million shapeless fragments. We shall look in vain for this order at the heart of the disorder in the novels that follow Stendhal. Already in Flaubert things no longer have a meaning contrary to that which they should have; they have very little, if any, sense at all. Women are no more, nor less, authentic than men; Parisians are no more, nor less, vain than provincials; the bourgeois are no more, nor less, energetic than the aristocrats.

In this universe of Flaubert's, spontaneous desire has not disappeared—it never completely disappears—but the exceptions have decreased in number and importance. Above all they no longer develop with the sovereign ease of Stendhal's hero. They always get the worst of the conflict, which puts them in opposition to society. The exception is a stunted blade of grass growing between huge paving stones.

It is not merely an author's whim or his particularly peevish humor which is responsible for curtailing the role of spontaneous desire in the universe of the novel; it is rather the progress of ontological sickness.

We have seen that spontaneous desire is still the rule in Cervantes; it became the exception in Stendhal. In Cervantes metaphysical desire stands out against the background of common sense; in Stendhal spontaneous desire stands out against a metaphysical background. Triangular desire has now become the most common form of desire. Admittedly we ought not to draw too rigorous conclusions from this technical reversal. We must not look for the expression of a statistical truth about desire in a novelistic work. The choice of a method depends on an infinite number of factors, not the least of which is a very legitimate regard for what would be effective. Every technique involves a certain exaggeration and its effects should not be confused with novelistic revelation in the proper sense.

Nevertheless the choice of opposite techniques in Cervantes and Stendhal is significant. As metaphysical desire spreads and intensifies it makes this reversal possible and even necessitates it. Metaphysical desire becomes more and more universal. In Cervantes, novelistic revelation is centered in the individual; in Stendhal and the other novelists of internal mediation the emphasis moves toward the collectivity.

From Flaubert on, except for a few other very special cases such as Dostoyevsky's *The Idiot*, spontaneous desire plays such a minor role it can no longer even serve to bring about the novelistic revelation. The exception in the case of Flaubert carries with it a certain indirect and negative social significance. In *Madame Bovary* the only exceptions are the peasant woman at the assembly whose very poverty puts her beyond the reach of bourgeois desire, and the great doctor who escapes it through his knowledge. These exceptions play, to some extent, the same role as in Stendhal: the old peasant woman provides a revealing contrast with the beaming bourgeois enthroned on the platform; similarly, the great doctor shows up Charles and Homais as nonentities, but his presence is too silent and episodic to bear the main weight of revelation. The exception now survives only in the completely eccentric regions of the novelistic universe.

The opposition between Mme de Rênal and her husband, and between Mme de Rênal and the citizens of Verrières is truly essential. The opposition between Emma and Charles, and between Emma and the citizens of Yonville is essential only in Emma's mind. When the contrasts remain, their power of revelation is slight. In most cases everything melts into a greyish uniformity. The progress of metaphysical desire merely increases the empty oppositions; it weakens the concrete oppositions or banishes them to the far boundaries of the novelistic universe.

This advance of metaphysical desire is made on two different fronts. The ontological sickness grows worse in the areas already contaminated, and it spreads to areas thus far spared. This invasion of virgin territory constitutes the real subject of *Madame Bovary*. In order to locate the heroine in the mainstream of a history of metaphysical desire we must turn again to the perceptive definition of one critic of Flaubert: "Madame Bovary is Madame de Rênal a quarter of a century later." This judgment is somewhat schematic but it reveals an essential aspect of Flaubertian desire. Mme Bovary belongs to the "upper" regions of triangular desire; she is suffering the first onslaught of a disease which makes its initial appearance through external mediation. Although chronologically it follows the works of Stendhal, Flaubert's novel should precede them in a theoretical discussion of metaphysical desire.

The evolution of metaphysical desire explains many differences between Stendhal and Flaubert. Every novelist finds himself faced with a particular moment of metaphysical structure; thus the technical problems never appear twice in the same terms.

Stendhal's conciseness and flashing irony are based on the network of exceptions running through the novelistic material. Once the reader has been given the clue to the oppositions, the slightest misunderstanding between two characters immediately suggests the pattern of passion-vanity and reveals metaphysical desire. Everything rests on the contrast between the rule and the exception. The transition from positive to negative is as rapid as the change from light to dark when one touches an electric switch. From one end of a Stendhalian novel to the other the lightning flashes of passion illuminate the shadows of vanity.

Stendhal's illumination is no longer available to Flaubert: the electrodes are separated and the current is interrupted. Flaubert's oppositions almost all belong to the Rênal-Valenod type and are even emptier and more headstrong. In Stendhal, the ballet of the two rivals unfolds before a witness who interprets it for us. Stendhal had only to show us Julien's "inner smile" to enlighten us on M. de Rênal's liberal conversion. In Flaubert this light is missing; there is no height from which to survey the plain. Thus we have to cross this immense bourgeois plain step by step.

THE EMPTINESS of the oppositions must be revealed with no outside help. This is the problem facing Flaubert. It is

one with that of stupidity—*la bêtise*—a major obsession
of his. To resolve the problem Flaubert invents the style
of false enumerations and false antitheses. No real operation is possible among the various elements of the novelistic universe. The elements do not go together, neither
are they in any concrete opposition to each other. They
confront each other symmetrically and then fall back into
the void; this impassive juxtaposition reveals the absurdity. The inventory grows longer but the total always remains zero. We constantly find the same empty oppositions between aristocrats and bourgeois, between the
devout and the atheists, reactionaries and republicans,
lovers and mistresses, parents and children, rich and poor.
The novelistic universe is a palace full of absurd orna-
ments and false windows which are there "for symmetry."

Flaubert's grotesque antitheses caricature the sublime
antitheses of Hugo or those categories on which the posi-
tivists base the classifications they believe to be definitive.
The bourgeois is delighted with his illusory riches. Prod-
ucts of internal mediation, these opposed concepts bear
the same relationship to authentic values as does the bizarre garden of *Bouvard et Pécuchet* to untouched nature. Flaubert's work is a *Discours sur le Peu de Réalité*
which is infinitely more daring than that of André Breton,
for the novelist is attacking science and ideology—the
very essence of the bourgeois conception of reality all-
powerful at that time. The "ideas" of Flaubert's characters
are even more devoid of significance than those of Stendhal's *vaniteux*. They remind us of the useless organs of
the body to be found frequently in the animal world,
monstrous appendices whose existence in one species
rather than another cannot be accounted for. One thinks
of certain herbivorous animals and their enormous horns,
whose only function is to entangle each other in endless
sterile fights.

The opposition is nourished by a double nullity, by an

equal spiritual poverty on both sides. Homais and Bournisien symbolize the two opposed but interdependent
halves of petty middle-class France. Flaubert's couples
even "think" in this grotesque coupling, like two drunks
who keep their balance only by trying to upset each other.
Homais and Bournisien lead each other on and finally fall
asleep, side by side, coffee cup in hand, before the body of
Emma Bovary. As Flaubert's novelistic genius ripens his
oppositions become more futile; the identity of the contraries is drawn more clearly. The evolution ends in
Bouvard and Pécuchet, who oppose and complement each
other as perfectly as two knick-knacks on a bourgeois
mantelpiece.

In that novel, modern thought loses what dignity and
strength remained, with the loss of continuity and stability. The rhythm of mediations is accelerated. Ideas and
systems, theories and principles confront each other in opposed pairs, which are always determined negatively.
Oppositions are devoured by symmetry; their role is now
merely decorative. Petty bourgeois individualism finally
ends in the ridiculous apotheosis of the Identical and the
Interchangeable.

CHAPTER VII

THE HERO'S *ASKESIS*

EVERY desire that is revealed can arouse or increase a rival's desire; thus it is necessary to conceal desire in order to gain possession of the object. Stendhal calls this concealment *hypocrisy*. The hypocrite suppresses everything in his desire which *can be seen,* in other words, every impulse toward the object. But desire is dynamic. It is almost identical with the impulse it provokes. The hypocrisy which triumphs in the universe of the *Black* attacks everything that is real in desire. Only this concealment of desire *for the sake of* desire can act as the basis of a "dialectic of master and slave." Here it is not a question of ordinary hypocrisy which deals with facts and beliefs: ordinary hypocrisy is within everyone's reach; it cannot become a test of an individual's inner strength.

The two partners in mediation copy one and the same desire; therefore this desire cannot suggest anything to one without suggesting it to the other as well. The dissimulation has to be perfect because the mediator's perspicacity is unlimited. Thus the author can no longer be content with describing gestures and repeating his characters' words—he must violate their consciousnesses, since words and gestures only lie. The hypocrite must resist every temptation because they all lie open to the gaze of the god. The model-disciple discerns the slightest movements of his disciple-model. Like the god of the Bible, the mediator "trieth the hearts and reins." Hypocrisy *for the sake of* desire requires as much will power as religious asceticism. It is a question of thwarting the same forces in both cases.

Julien's career in the universe of the *Black* is as demanding as a military career in the universe of the *Red;* there has been a change, however, in the direction of the effort. In a universe where desire must always pass through Another, truly successful action is directed toward the Self. It is totally interior. The fools in Verrières and elsewhere imagine that the little seminarian owes his brilliant rise in the world to chance or to Machiavellian calculation, but the reader who follows Stendhal in his penetration of Julien's consciousness must give up this simplistic view. Julien Sorel owes his success to a strange strength of soul which he cultivates with the passion of a mystic. This strength is dedicated to the service of the Self just as true mysticism is dedicated to the service of God.

As a child Julien Sorel is already practicing *askesis* for the sake of desire. He keeps his arm in a sling for a whole month as a punishment for having revealed his true thoughts concerning Napoleon. The critics perceive the ascetic meaning of the arm-in-a-sling but they see in it only "a character trait." They do not understand that the whole universe of the *Black* is implicit in this childish gesture. The arm-in-a-sling is the ransom for one moment of frankness—one moment of weakness. At the other end of the novel Julien's heroic indifference to Mathilde is the ransom for a second moment of frankness. Julien let Mathilde see the desire he felt for her. The mistake is analogous, the self-punishment is no less so. Every infraction of the code of hypocrisy is atoned for by an increase in ascetic dissimulation.

We do not perceive the identity of the two actions because the arm-in-a-sling achieves no concrete result whereas the heroic indifference wins back Mathilde. The arm-in-a-sling seems "irrational" to us but we see the feigned indifference as an "amorous tactic." The second ascetic gesture takes place in the down-to-earth and reassuring universe of novelistic "psychology." Julien's success makes us believe in the positive nature of his enterprise. We persuade ourselves without difficulty that the child's gesture is completely irrational while that of the adult is a result of lucid calculation; but Stendhal does not present things this way. The two acts belong to the same shadowy area of the consciousness. The instinct which moves Julien, the instinct of hypocrisy, is never rational but it is infallible. Julien will owe all his triumphs to it.

The arm-in-a-sling constitutes the first moment of underground *askesis*—absolute gratuitousness. Moreover this gratuitousness is inseparable from the very idea of *askesis*. The winning back of Mathilde constitutes the second moment, reward. To perceive the identity of the two acts is to pose the problem of *askesis* for the sake of desire in its fullest sense. The winning back of Mathilde proves that this *askesis* is not merely an absurdity superimposed on the initial and fundamental absurdity of metaphysical desire. Renunciation *for the sake of* desire is wholly consonant with this desire. In internal mediation it is precisely the mediator-rival's desire which separates subject from object; but this mediator's desire is itself copied from the subject's desire. *Askesis* for the sake of desire discourages imitation; thus it alone can open the road to the object.

Just as the mystic turns from the world in order that God may turn toward him and give him the gift of His grace, Julien turns away from Mathilde in order that Mathilde may turn toward him and make him the object of her own desire. *Askesis* for the sake of desire is just as legitimate and productive, in the triangular context, as "vertical" *askesis* is in the framework of religious vision. The analogy between deviated transcendency and vertical transcendency is even closer than we at first suspected.

Like Stendhal, Dostoyevsky constantly stresses this analogy betweeen the two transcendencies. Dolgorouki, the hero of *A Raw Youth,* practices an asceticism somewhat similar to Julien's. Dolgorouki, like Julien, has his "idea," that is, his model which he copies religiously. This model is no longer the victorious Napoleon but Rothschild, the millionaire. Dolgorouki wants to make his fortune by an existence of heroic self-denial. After he has made his fortune he plans to renounce it in order to show Others his tremendous disdain. He prepares himself for the austere existence ahead of him by throwing out of the window the meals a devoted servant brings him. For more than a month he lives on bread and water, cursing the old woman who "thinks only of his health."

This is very close to Julien's arm-in-a-sling. And when the wandering Makar describes the life of privation led by the hermit saints in the desert, Dolgorouki, the same Dolgorouki who throws his meals out of the window, is loud in his condemnation of a way of existence which is "useless to society." Unable to recognize the disturbing analogy between religious *askesis* and his own conduct, he settles the question of monasticism in peremptory tones, as a *modern* and *lucid* man, a man who knows that "two and two make four." The rationalist does not want to perceive the metaphysical structure of desire: he contents himself with ridiculous explanations, he appeals to "good sense" and "psychology." His confidence is not at all weakened by the fact that he himself more or less consciously practices *askesis* for the sake of desire. Incapable of self-analysis and led on by his pride, he instinctively applies the precepts of underground mysticism which are always analogous to, but the inverse of, the principles of Christian mysticism: *"Do not ask and you will be given; do not search and you will find; do not knock and it will be opened."* The further man strays from God, Dostoyevsky tells us, the deeper he plunges into the irrational, at first in the name of reason and finally in his own name.

The ambiguity of the priest in Stendhal is linked with the two directions which renunciation can take. The most profound hypocrisy can be distinguished from virtue only by its poisoned fruit. The contrast between a good and bad priest is total but subtle. For a long time Julien does not learn to distinguish the Abbé Pirard from the scoundrels around him.

Nietzsche, who claims to owe so much to Stendhal in the field of "psychology," regards the soldier as the least vulnerable to *ressentiment,* and the priest the most. In the universe of the *Red,* where violence is not impossible, passion flourishes openly. In the universe of the *Black,* on the contrary, passions are concealed. The priest obviously is at a great advantage since he makes a profession of controlling his desires. His self-control is as deadly in evil as it can be supreme in good. Stendhal deems the role of the Church under the Restoration important because he recognizes the ascetic exigencies of internal mediation. The underground action of the *Congrégation* is a result of this mediation. The "religious" vocation of Julien cannot be entirely explained by opportunism. It is already rooted in the inverted religion implanted in the universe of the *Black.*

Far from discouraging any comparison with Dostoyevsky, Stendhal's anticlericalism expresses in its own fashion an essentially Dostoyevskian idea: the analogy between two transcendencies. This anticlericalism has no connection with that of Rabelais or Voltaire. The novelist is not denouncing the abuses of a sensual and medieval cleric.

Quite the contrary. Religious hypocrisy conceals double
mediation. Stendhal often gave way to the pleasure of
scandalizing but he never really confused the Church, nor
Christianity, with the caricatures of them used as authori-
ties by the reactionaries under the Restoration. We must
not forget that in Stendhal's society the Church was "fashionable;" in Dostoyevsky's this was no longer so.

In Dostoyevsky's universe deviated transcendency is no
longer hidden behind religion. But we must not think that
the characters in *The Possessed* are showing us their real
faces in becoming atheists. The possessed are no more
atheists than Stendhal's devout are believers. The victims
of metaphysical desire always choose their political, philosophical, and religious ideas to fit their hatred; thought is
no more than a weapon for an affronted consciousness.
Never has it seemed so important, yet in actual fact it no
longer has any importance at all. It is completely dominated by metaphysical rivalry.

Askesis for the sake of desire is an inevitable conse-
quence of triangular desire. It can therefore be found in
the work of all the novelists of that desire. It is present as
early as Cervantes. Don Quixote does amorous penance
after the fashion of Amadis. Although there is no reason to
reproach Dulcinée, he strips off his clothes and throws
himself on the pointed rocks of the sierra. As usual the
gross farce hides a profound idea. Proust's narrator also
practices *askesis* for the sake of desire in his relations
with Gilberte. He resists the temptation to write to her and
does everything he can to master his passion.

Hegel's unhappy consciousness and Sartre's *projet* to be
God are the outcome of a stubborn orientation toward the
transcendent, of an inability to relinquish religious pat-
terns of desire when history has outgrown them. The novelistic consciousness is also unhappy because its need for
transcendency has outlived the Christian faith. But there

the resemblances end. In the eyes of the novelist, modern man suffers, not because he refuses to become fully and totally aware of his autonomy, but because that awareness, whether real or illusory, is for him intolerable. The need for transcendency seeks satisfaction in the human world and leads the hero into all sorts of madness. Stendhal and Proust, even though they are unbelievers, part company at this point with Sartre and Hegel to rejoin Cervantes and Dostoyevsky. Promethean philosophy sees in the Christian religion only a humanism which is still too timid for complete self-assertion. The novelist, regardless of whether he is a Christian, sees in the so-called modern humanism a subterranean metaphysics which is incapable of recognizing its own nature.

THE NEED for dissimulation peculiar to internal mediation has particularly deplorable results in the domain of sexuality. The subject's desire is aimed at the body of the mediator. The mediator thus is absolute master of that object; he can grant or refuse possession according to his whim. The meaning of this whim can easily be anticipated if this mediator is also incapable of desiring spontaneously. As soon as the subject reveals his desire for possession the mediator copies that desire. He will desire his own body; in other words, he will accord it such value that to yield possession would appear scandalous to him. Even if the mediator does not imitate the subject's desire, he will not respond to that desire; the victim of ontological sickness despises himself too much, in fact, not to despise the being who desires him. Double mediation in the sexual domain as in all others is incompatible with any reciprocity between the Self and the Other.

Surrender to sexual desire always has formidable consequences for the lover. He can only hope to draw the de-

sires of his beloved toward himself by feigning indifference; but he can hide his desire only by suppressing everything that is real and concrete in his sexual drive.

Thus sexuality too has its *askesis* for the sake of desire,
but the will never intervenes in erotic activity without
danger. In Julien Sorel *askesis* for the sake of desire still
results from a free decision. As the mediator comes closer,
the situation changes. Consciousness loses its control over
the process. Resistance to desire becomes increasingly
painful but it no longer depends on a voluntary decision.
Torn by two forces pulling in opposite directions, the subject becomes prey to fascination. Originally he refused to
yield to desire for tactical reasons; now he finds he is incapable of such a surrender. The marvelous self-control of
which the modern Don Juan is so proud leads directly to
the Stendhalian "fiasco." All our contemporary literature
bears witness more or less consciously to the agonizing
proximity of the two themes. André Malraux's conquerors
are all haunted by sexual impotence. Ernest Hemingway's
work would be more truthful if Jake, in *The Sun Also
Rises,* instead of being a war cripple, simply presented *the
other side* of those marvelously flegmatic beings whose
superb virility we admire in the other novels.

The calculating Julien Sorel, and Octave de Malivert,
the impotent hero of *Armance,* are without a doubt related to each other. Desire can be released from the inter-
dict only if the beloved, for some reason or other, is unable to *see* her lover and feel his caresses. This lover
need no longer fear that he may reveal to his beloved the
humiliating spectacle of his own desire. Julien would like
to destroy Mathilde's consciousness when she finally falls
into his arms: "Ah! If only I could kiss these pale cheeks
without your being aware." Similar traits can be found in
the work of later novelists. The only moment of pleasure

enjoyed by Proust's narrator is when Albertine is *asleep.* For Dostoyevsky's lovers the homicidal act, which would close the eyes of the beloved and thus deliver her to them —not so much defenseless as without consciousness—is a perpetual temptation. By a revealing contradiction the desiring subject ends up destroying this consciousness with which he cannot become one.

Many characteristics of so-called *modern* eroticism, once they have been cleansed of their romantic make up, are seen to be connected with the triangular structure of desire. An essentially metaphysical and contemplative eroticism, it flourishes in eighteenth- and nineteenth-century literature as well as in the cinema. It is constantly increasing its means of suggestion and is gradually sinking into pure imagination. Once defined as an exaltation of the will, it has degenerated into onanism. This ultimate tendency is becoming increasingly obvious in certain contemporary neoromantic works.

Sexuality mirrors the whole of existence; fascination is everywhere in our political, social, and private lives but is never acknowledged; it tries to pass either for detachment or for its opposite, "engagement." The paralytic likes to pretend that his immobility is of his *own choice.* We ought to study the sexual obsessions of contemporary literature. They will most certainly reveal a double inaptitude to communion and to solitude which characterizes all the activities of the desiring subject at the paroxystic stage of internal mediation. Paralyzed by the mediator's observation the hero tries to elude his gaze. From now on his whole ambition is confined to looking without being seen; this is the theme of the *voyeur,* which has already assumed such importance in Proust and in Dostoyevsky and which becomes even more important in the so-called "nouveau roman" of contemporary fiction.

Dandyism is closely connected with the important question of *askesis* for the sake of desire, and thus we might have expected that dandyism would interest Stendhal. It also interests Baudelaire but the poet's interpretation is very different from that of the novelist. The romantic poet treats dandyism as a "remnant of aristocratic times" whereas the novelist regards it as a product of modern times. The dandy belongs totally to the universe of the *Black*. The victory of mournful over gay vanity enables him to acclimate himself to Paris. The dandy comes from England where metaphysical desire is more advanced than in France. Completely dressed in black, he has nothing in common with the *gentilhomme* of the *ancien régime* who was not afraid to be surprised, to admire, to desire, and even to burst into laughter.

The dandy is distinguished by his affectation of cold indifference. But his is not the coldness of the stoic; it is calculated to stir up desire, a coldness which is always saying to the Others: "I am self-sufficient." The dandy wants to make Others imitate the desire he pretends to feel for himself. He exhibits his indifference in public places as one might draw a magnet through iron filings. He universalizes, industrializes asceticism for the sake of desire. There is nothing less aristocratic than this undertaking; it reveals the bourgeois soul of the dandy. This high-mannered Mephistopheles would like to be the capitalist of desire.

Thus in slightly different forms the dandy will be found in the works of all the novelists of internal mediation. Stendhal, Proust, and even Dostoyevsky created dandys. When Karmazinov asks him who Stavrogin is, Verhovenski answers: "He is a kind of Don Juan." Stavrogin is the most monstrous and satanic incarnation of novelistic dandyism. A supreme dandy, supremely successful, only for his greater misery, Stavrogin is beyond desire. It is not clear whether he no longer desires because Others desire him or whether Others desire him because he no longer desires. Thus is formed a vicious circle from which Stavrogin cannot escape. No longer having a mediator himself, he becomes the magnetic pole of desire and hatred. All the characters in *The Possessed* become his slaves; they gravitate around him tirelessly; they exist only for him, they think only through him.

But it is Stavrogin,[1] as his name suggests, who bears the heaviest cross. Dostoyevsky wants to show us just what the "success" of the metaphysical undertaking would entail. Stavrogin is young, good-looking, rich, strong, intelligent, and noble. Dostoyevsky does not endow his character with all these qualities because he feels a secret sympathy for him, as suggested by so many avantgarde critics. Stavrogin illustrates a theoretical case. He has to unite in his own person all the conditions for metaphysical success in order that the "struggle of master and slave" should always turn to his advantage. Stavrogin has no need to put out his hand that everybody, men and women alike, fall at his feet and surrender to him. Stavrogin is the victim of *ennui;* he is rapidly reduced to the most horrible caprices and ends by committing suicide.

Prince Myshkin is at the other end of the Dostoyevskian scale and he plays, in his novelistic universe, a role somewhat similar to that played by Stavrogin in his, but for contrary reasons. The Prince is not without desires but his dreams pass far over the heads of the other characters in *The Idiot.* He is the man with the most remote desire in the universe of the nearest desire. As far as those around him are concerned it is exactly as if he had no desire. He does not let himself be trapped in the triangles of others. Envy, jealousy, and rivalries abound in his presence but he is not contaminated. He is not indifferent—far from

---

[1] The name in Russian signifies "iron bearer."

it—but his charity and pity are not as binding as desire. He never offers other characters the support of his vanity and they are always stumbling around him. For this reason he is to a certain extent responsible for the death of General Ivolgin for he lets the wretched man enmesh himself in his own lies. A Lebedeff would have been forced by his own pride to interrupt the general; by doubting his word he would have given him a way out through indignation.

Myshkin offers no hold for pride or shame; his sublime indifference can only irritate the vain desires crisscrossing around him. His authentic renunciation has the same results as the dandy's false renunciation. Like Stavrogin, Myshkin acts as a magnet for unattached desires; he fascinates all the characters in *The Idiot*. The "normal" young people are unable to decide between two conflicting opinions of him—they wonder whether he is an idiot or a consummate tactician, a superior kind of dandy. The author himself seems to have doubts. Myshkin is not truly incarnate. The character remains problematic.

The triumph of evil is so complete in Dostoyevsky's universe that a Myshkin's humility, his stubborn attempt to transfigure his neighbor's existence by love, bears the same poisoned fruits as the frightful aridity of pride. We can understand why the Prince and Stavrogin have the same point of departure in the author's rough draft. This common origin does not prove that Dostoyevsky hesitates between the devil and God. It surprises us because, under the influence of romanticism, we attach too much importance to the individual hero. The novelist's fundamental concern is not the creation of characters but the revelation of metaphysical desire.

THE DESIRING subject, when he takes possession of the object, finds that he is grasping a void; thus, in the final reckoning, the master ends up as far from his aim as the slave. By pretending and dissimulating desire, he succeeds in exerting control over the Other's desire. He possesses the object but that object loses its value in the very act of being possessed: once he has won Mathilde's love Julien rapidly loses interest in her; Proust's narrator wants to rid himself of Albertine as soon as he thinks she is faithful to him; Lizaveta Nicolaevna has only to give herself to Stavrogin to have him turn away from her. The slave immediately becomes a part of the kingdom of the banal of which the master is the center. Each time the master renews his desire and advances on his object, he thinks he has left his prison but he carries it with him, as the saint carries his halo. The master thus pursues his sad exploration of reality indefinitely, like the positivist scholar who hopes to attain supreme knowledge by an exhaustive analysis of the "facts."

The master is doomed to disillusionment and boredom. To listen to him, one would think that he recognizes the absurdity of metaphysical desire. But he has not renounced *every* desire. He has only renounced those desires which experience proves do not live up to expectations; he renounces easy desires and beings who surrender without a fight. Only the threat, or rather the promise of a victorious resistance, attracts him from now on. De Rougemont, in *Love in the Western World*, perceived this fatality of romantic passion: "New obstacles have to be found in order to desire again and in order to exalt that desire to the proportions of a conscious, intense and continually interesting passion."

The master is not cured, he has become blasé. His cynicism is the opposite of true wisdom. He has to come nearer and nearer to slavery in order to shake off his boredom. He is like the driver who races his car a little faster every lap and must end up overturning.

Tolstoy's Napoleon offers an example of a great self-control headed for slavery. Like all bourgeois, Napoleon is a parvenu who owes his success to the ascetic instinct of internal mediation. Like all bourgeois, he confuses this ascetic instinct with the categorical imperative of an absolutely disinterested ethic. But in the midst of his triumph Napoleon discovers that nothing in him has changed and this discovery plunges him into despair. He wants to track down in another's gaze a reflection of that divinity which still eludes him. He wants to be emperor by "divine right," to proclaim his will *urbi et orbi*, to demand obedience from the entire world.

The master seeks the object which will resist him. Stavrogin does not find it; Napoleon finally does. There are many more Napoleons than Stavrogins in the universe of internal mediation. The ambitious man is not persecuted by a blind fate; it is the dialectic of pride and shame which is always present even at the height of glory. The soul of the great man is constantly being hollowed out by the abyss of nothingness.

The novelistic dialect of master and slave throws light on the Tolstoian concept of history. Napoleon condemns himself, for in this universe of internal mediation one must always choose either the sterile self-control of the dandy or the most abject slavery. Isaiah Berlin, in his brilliant essay *The Hedgehog and the Fox,* shows that there is no historic determinism in Tolstoy, in the usual sense of the term. The novelist's pessimism is not based on an inexorable chain of causes and effects, nor on a dogmatic conception of "human nature," nor on any other data immediately accessible to the investigations of the historian or sociologist. Like every object of desire history is ephemeral. With equal ease it frustrates the conjectures of scientists and the calculations of men of action who think they have tamed it. In the universe of internal mediation desire for omnipotence, like the desire for omniscience, contains within itself the germs of its own failure. Desire misses its object at the very moment when it seems to attain it, for by becoming visible it arouses rival desires that stand between the hero and his object. Each individual's activity is restrained by the Others and the more spectacular the activity the more effective the restraint. Now the master is drawn relentlessly, from desire through desire, toward the supreme spectacle of his own omnipotence. He always moves, therefore, toward his own destruction.

EVERY startling success in the universe of double mediation results from real or feigned *indifference*. It is Père Sorel's indifference which enables him to get the better of M. de Rênal; indifference assures La Sanseverina's triumph at the Court of Parma and M. Leuwen's in the Chamber of Deputies. The whole secret consists of displaying indifference without giving away one's game. The banker's politics in *Lucien Leuwen* could be considered a parliamentary dandyism; Kutuzov's victory, in *War and Peace*, could be considered strategic dandyism. Compared with Napoleon and the young officers of the Russian army who desire victory too much to win it, the old general is the incarnation not so much of military genius as of superior self-control.

Askesis for the sake of desire is equally well illustrated in the work of Balzac but the metaphysical game does not unfold with the same geometric exactness as in Stendhal, Proust, or Dostoyevsky. Some of Balzac's heroes triumph over every obstacle by brute courage and an activity mostly concerned with the external world. The windmills do not overthrow the men, but the men the windmills. The laws of triangular desire do not always provide an interpretation of the career of Balzac's ambitious characters.

These characters take the objects of their desire by

storm and then settle down to a real and lasting enjoyment of them. Rastignac is perfectly happy in his box at the theater; the audience in the orchestra looks on him as he looks on himself. This is the happiness dreamed of by the dandy or the businessman. Everyone in the universe of internal mediation heaves on the chain of desire and dreams of the retirement he will enjoy, not out of the world, but in a world he has finally conquered, a world possessed and still desirable. Rastignac's destiny does not reveal metaphysical desire, it reflects it.

Balzac is the epic poet of bourgeois desire and his novels remain imbued with it. His vituperations against modern society share the ambivalence of certain contemporary denunciations, such as those of the early Dos Passos, for example. There is always some ambiguity in them. It is hard to distinguish indignation from complaisance. There are in Balzac many intuitions parallel to those of the novelists studied in this book. But the web in which the desiring subject is trapped is full of rents through which often enough the author himself or his personal representatives slip. In the novelists we have chosen to study the cloth is so closely woven, the thread so strong that it is impossible for anyone to escape the unyielding laws of desire without escaping the desire itself.

In DOUBLE mediation, as we have said, mastery is always the reward of the partner who has best concealed his desire. The strategy of high society and of love in Proust's universe always conforms to this law. Only indifference can open the doors of the salon to the snob: "The lights of high society are so used to being sought after that one who shuns them seems to them a phoenix."

Askesis for the sake of desire is a universal requirement in the novels of internal mediation. Far from reducing all the heroes to a single type, this law enables us to define certain differences—for example, between Julien Sorel and Proust's narrator. Marcel is condemned to slavery because he is incapable of going all the way with sacrifice *for the sake of* desire:

> But the disastrous manner in which the psychopathic universe is constructed has decreed that the clumsy action, the action which we ought most carefully to have avoided, should be precisely the action that will calm us. . . . when the pain is too keen, we dash headlong into the blunder that consists in writing, sending somebody to intercede, going in person, proving that we cannot get on without the woman we love.

Marcel gives in to all the temptations over which Julien triumphs. Someone is indeed vanquished in *The Red and the Black* but it is not Julien, it is Mathilde. There are indeed conquerors in *Remembrance of Things Past* but they are never Marcel, Swann, or Charlus; they are Gilberte, Albertine, Odette, and Morel. A mechanical comparison between Stendhal's and Proust's heroes will never reveal the unity of metaphysical desire nor the close connection between the two novelists, for the principal heroes of the two novels represent opposite moments of the same dialectic.

The laws of desire are universal but they do not entail a uniformity of the novels, even at those points where their application is most precise. The law is the foundation of the diversity and makes it intelligible. Julien Sorel is a hero-master, Marcel is a hero-slave. The unity of the novel can be seen only if we cease to regard the character—the sacrosanct individual—as a completely autonomous entity, if we disengage the laws that govern the relationships between all the characters.

In *The Red and the Black* it is almost always the master

who contemplates the universe of the novel. We penetrate the consciousness of a free, indifferent, and haughty Mathilde. After Mathilde becomes a slave we see her only from the outside, through the eyes of the master who, henceforth, is Julien. Novelistic insight is usually found in the consciousness of a master; when this consciousness loses its mastery, it also loses that insight which then passes to the conqueror. It is the reverse in Proust: the consciousness which filters the light of the novel and gives to it its specifically Proustian quality is almost always the consciousness of a slave.

The transition from mastery to slavery throws light on many of the contrasts between Stendhal on the one hand and Proust and Dostoyevsky on the other. We know that the future for mastery is slavery. True in theory, this principle is also true in the evolution of the novels. Slavery is the future of mastery; Proust and Dostoyevsky are therefore Stendhal's future; their novels are *the truth* of Stendhal's work.

This movement toward slavery is one of the basic principles of novelistic structure. Every authentic development in the novel, no matter how broad its scope, can be defined as a transition from mastery to slavery. This law is confirmed by novelistic literature considered in its totality; it is equally well confirmed by the complete works of one author, or one novel in particular, or even one episode within that novel.

First let us look at the case of an author's works as a whole. We defined Stendhal as a novelist of mastery compared with later novelists. If we look at each work of Stendhal's individually we shall find the evolution from master to slave reflected in the difference between his first and last works. In *Armance* real slavery does not as yet appear in any form; unhappiness remains essentially romantic and poses no threat to the autonomy of the characters. In *The Red and the Black* slavery is present but it almost always remains unessential. In *Lucien Leuwen* its importance grows with the character of Dr. du Périer. In *The Charterhouse of Parma* the novel's camera dwells more and more complaisantly on servile characters and situations: the jealousy of Mosca and La Sanseverina, the terror of the Prince of Parma, the meanness of the prosecutor Rassi. Finally, in *Lamiel,* Stendhal creates for the first time a hero-slave in the person of Sansfin, a bourgeois precursor of the underground hero.

We find a similar movement toward slavery in Proust. Jean Santeuil never loses his freedom; he is not a snob but the world around him is crawling with snobs. *Jean Santeuil* is a novel of mastery. *Remembrance of Things Past* is a novel of slavery.

Let us now consider a single novel. We have said that Julien Sorel is a hero-master. This is true but the further one reads in the novel the closer is Julien's contact with slavery. The danger is greatest in the episode with Mathilde, i.e., in the section immediately preceding the conclusion which brings release. (The latter interrupts and reverses the movement toward slavery. The conclusion is still outside the scope of the present analysis.)

We find the same movement toward slavery in *Remembrance of Things Past* but the point of arrival is much lower than in *The Red and the Black*. At the time of his first love Marcel still shows a certain amount of ascetic will power: he stops seeing Gilberte when he realizes that she is turning away from him, and he successfully resists the temptation to write to her. But his will power and hypocrisy are not sufficient to win back his beloved; he is not as strong as Julien, but he is still strong enough to escape enslavement. However in *The Captive* and *The Fugitive* he surrenders completely to slavery. The lowest point of this "descent into hell" is situated, as in Stendhal, in that part of the work immediately before the redeeming conclusion.

Similarly the psychological and spiritual evolution of the secondary characters is also an advance toward slavery, which this time is not interrupted by the novel's conclusion. Charlus for example continues to decline and fall from one end of the novel to the other.

This movement toward slavery is indistinguishable from the *fall* which we described at the end of Chapter III. We are merely presenting the phenomenon from a different angle in order to make explicit certain modalities such as the dialectic of master and slave; moreover, this dialectic belongs only to the upper regions of internal mediation. When the two rivals are very close to each other, double mediation ends in double fascination. *Askesis* for the sake of desire becomes involuntary and causes paralysis. The two partners are faced with very similar concrete possibilities; they thwart each other so successfully that neither of them is able to approach the object. They remain opposite each other, immobilized in an opposition that absorbs them totally. Each is for the other his own image emerging from the mirror to bar his way. Mastery, a secondary figure, has vanished.

Old Karamazov and his children offer an example of this ultimate stage of internal mediation. Varvara Petrovna and Stepan Trofimovitch, in *The Possessed*, are equally fascinated by each other. Inspired by these examples André Gide tried in *The Counterfeiters* to incarnate this image of desire in the elderly La Pérouse couple.

WE HAVE sketched the theoretic development of double mediation. We have seen desire grow and intensify without the intervention of any external element in the two superimposed triangles. Double mediation is a figure turned in upon itself; desire circulates in it and feeds on its own substance. Thus double mediation constitutes a veritable "generator" of desire, the simplest possible. For this reason we chose it for our theoretical discussion. Beginning from the standpoint of double mediation, it is easy to imagine more complex figures, equally autonomous, which give birth to ever more vast *novelistic worlds*. Frequently, concrete situations correspond to these more complex figures. Instead of selecting his own slave for his mediator, the subject may choose a third individual, and the latter a fourth—Saint-Loup is the slave of Rachel, who in turn is the slave of the polo player, who in turn is André's slave—thus we have a "chain" of triangles. The character who plays the part of mediator in a first triangle may play the part of slave in a second triangle and so on.

Racine's *Andromaque* provides a good example of this chain of triangles. Orestes is slave to Hermione; Hermione is slave to Pyrrhus; Pyrrhus is Andromaque's slave, who is herself faithful to a dead man's memory. All these characters keep their eyes fixed on their mediator and show absolute indifference toward their slaves. They all resemble each other in their sexual pride, their anguished isolation, and their unconscious cruelty. *Andromaque* is the tragedy of the courtier and belongs to a very modern type of mediation.

Racine's tragedy before *Phèdre* reflects rather than reveals metaphysical desire. The novelist would emphasize the analogies between the characters; the tragedian tries to hide them. The critics never fail to comment on Racine's "mistake," from the point of view of tragedy, in creating these characters who are too alike.

The novelistic universe of *The Princess of Clèves* is quite similar to that of Racine. Love is always unhappy in it. The sad stories of Mme de Tournon and Mme de

Thémines are a warning to Mme de Clèves. But the heroine, right up to the conclusion, is unable to make the connection between the fate of these poor women and her own future. She sees only the vernal side of love in the features of the Duke de Nemours. Her pride identifies with this mirage and rejects the other side as being reserved for *other* women. But the Princess does escape from desire. Toward the end of the novel she has the terrible experience of realizing that she is no different from those other women who are lost through love. No character in *Andromaque* experiences this. Let us listen to Mme de Clèves when she discovers that Nemours has betrayed her secret. The Duke has boasted to his friends that the Princess loved him: "I was wrong," Mme de Clèves remarks bitterly, "to think that there was a man who could keep secret something which flattered his pride. . . . Yet this man whom I believed so different from other men has put me in the same position as other women whom I was so far from resembling." In one sentence the Princess sums up the whole operation of metaphysical desire. The subject clings to a mediator who is transfigured by his desire. He thinks he is heightening his individuality by desiring this being, whereas in reality he is losing it, for everyone is the victim of the same illusion. Every woman has her Nemours.

The Princess of Clèves must be compared with the great novels of literature since it reveals certain aspects of metaphysical desire. Racine's tragedy points to the hand of fate in the disharmony of love but Mme de la Fayette questions the meaning of desire and finally, in the conclusion, puts her finger on the grotesque and painful mechanism of passional conflict. Mme de Clèves has just granted a last interview to the Duke de Nemours:

> M. de Clèves was perhaps the only man in the world capable of preserving his love in marriage. But my

fate would not let me profit from this happiness; perhaps too his passion subsisted only because he thought I was without passion. But I would not have the same means of preserving yours; I even believe that it is the obstacles which have kept you constant.

The novel's "message" is not sacrifice to the memory of a dead husband, as has been so frequently repeated, until recent years, by critics imbued with masculine and bourgeois prejudices. Nor has the conclusion any connection with Corneille's static glory. Mme de Clèves finally perceives the future which lies ahead of her. She refuses to take part in the infernal game; by leaving the Court she is escaping from the world of the novel and its metaphysical contagion.

CHAPTER VIII

MASOCHISM AND SADISM

THE MASTER has learned from his many different experiences that an object which can be possessed is valueless. So in the future he will be interested only in objects which are forbidden him by an implacable mediator. The master seeks an insurmountable obstacle and he almost always succeeds in finding one.

A man sets out to discover a treasure he believes is hidden under a stone; he turns over stone after stone but finds nothing. He grows tired of such a futile undertaking but the treasure is too precious for him to give up. So he begins to look for a *stone which is too heavy to lift*—he places all his hopes in that stone and he will waste all his remaining strength on it.

The *masochist,* for that is whom we have been describing, may be originally a master who has become blasé. Continual success, or rather continual disappointment, makes him desire his own failure; only that failure will indicate an authentic deity, a mediator who is invulnerable to his own undertakings. As we know, metaphysical desire always ends in enslavement, failure, and shame. If these consequences are too long delayed, the subject's bizarre logic will force him to hasten their arrival. The masochist hastens the course of his own destiny and gathers into one single moment the various phases of the metaphysical process which until now have been separated. In the course of "ordinary" desire the obstruction was a result of imitation; now imitation is the result of obstruction.

Enslavement leads to masochism even more directly than mastery. The victim of internal mediation always sees, we may recall, a hostile intention in the mechanical obstacle which the desire of the mediator places in his path. The victim is loud in his indignation but at heart he believes he deserves the punishment inflicted on him. The mediator's hostility always seems somewhat legitimate, since by very definition the victim feels inferior to the person whose desire he copies. Thus contempt and obstruction only redouble desire because they confirm the superiority of the mediator. From this point it is but a short step to choosing the mediator, not because of his seemingly positive qualities but because of the *obstruction he can provide;* and the more a subject despises himself the more easily he makes this step.

Even in "ordinary" desire there was no act of the subject which did not eventually work against him, yet he remained unaware of any connection between his misfortunes and his desire. The masochist perceives the *necessary* relation between unhappiness and metaphysical desire, but he nevertheless does not renounce his desire. By a misunderstanding even more remarkable than those which preceded it, he now chooses to see in shame, defeat, and enslavement not the inevitable results of an aimless faith and an absurd mode of behavior but rather the *signs* of divinity and the preliminary condition of all metaphysical success. Henceforth the subject bases his enterprise of autonomy on failure; he founds his *projet* of being God on an abyss.

De Rougemont in *Love in the Western World* recognizes that every passion feeds on the obstacles placed in its way and dies in their absence. From this De Rougemont concludes that desire should be defined as a desire of the obstacle. The observations in *Love in the Western World* are remarkable but the explanatory synthesis at this stage seems inadequate. Any synthesis is incomplete which ends in an object or an abstract concept and not in a living relationship between two individuals. The obstacle, even in the case of masochism where it alone is directly sought, cannot be primary. The quest for the mediator has ceased to be immediate, but it is this quest which is being pursued through the intermediary of the obstacle.

In the lower stages of internal mediation the subject despises himself so much that he has no confidence in his own judgment. He believes he is infinitely far from the supreme Good he is pursuing; he cannot believe that the influence of that Good can reach as far as himself. He is thus not sure he can distinguish the mediator from ordinary men. There is only one thing whose value the masochist thinks himself capable of judging—himself, and his value is nil. The masochist will judge other men according to their perceptiveness with regard to himself: he will reject those who feel tenderness and affection for him, whereas he turns eagerly to those who show, by their contempt for him, real or apparent, that they do not belong, like him, to the race of the accursed. We are masochists when we no longer choose our mediator because of the admiration which he inspires in us but because of the disgust we seem to inspire in him. From the standpoint of a metaphysical hell the masochist's reasoning is irreproachable. It is a model of scientific induction; it may even be the archetype of inductive reasoning.

We have already seen, in Chapter II, examples of masochism in which humiliation, impotence, and shame, i.e., the obstacle, determined the choice of mediator. It is the *noli me tangere* of the Guermantes which unleashes in

Marcel a furious desire to "be received." It is the same process in the case of the underground man and that of Zverkov's buddies. In the episode of the officer there is in the most literal sense of the word an obstacle: the underground man is actually forced off the sidewalk by the officer's insolence. In every case, in the works of the novelists of internal mediation, we can confirm the accuracy of De Rougemont's observations: "The most serious obstruction is thus the one preferred above all. It is the one most suited to intensifying passion." The description is correct but we should add that the most impassable obstacle has this value only because it indicates the presence of the most divine mediator. Marcel imitates Albertine's language and manners; he even adopts her tastes. The underground man strives in a grotesque fashion to copy the impudent boasting of the man who insulted him. Isolde would be less attractive if she were not the promised wife of the King, for it is to royalty, in the most absolute sense of the word, that Tristan aspires. The mediator remains hidden, because the myth of Tristan is one of the first romantic poems. The great novelists, on the other hand, in their revelation of the completely imitative existence of the passionate being, illuminate the darkest depths of the Western soul.

The masochist is at once more lucid and more blind than other victims of metaphysical desire. He is more lucid in that he possesses that lucidity, increasingly prevalent in our time, which permits him alone among all desiring subjects to perceive the connection between internal mediation and the obstacle; he is more blind because, instead of following out the implications of this awareness to their necessary conclusion, instead of giving up misdirected transcendency, he tries paradoxically to satisfy his desire by rushing toward the obstacle, thus making his destiny one of misery and failure.

The source of this ill-starred lucidity which characterizes the last stages of ontological sickness is not difficult to discover. It is the increased proximity of the mediator. Enslavement is always the final result of desire, but at first it is very distant and the desiring subject cannot perceive it. The eventual result becomes increasingly clear as the distance between mediator and subject decreases and the phases of the metaphysical process are accelerated. Every metaphysical desire thus tends toward masochism, because the mediator is always growing nearer and the enlightenment which he brings with him is incapable, by itself, of curing ontological sickness; this insight only provides the victim with the means of hastening the fatal evolution. Every metaphysical desire proceeds toward its own truth and toward the desiring subject's awareness of this truth; masochism occurs when the subject himself enters into the light of this truth and eagerly collaborates in its advent.

Masochism is founded on a profound but still insufficient intuition of metaphysical truth, a deviated and perverted intuition whose effects are even more harmful than the innocence of previous stages. When the desiring subject perceives the abyss that desire has hollowed out beneath his feet, he voluntarily hurls himself into it, hoping against hope to discover in it what the less acute stages of metaphysical sickness have not brought him.

In practice it is sometimes difficult to distinguish true masochism from the unconscious and diffuse masochism found in all forms of metaphysical desire. It is a fact that Don Quixote and Sancho are never happy unless they are being beaten black and blue. "Idealistic" readers hold Cervantes responsible for the prodigious beatings his hero receives; modern readers, more "lucid," more "realistic" than the first romantics, are wont to consider Don Quixote a masochist. The two contrary opinions are opposite twin forms of the romantic error. Don Quixote is no more a masochist, in the strict sense of the word, than Cervantes is a sadist; he is imitating his mediator Amadis of Gaul. In the case of Julien Sorel there is already more reason for doubt. The adolescent could live in comfort with his friend Fouqué but instead he comes to the Hotel de la Mole to expose himself to the scorn of aristocrats who are inferior to him. Again, what is the meaning behind the furious passion which derives solely from Mathilde's disdain and cannot outlive it?

Between the desiring subject who submits with resignation to the unpleasant consequences of mediation and the subject who seeks them out avidly, not because they give him pleasure but because for him they have the value of a *sacrament*, all shades of the spectrum are possible. There is no clear division between the premasochism of Don Quixote and the unquestionable masochism of Marcel or the underground hero; above all, one cannot be classified as "normal" and the other as "pathological." The dividing line between sickness and health is always arbitrary and is drawn by our own desires. The great novelists erase this line and thus abolish yet another barrier. No one can say where a repulsive masochism begins and so-called "legitimate" ambition and a noble hunger for what is risky leave off.

Every reduction of the distance between the mediator and the subject is a step in the direction of masochism. The passage from external to internal mediation has itself masochistic implications. Unsatisfied with a mediator who is only a figurehead, men choose like the frogs of the fable an active mediator who slashes them to pieces. Enslavement always implies masochism since it is based on the obstacle which a rival's desire puts in our way, since the slave is glued to that obstacle like a limpet to a rock.

Masochism clearly reveals the contradiction which

forms the basis of metaphysical desire. The impassioned person is seeking the divine through this insuperable obstacle, through that which, by definition, cannot be crossed. It is this metaphysical meaning which has escaped most psychologists and psychiatrists. Often the subject is said simply to desire shame, humiliation, and suffering. No one has ever desired any such thing. Every victim of metaphysical desire, including the masochist, covets his mediator's divinity, and for this divinity he will accept if necessary—and it is always necessary—or even seek out, shame, humiliation, and suffering. He hopes that misery and suffering will reveal to him the person whom he should imitate in order to free himself of his wretched condition. But these deluded people never desire, purely and simply, shame, humiliation, and suffering. The masochist cannot be understood unless we recognize the triangular nature of his desire. The conception has always been of a linear desire and, starting from the subject, the sempiternal straight line is traced; and this line always runs into the familiar disappointments. These in turn are thought to be the *object* of his desire; it is asserted in short that the masochist desires what *we* would never desire.

Another difficulty with this definition is that it renders impossible any distinction, even theoretical, between metaphysical desire in general and masochism in the proper sense of the term. Masochism is diagnosed, in fact, any time the observer sees the connections between desire and its disastrous results. And it is taken for granted that this connection is perceived by the subject, even though in the higher and earlier stages of mediation he is completely unaware of it. Only when the subject is aware of the connection can we speak of masochism, if the term is to retain an exact theoretical meaning.

To make suffering—the simple result of desire, or, in

masochism, its preliminary condition—the actual *object* of that desire is a particularly revealing "mistake." Like other mistakes of the same type, it is not due to an unfortunate accident or to a lack of scientific precautions by the observer. This observer *does not want* to delve into the truth of desire to the point where he himself would be just as much involved as the subject of his observations. By restricting the deplorable consequences of metaphysical desire to an object which the masochist, and he alone, would desire, one makes an exceptional being of him, a monster whose sentiments have nothing in common with those of "normal" people, i.e., our own. The masochist is supposed to desire the *opposite* of what we desire. The contradiction which ought to be perceived as being desire itself at its most intense becomes an individual's idiosyncrasy; it becomes a barrier between the observer and this masochist whom it would be dangerous to understand entirely.

Let us note that contradictions which in reality are the very basis of our psychic life always appear as "differences" between Others and ourselves. The connections established by internal mediation vitiate many would-be "scientific" observations. We dehumanize every desire whose harmful consequences we perceive in order not to recognize the image, or caricature, of our own desires. Dostoyevsky accurately observes that by having our neighbor confined to a mental institution we convince ourselves of our own sanity. What could we have in common with this awful masochist whose desire has for its end the very essence of the nondesirable? It is preferable, of course, not to know that the masochist desires exactly what we ourselves desire: autonomy and a god-like self-control, his own self-esteem and the esteem of others; but by an intuition of metaphysical desire more profound than his doctors possess—although it is still tragically imperfect—he no longer hopes to find these inestimable treasures except at the side of a master whose humble slave he will be.

CLOSELY related to the existential masochism we have just described is the purely sexual masochism and sadism, which play an important role in the works of Proust and Dostoyevsky.

The sexual masochist tries to reproduce in his erotic life the conditions of an extremely intense metaphysical desire. Ideally his partner and mediator would be the same person. But this ideal cannot, by definition, be achieved, for if it were it would cease to be desirable, the mediator having lost his divine powers. Thus the masochist is reduced to imitating his impossible ideal. He wants to act with his sexual partner the role which he would play—or so he thinks—with his mediator. The brutalities demanded by the masochist are always associated in his mind with those to which a truly divine model would probably subject him.

Even in this purely sexual masochism, therefore, it cannot be said that the subject "desires" suffering. What he desires is his mediator's presence, contact with the sacred. He can evoke the image of this mediator only by recreating the actual or imagined atmosphere of his relations with him. Suffering which does not remind him of the mediator is of no erotic value to the masochist.

Sadism is the "dialectical" reverse of masochism. Tired of playing the part of the martyr, the desiring subject chooses to become the tormentor. The triangular conception of desire reveals the relationship of the two attitudes and their frequent alternation.

Sexual activity mirrors the whole of existence. It is a stage upon which the masochist plays his own part and imitates his own desire; the sadist plays the role of the mediator himself. This change of roles should not surprise us. We know that all victims of metaphysical desire seek to appropriate their mediator's being by imitating him. The sadist wants to persuade himself that he has already attained his goal; he tries to take the place of the mediator and see the world through his eyes, in the hope that the play will gradually turn into reality. The sadist's violence is yet another effort to attain divinity.

The sadist cannot achieve the illusion of *being* the mediator without transforming his victim into a replica of himself. At the very moment of redoubling his brutality he cannot help recognizing himself in the other who is suffering. This is the meaning of that strange "communion" between the victim and his tormentor so often observed.

It is frequently said that the sadist persecutes because he feels he is being persecuted. This is true but it is not quite the whole truth. In order to desire to persecute we must believe that the being who persecutes us thereby attains a sphere of existence infinitely superior to our own. One cannot be a sadist unless the key to the enchanted garden appears to be in the hands of a tormentor.

Sadism reveals once again the immense prestige of the mediator. The face of the man now disappears behind the mask of the infernal god. Horrible as the madness of the sadist is, it has the same meaning as previous desires. And if the sadist resorts to desperate measures it is because the hour of despair has struck.

Dostoyevsky and Proust recognize the imitative character of sadism. After the banquet at which he has degraded and humiliated himself, where he thought he was tormented by petty persecutors, the underground man actually tortures the unfortunate prostitute who falls into his hands. He imitates what he thinks was the conduct of

Zverkov's crew toward himself; he aspires to the divinity with which in his anguish he has clothed his petty fellow-actors in the previous scenes.

The sequence of episodes in *Notes from the Underground* is of some importance. First comes the banquet and then the scenes with the prostitute. The existential aspects of the masochistic-sadistic structure precede its sexual aspects. Far from laying the emphasis on the latter as do so many doctors and psychiatrists, the novelist stresses the basic individual *projet*. The problems presented by sexual masochism and sadism can be understood only if their phenomena are regarded as a reflection of the whole of existence. Every reflection obviously comes after the thing it reflects. Sexual masochism is a mirror for existential masochism and not the reverse. Once more it must be said—current interpretations always reverse the true meaning and hierarchy of the phenomena. In the same way that sadism is put before masochism—we speak of sado-masochism instead of masochism-sadism—the sexual elements are systematically given priority over the existential elements. This reversal is so constant that it can by itself serve to define the transition from the true order which is metaphysical to these "psychologies" and "psychoanalyses" which are often the very opposite of the truth.[1]

[1] Hurling insults at Freud is a popular pastime among literary critics. It makes us feel that we have solved, once and for all and at very little cost, the problem posed by psychoanalysis. The passage above is a good example of these futile exercises in tribal exorcism. Honesty demanded that it be maintained and that it be disavowed in the present footnote. The author is aware that he may thus lose the sympathy of those who see his anti-Freudianism as the one redeeming feature in his thought.

Attempts to dismiss literature through a summary psychoanalytical diagnosis have been justly ridiculed. But these attempts were not representative of the best psychoanalytical thought. From a Freudian viewpoint, the original triangle of desire is, of course, the Oedipal triangle. The story of "mediated" desire is the story of this

Sexual masochism and sadism are second-degree imitations; they are imitations of an imitation since the subject's existence in metaphysical desire is already an imitation. Like Dostoyevsky, Proust realized that sadism is a copy, a play of passion performed for oneself and for a magic end. Mlle Vinteuil tries to imitate the "wicked"; her desecration of her father's memory is both crude and naïve:

> A "sadist" of her kind is an artist in evil, which a wholly wicked person could not be, for in that case the evil would not have been external, it would have seemed quite natural to her, and would not even have been distinguishable from herself . . . they [these artists] endeavour to impersonate, to assume all the outward appearance of wicked people . . . so as to gain the momentary illusion of having escaped beyond the control of their own gentle and scrupulous natures into the inhuman world of pleasure.

The sadist never ceases to identify with the victim, that is with persecuted innocence, even during the very perpe-

---

Oedipal desire, of its essential permanence beyond its ever changing objects. Freud's article on Dostoyevsky is essential but Freud does not perceive that, in his last and greatest work, *Brothers Karamazov*, Dostoyevsky's insight into the essence of desire is no less acute for being couched in a different language than the psychoanalyst's. Psychoanalysis is exclusively regressive, whereas the novel is both regressive and progressive. One of the tasks facing criticism is the establishment of a genuine dialogue with Freud. If the original triangle is that of Oedipus, so is perhaps the original "romanesque" revelation. In the conclusion of *Oedipus the King*, the hero discovers that the culprit he was looking for is none but himself. So does the novelist when he says, "Madame Bovary c'est moi, Julien Sorel c'est moi." The Self discovers that the Other, who has become the hated Double, is really identical to himself in those very features which make him appear most hateful. Sophocles' tragedy, and other works of art, do more than "prefigure psychoanalysis." They suggest other dimensions which cannot be interpreted, either, through the Aristotelian *catharsis*, unless we agree that the word catharsis simply names the problem rather than provides the solution.

tration of evil. He is the incarnation of Good and his mediator of Evil. The romantic and "Manichean" division between Self and Others is always present and even plays an essential role in sado-masochism.

Deep in his heart, the masochist cannot stand the Good to which he thinks he is condemned, and he worships the persecuting Evil, for his mediator personifies Evil. This fact is particularly clear in Proust. Among his fellow students in high school, Jean Santeuil seeks the companionship of the brutal ones, who look on him as an object of ridicule. The narrator of *Remembrance of Things Past* defines the desired being as "the unreal and diabolic objectivation of the temperament which is opposed to my own, of the almost barbarous and cruel vitality which is so lacking in my weakness, my extremes of painful sensibility and intellectuality." Most of the time the subject himself is not aware of his passion for Evil. The truth only appears in flashes in his sexual life and in certain remote areas of existence. The gentle Saint-Loup is cruel only in his relations with the servants. His clear perception is totally taken up with the defense of Good. On this level the aggravation of desire often shows up in the form of aggravation of the moral sense, of delirious philanthropy, and of a virtuous enrollment in the forces of Good.

The masochist identifies with all the "insulted and the injured," with all the real and imaginary misfortunes that vaguely remind him of his own destiny. The masochist has a grudge against the very Spirit of Evil. And yet he does not want to crush the wicked so much as to *prove* to them their wickedness and his own virtue; he wants to cover them with shame by making them look at the victims of their own infamy.

At this stage of desire the "voice of conscience" is indistinguishable from the hatred aroused by the mediator. The masochist turns this hatred into a duty and condemns everyone who does not hate along with him. This hatred allows the desiring subject to keep his eyes constantly on his mediator. The masochist is all the more eager to destroy the delicious Evil because he believes himself incapable of piercing that impenetrable armour and reaching the divinity. Thus he has passionately renounced Evil; like the underground man he is the first to be astonished at certain displeasing phenomena which he observes in himself and which seem to contradict the whole of his moral life. The masochist is fundamentally a pessimist. He knows that Evil is destined to triumph. It is despairingly that he fights on the side of the Good; the fight is therefore all the more "commendable."

For cynical moralists, and in a different way for Nietzsche, all altruism, every identification with weakness and impotence, results from masochism. For Dostoyevsky, on the contrary, the masochistic ideology, like all the other fruits of metaphysical desire, is an inverse image of vertical transcendency. This terrible caricature testifies in favor of the original.

All the values of Christian morality can be found in masochism but their hierarchy is inverted. Compassion is never a principle but a result. The principle is hatred of the triumphant wicked. Good is loved in order that Evil be hated more. The oppressed are defended for the sake of overwhelming the oppressors.

The masochistic vision is never independent. It is always in opposition to a rival masochism which is organizing the same elements into a symmetrical and inverse structure. What is defined as Good on one leaf of the diptych is automatically defined as Evil on the other, and vice versa.

Dostoyevsky suggests, in *The Possessed*, that all modern ideologies are penetrated by masochism. The unfortunate Shatov tries desperately to escape the revolutionary

ideology but generally ends up with a reactionary ideology. Evil triumphs even in the efforts Shatov makes to rid
himself of it. The wretched man seeks an affirmation but
attains only the negation of a negation. Like others, the
slavophile ideology is a result of the modern spirit. These
new ideas are suggested to Shatov by Stavrogin.

The character of Shatov destroys the hypothesis of a
purely reactionary Dostoyevsky. Slavophilism in Dostoyevsky, like certain forms of revolutionary spirit in
Stendhal, is a remnant of romanticism, which the author
has not yet completely transcended. Shatov is Dostoyevsky meditating on his own ideological evolution, on
his own inability to free himself of negative ways of thinking. And it is in this very meditation that Dostoyevsky
transcends the slavophile ideology. The partisan spirit
still triumphs in *An Author's Notebook* but Dostoyevsky
crushes it in *The Brothers Karamazov.*

It is in this surpassing of the slavophile ideology that
we find the finest moment of Dostoyevsky's genius.

Do not hate the atheists, the professors of evil, the ma-
terialists, or even the wicked among them, for many are
good, especially in our time.

Dostoyevsky, in everything prior to *The Brothers*
Karamazov, and Proust, throughout his work, sometimes
yield to a common temptation: they endow certain characters with an essential wickedness, with a cruelty which
at first is not a response to another cruelty, or to an illusion of cruelty. These passages reflect the sado-masochis-
tic structure of experience; they do not reveal it.

Novelistic genius is based on the ability to transcend
and reveal the metaphysical desire but some dark corners
remain, certain obsessions resist the novel's insight. This
ability to *go beyond* is the fruit of an interior struggle and

the novels always bear the traces of this struggle. Novelistic genius is like the tide rising over uneven ground. Some little islands remain after the rest is submerged. There is always a critical zone in the extreme areas of metaphysical desire explored by the novelist. In Proust, some of the aspects of homosexual desire belong in this zone which novelistic revelation is rather slow to penetrate and in which it cannot always definitively assert itself.

In his greatest moments, however, which are often the *last* moments, the novelist triumphs over the supreme obstacles, he recognizes finally that the fascinating Evil is no more real than the Good with which the masochist automatically identifies:

> Perhaps she would not have thought of wickedness as a state so rare, so abnormal, so exotic, one which it was so refreshing to visit, had she been able to distinguish in herself, as in all her fellow men and women, that indifference to the sufferings they cause which, whatever names else be given it, is the one true, terrible and lasting form of cruelty.

That sentence seems even more wonderful when one considers the length of the spiritual journey stretching behind it. The sado-masochist's nightmare is as blatant a lie as Don Quixote's dream or the insipid illusion of the bourgeois. Basically, it is the same lie. The adorable persecutor is neither god nor demon; he is merely a person like ourselves, the more eager to hide his own suffering and humiliation because they are more intense. Albertine turns out to be insignificant. Zverkov is nothing but a boring idiot. The sado-masochist's mistake would make us laugh as much as Don Quixote's were the results of mediation not so terrible.

In Cervantes' eyes, Don Quixote is a man who neglects his duty. But his madness does not as yet place him in any radical opposition to the values of civilized Christian society. The illusion is very spectacular but its effects are harmless. It could be said without any paradox that among heroes of novels Don Quixote is the least mad. But the lie becomes more blatant and the consequences more serious as the mediator approaches. If we still doubt that this is true it is because we are prejudiced in favor of the dull, the mediocre or even the sordid and terrible, at least in the sense that we make these very characteristics our criteria of truth. An irrational but significant preference —itself the result of an increasingly intense mediation— leads us to consider the underground more "real," more "true" than the "beautiful and the sublime" of early romanticism. De Rougemont denounced this astonishing prejudice in *Love in the Western World:* "That which is most base seems to us most true. It is the superstition of our time." Fundamentally to be a *realist* is to tip the scales of probability in favor of the worst. But the realist makes an even more serious error than does the idealist. Not truth but falsehood advances as the "crystal palaces" are transformed into a vision of hell.

The genius of the novel rises above the oppositions that stem from metaphysical desire. It tries to show us their illusory character. It transcends the rival caricatures of Good and Evil presented by the factions. It affirms the identity of the opposites on the level of internal mediation. But it does not end in moral relativism. Evil exists. The tortures inflicted by the underground man on the young prostitute are not imaginary. The suffering of Vinteuil is only too real. Evil exists and it is metaphysical desire itself—deviated transcendency—which weaves man's thread in the wrong direction, thus separating what it claims to unite and uniting what it claims to separate. Evil is that negative pact of hatred to which so many men strictly adhere for their mutual destruction.

CHAPTER IX

THE WORLDS OF PROUST

COMBRAY is a closed universe. In it the child lives in the shadow of his parents and the family idols with the same happy intimacy as the medieval village in the shadow of the belfry. Combray's unity is primarily spiritual rather than physical. Combray is the vision shared by all the members of the family. A certain order is superimposed on reality and becomes indistinguishable from it. The first symbol of Combray is the magic lantern whose images take on the shape of the objects on which they are projected and are returned in the same way to us by the wall of the room, the lamp shades, and the doorknobs.

Combray is a closed culture, in the ethnological sense of the word, a *Welt* as the Germans would say, "a little closed world" the novelist calls it. The gulf between Combray and the rest of the world is on the level of perception. Between the perception of Combray and that of the "barbarians" there is a specific difference which it is the essential task of the novelist to reveal. The two bells at the entrance provide us with only a symbol, rather than an illustration of that difference. The bell which "any person of the household . . . put . . . out of action by coming in 'without ringing'" and "the double peal—timid, oval, gilded—of the visitors' bell" evoke two totally incommensurable universes.

At a very superficial level Combray is still capable of

making out the difference in perceptions. Combray notices the difference between the two bells; Combray is not unaware that *its* Saturday has a color, a tonality all its own. Lunch is moved up an hour on that day.

> The return of this asymmetrical Saturday was one of those petty occurrences, intra-mural, localised, almost civic, which, in uneventful lives and stable orders of society, create a kind of national unity, and become the favourite theme for conversation, for pleasantries, for anecdotes which can be embroidered as the narrator pleases; it would have provided a nucleus, ready-made, for a legendary cycle, if any of us had had the epic mind.

The members of Combray feel a certain solidarity and brotherliness when they discover something which distinguishes them from the outside world. Françoise, the maid, particularly enjoys this feeling of unity. Nothing causes her more amusement than the little misunderstandings occasioned by the family's forgetting, not that Saturdays are different, but that outsiders are not aware of that fact. The "barbarian" amazed at the change in schedule of which he was not forewarned appears slightly ridiculous. He is not *initiated* into the truth of Combray.

"Patriotic" rites spring up in that intermediate zone where the differences between ourselves and others become perceptible without being completely effaced. The misunderstanding is still half voluntary. On a more profound level it is not voluntary at all, and only the author-narrator can bridge the abyss between the divergent perceptions of a *single* object. Combray is incapable, for example, of understanding that apart from the bourgeois, domestic Swann to whom it is accustomed, there exists another aristocratic and elegant Swann, perceived only by high society.

And so, no doubt, from the Swann they had built up for their own purposes my family had left out, in their ignorance, a whole crowd of the details of his daily life in the world of fashion, details by means of which other people, when they met him, saw all the Graces enthroned in his face and stopping at the line of his arched nose as at a natural frontier; but they contrived also to put into a face from which its distinction had been evicted, a face vacant and roomy as an untenanted house, to plant in the depths of its unvalued eyes a lingering sense, uncertain but not unpleasing, half-memory and half-oblivion, of idle hours spent together.

The novelist is trying to make us see, touch, and feel what men by definition never see, touch, or feel: two perceptive events which are as imperative as they are contradictory. Between Combray and the outside world there is only an appearance of communication. The misapprehension is total but its results are more comic than tragic. We are provided with another example of comic misunderstanding in the imperceptible thanks which Aunt Céline and Aunt Flora give Swann for a present he sent them. The allusions are so vague and distant that no one notices them, but the two old ladies do not for a moment suspect that they may not have been understood.

What is the origin of this inability to communicate? In the case of the "two Swanns" it would seem that it can all be traced to intellectual causes, to a simple lack of information. Certain of the novelist's expressions seem to confirm this hypothesis. The family's *ignorance* creates the Swann of Combray. The narrator sees in this familiar Swann one of the charming *errors* of his youth.

The error is usually accidental. It disappears as soon as the attention of the person involved is drawn to it, as soon as the means of correcting it are provided. But, in the case of Swann the evidence piles up, the truth about him comes in from all sides without the opinion of the family, and especially that of the great-aunt, being in the least affected. It is learned that Swann frequents the aristocracy; *Le Figaro* mentions paintings in "the collection of Charles Swann." But the great-aunt never swerves in her belief. Finally it is discovered that Swann is the friend of Mme de Villeparisis; far from causing the great-aunt to think more highly of Swann, however, this bit of news has the effect of lowering her opinion of Mme de Villeparisis: "How should she know Swann?" says the great-aunt to the grandmother, "A lady who, you always made out, was related to Marshal MacMahon!" The truth, like a bothersome fly, keeps settling on the great-aunt's nose only to be flicked away.

Thus the Proustian error cannot be reduced to its intellectual causes. We must take care not to judge Proust on the basis of one isolated expression, and especially of the particular meaning to which a particular philosopher might limit that expression. We must go beyond the words to the substance of the novel. The truth about Swann does not penetrate Combray because it contradicts the family's social beliefs and its sense of bourgeois hierarchies. Proust tells us that facts do not penetrate the world where our beliefs reign supreme. They neither gave rise to them nor can they destroy them. Eyes and ears are closed when the well-being and integrity of the personal universe are involved. His mother observes his father, but not too closely, for she does not want to understand "the secret of his superiorities." The aunts Céline and Flora possess to an even higher degree the precious ability of not perceiving; they stop listening the moment the conversation changes in their presence to something which does not interest them.

> Their sense of hearing . . . would leave its receptive
> channels unemployed, so effectively that they were
> actually becoming atrophied. So that if my grandfa-
> ther wished to attract the attention of the two sisters,
> he would have to make use of some such alarm sig-
> nals as mad doctors adopt in dealing with their dis-
> tracted patients; as by beating several times on a
> glass with the blade of a knife, fixing them at the
> same time with a sharp word and a compelling
> glance.

These defense mechanisms are obviously the result of
mediation. When the mediator is as distant as in the case
of Combray, they cannot be considered Sartrean "bad
faith," but rather what Max Scheler in *Ressentiment* calls
"organic falsehood." The falsification of experience is not
carried out consciously, as in a simple lie; rather the process begins in advance of any conscious experience at the
point at which representations and feelings about value
are first elaborated. The "organic falsehood" functions
every time someone wishes to *see* only that which serves
his "interest" or some other disposition of his instinctive
attention, whose object is thus modified even in memory.
The man who deludes himself in this way no longer needs
to lie.

Combray shies away from dangerous truths as a
healthy organism refuses to digest something which
would harm it. Combray is an eye which blinks out the
particles of dust which might irritate. Everyone at Combray is therefore his own censor; but this self-censorship,
far from being painful, blends with the peace of Combray,
with the happiness of being a part of Combray. And in its
original essence, it is identical with the pious watchful-
ness with which Aunt Léonie is surrounded. Everyone
makes an effort to keep from her anything which might

disturb her tranquillity. Marcel earns a reprimand for his lack of consideration when he tells her that during the course of a walk they had met "someone they didn't know."

In the child's eyes, Aunt Léonie's room is the spiritual center, the holy of holies of the family house. The night-table crowded with *eau de Vichy*, medicines, and religious pamphlets is an altar at which the high-priestess of Combray officiates with the aid of Françoise.

The aunt seems not to be active but it is she who is responsible for the metamorphosis of the heterogeneous data; she transforms it into "Combray lore." Out of it she makes a rich, tasty, and digestible food. She identifies passers-by and strange dogs; she reduces the unknown to the known. Combray owes all its knowledge and truth to her. Combray, "which a fragment of its medieval ramparts enclosed, here and there, in an outline as scrupulously circular as that of a little town in a primitive painting," is a perfect sphere and Aunt Léonie, immobile in her bed, is the center of the sphere. She does not join in the family activities but it is she who gives them their meaning. It is her daily *routine* which makes the sphere revolve harmoniously. The family crowds around the aunt like houses of the village around the church.

THERE ARE striking analogies between the organic structure of Combray and the structure of the fashionable salons. There is the same circular vision, the same internal cohesion sanctioned by a system of ritual gestures and words. The Verdurin salon is not simply a meeting-place, it is a way of seeing, feeling, judging. The salon is also a "closed culture." Thus the salon will reject anything which threatens its spiritual unity. It possesses an "eliminative function" similar to that of Combray.

The parallel between Combray and the Verdurin salon can be followed all the more easily since the "foreign body" in both cases is the unfortunate Swann. His love for Odette draws him to the Verdurins. His crossing of social lines, his cosmopolitanism, and his aristocratic relations appear even more subversive at the Verdurins than at Combray. The "eliminative function" is exercised with great violence. The great-aunt is satisfied with a few relatively inoffensive sarcasms in reaction to the general feeling of uneasiness caused by Swann. There is no threat to good-neighborly relations; Swann remains *persona grata.* The situation evolves differently in the Verdurin salon. When the "patroness" realizes that Swann cannot be assimilated, the smiles turn to grimaces of hatred. Absolute excommunication is pronounced, the doors of the salon are closed with a bang. Swann is banished to the outer darkness.

There is something strained and rigid about the spiritual unity of the salon which is not present at Combray. This difference is particularly finely drawn at the level of the religious images expressing that unity. The images used to describe Combray are generally borrowed from the primitive religions, from the Old Testament, and from medieval Christianity. The atmosphere is that of young societies in which epic literature flourishes, faith is naïve and vigorous, and foreigners are always "barbarians" but are never hated.

The imagery of the Verdurin salon is completely different. The dominant themes belong to the Inquisition and the witch-hunts. Its unity seems constantly threatened. The patroness is always standing in the breach ready to repulse the attack of the infidels; she nips schisms in the bud; she keeps constant watch over her friends; she disparages distractions which are found beyond her influence; she demands an absolute loyalty; she roots out any sectarian and heretical spirit which compromises the orthodoxy of her "little clan."

How can we account for the difference between the two different types of the sacred which give unity, the one to the Verdurin salon, the other to Combray? Where are the gods of Combray? Marcel's gods, as we have already seen, are his parents and the great writer Bergotte. They are "distant" gods with whom any metaphysical rivalry is completely out of the question. If we look around the narrator, we find this *external mediation* everywhere. Françoise's gods are the family and especially Aunt Léonie; god for Marcel's mother is his father whom she does not examine too closely in order not to cross the barrier of respect and adoration between him and her; the father's god is the friendly but Olympian M. de Norpois. These gods are always accessible, always ready to answer the call of their faithful, always ready to satisfy reasonable demands, but they are separated from mortals by an insuperable spiritual distance, a distance which prohibits any metaphysical rivalry. In one of the passages of *Jean Santeuil* which present a sketch of Combray can be found a veritable allegory of this collective external mediation. A swan symbolizes the mediator in the almost feudal universe of middle-class childhood. In this closed and protected universe the prevailing impression is one of joy:

> Nor from that general rapture was the swan [excepted], moving slowly on the river bearing, he too, the gleam of light and happiness on his resplendent body . . . never, for a moment, disturbing the happiness about him, but showing by his joyful mien that he, too, felt it though not by a jot changing his slow, majestic progress, as a noble lady may watch with pleasure her servants' happiness, and pass near to them, not despising their gaiety, not disturbing it, but taking in it no part herself save by a show of gracious

kindliness and by the presence of a charm shed by her dignity on all around.

Where, then, are the gods of the Verdurin salon to be found? The answer seems easy. In the first place there are the lesser divinities, painters, musicians, and poets, who frequent the salon: more or less ephemeral incarnations of the supreme divinity—ART—whose slightest emanations are enough to throw Mme Verdurin into ecstasies. There is no danger of the official cult going unnoticed. In its name the "Boetians" and the "bores" are banished. Sacrilege is punished more severely than at Combray; the slightest heresy can provoke a scandal. The temptation is to draw the conclusion that faith is more vigorous at the Vendurins than at Combray.

The difference between the two "closed worlds," the more rigid restriction of the salon, would therefore seem to be explained by a strengthening of *external* mediation; at any rate this is the conclusion suggested by appearances. But appearances are deceptive and the novelist rejects this conclusion. Behind the gods of external mediation who no longer have any real power at the Verdurins, there are the true, hidden gods of *internal* mediation, no longer gods of love, but of hate. Swann is expelled in the name of the official gods but in reality we must see here a reprisal against the implacable mediator, against the disdainful Guermantes who close their doors to Mme Verdurin and to whose world Swann suddenly reveals that he belongs. The real gods of the patroness are enthroned in the salon of the Guermantes. But she would rather die than openly or even secretly worship them as they demand. This is why she carries out the rites of her false aesthetic religion with a passion as frenetic as it is mendacious.

From Combray to the Verdurin salon the structure of the "closed little world" does not seem to have changed.

The most obvious traits of this structure are merely strengthened and emphasized; the appearances are, if we might be permitted such an expression, more apparent than ever. The salon is a caricature of the organic unity of Combray, just as a mummified face is a caricature of a living face and accentuates its traits. On closer examination it is seen that the elements of the structure, identical in both cases, have a different hierarchy. At Combray the rejection of the barbarians is subordinate to the affirmation of the gods. At the Verdurins it is the reverse. The rites of union are camouflaged rites of separation. They are no longer observed as a means of communion with those who observe similar rites but as a means of distinction from those who do not observe them. Hatred of the omnipotent mediator supersedes love of the faithful. The disproportionate place the manifestations of this hatred hold in the existence of the salon provides the single but irrefutable indication of metaphysical truth: the hated outsiders are the true gods.

The almost identical appearances conceal two very different types of mediation. We are now observing the transition from external to internal mediation not on the level of the individual but on that of the "closed little world." The childhood love of Combray yields to the adult rivalry in hatred, the metaphysical rivalry of snobs and lovers.

Collective internal mediation faithfully reproduces the traits of individual mediation. The happiness of being "among one's friends" is as unreal as the happiness of being oneself. The aggressive unity presented by the Verdurin salon to the outside world is simply a façade; the salon has only contempt for itself. This contempt is revealed in the persecution of the unfortunate Saniette. This character is the faithful of the faithful, the pure soul of the Verdurin salon. He plays, or would play if the salon were really all that it pretends to be, a role somewhat similar to Aunt Léonie's at Combray. But instead of being honored and respected, Saniette is buried under insults; he is the butt of the Verdurins. The salon is unaware that it despises itself in the person of Saniette.

The distance between Combray and the life of the salon is not the distance separating "true" from "false" gods. Nor is it the distance that separates a pious and useful lie from the cold truth. Nor can we agree with Heidegger that the gods have "withdrawn." The gods are nearer than ever. Here the divergence between neoromantic thought and novelistic genius becomes absolutely clear. Neoromantic thinkers loudly denounce the artificial character of a cult confined to accepted values and faded idols in the bourgeois universe. Proud of their perceptiveness, these thinkers never go beyond their first observations. They believe that the source of the sacred has simply dried up. They never stop to wonder what might be hidden behind middle-class *hypocrisy*. Only the novelist looks behind the deceptive mask of the official cult and finds the hidden gods of internal mediation. Proust and Dostoyevsky do not define our universe by an absence of the sacred, as do the philosophers, but by the perversion and corruption of the sacred, which gradually poisons the sources of life. As one goes further from Combray the positive unity of love develops into the negative unity of hate, into the false unity which hides duplicity and multiplicity.

That is why only one Combray is necessary while there must be several rival salons. At first there are the Verdurin and Guermantes salons. The salons exist only as functions of each other. Among the collectivities that are simultaneously separated and united by double mediation we find a dialectic of master and slave similar to that which controls the relations of individuals. The Verdurin salon and the Guermantes salon carry on an underground struggle for mastery of the world of fashionable society. For most of the novel the Duchess of Guermantes retains her mastery. Haughty, indifferent, and contemptuous, the hawk-faced Duchess is so dominant that she almost seems the universal mediator of the salons. But like all mastery it proves empty and abstract. Naturally Mme de Guermantes does not see her salon with the eyes of those who long for admittance. If the bourgeois Mme Verdurin, who is supposed to be such an art lover, secretly longs only for aristocracy, the aristocratic Mme de Guermantes dreams only of literary and artistic glories.

For a long time Mme Verdurin is the underdog in the struggle with the Guermantes salon. But she refuses to humble herself and obstinately conceals her desire. Here as elsewhere the "heroic" lie finally wins its reward. The working of internal mediation demands Mme Verdurin's ultimate arrival in the residence of the Prince de Guermantes. As for the Duchess, whose *mastery* has been too blasé, she abuses her power and squanders her prestige. In the end she loses her position in society. The laws of the novel necessitate this double reversal.

COMBRAY is always described as a patriarchal regime; it is impossible to say whether it is authoritarian or liberal since it functions all by itself. The Verdurin salon, on the other hand, is a frenzied dictatorship; the patroness is a totalitarian head of state who rules by a skillful mixture of demagoguery and ferocity. When Proust evokes the loyalist sentiments inspired by Combray, he speaks of *patriotism;* when he turns to the Verdurin salon he speaks of *chauvinism.* The distinction between patriotism and chauvinism is an accurate expression of the subtle yet radical difference between Combray and the salons. Patriotism is the result of external mediation while chauvinism is rooted in internal mediation. Patriotism already contains elements of self-love and therefore self-contempt but it is still a sincere cult of heroes and saints. Its fervor is not dependent upon rivalry with other countries. Chauvinism, on the contrary, is the fruit of such rivalry. It is a negative sentiment based on hatred, that is to say, on the secret adoration of the Other.

Proust's remarks on the First World War, despite their extreme caution, betray a profound disgust. Rose colored chauvinism is the product of a mediation similar to that of snobbism. The chauvinist hates a powerful, belligerent, and well-disciplined Germany because he himself is dreaming of war, power, and discipline. The revengeful nationalist feeds on Barrès and praises "the earth and the dead" but the earth and the dead are not important to him. He thinks that his roots go deep but he is floating in an abstraction.

At the end of *Remembrance of Things Past* war breaks out. The Verdurin salon becomes the center of the "fight to the bitter end" attitude in society. All the faithful fall in with the patroness's martial step. Brichot writes a belligerent column in a big Paris newspaper. Everyone, even the violinist Morel, wants to "do his duty." Society's chauvinism finds its complement in civic and national chauvinism. The appearance of chauvinism is thus much more than just appearance. Between the microcosm of the salon and the macrocosm of the nation at war there is only a difference of scale. The desire is the same. The metaphors which continually transport us from one dimension to the other draw our attention to this identity of structure.

France is to Germany what the Verdurin salon is to the Guermantes salon. Now Mme Verdurin, the sworn enemy of the "bores," ends by marrying the Prince of Guermantes and removing her arms and baggage into the enemy camp. The rigorous parallelism between social and national chauvinism suggests that we should seek in the order of the macrocosm a parallel to the dramatic reversal in the microcosm, a reversal which can without exaggeration be considered to touch on "treachery." If the novel does not provide this parallel it is simply because it ends too soon. Twenty more years and a second world war are needed to produce the event which would have allowed Proust to round out his metaphor. In 1940 a certain kind of abstract chauvinism embraced the cause of triumphant Germany after years of fulminating against those who timidly suggested a *modus vivendi* with an "hereditary" enemy not yet gone mad and still confined within his own frontiers. Similarly, Mme Verdurin inspires terror in her "little clan" and excommunicates the "faithful" at the slightest sign of weakness toward the "bores," right up to the day when she marries the Prince of Guermantes, closes the doors of her salon to the "faithful," and opens them wide to the worst snobs of the Faubourg Saint-Germain.

Naturally some critics see in the social about-face of Mme Verdurin proof of her "freedom." We are lucky if they do not make use of this so-called freedom to "rehabilitate" Proust in the eyes of current thinkers and to cleanse the novelist of the terrible suspicion of "psychologism." "Look," they say, "Mme Verdurin is capable of abandoning her principles; this character therefore is certainly worthy of participating in an existential novel and Proust, too, is a novelist of *freedom!*"

Obviously these critics are making the same mistake as Jean Prévost when he mistook the political conversion of M. de Rênal for a spontaneous gesture. If Mme Verdurin is "spontaneous" then the enthusiastic "collaborators" are also, since they were fanatical nationalists only a short time before. In reality no one is spontaneous: the laws of double mediation are at work in both cases. The spectacu-

lar reprisals against the persecuting divinity always give
way to an attempt at "fusion" when circumstances appear
favorable. Thus the underground man interrupts his plans
of vengeance to write a passionate, raving letter to the
officer who insulted him. None of these apparent "conversions" contributes anything new. Here we have no freedom
asserting its omnipotence by an authentic break with the
past. The convert has not even changed his mediator. We
have the illusion of change because we had not recognized a mediation whose only fruits were "envy, jealousy,
and impotent hatred." The bitterness of these fruits concealed from us the presence of the god.

THE STRUCTURAL identity of the two chauvinisms is again
revealed in the expulsion of Baron de Charlus. The affair
is a more violent version of Swann's misadventure.
Charlus is drawn to the Verdurins by Morel; Swann was
attracted by Odette. Swann was the friend of the Duchess
of Guermantes; Charlus is her brother-in-law. Thus the
Baron is eminently a "bore" and subversive. The "eliminative function" of the salon is exerted against him with
particular savagery. The oppositions and contradictions
aroused by metaphysical desire are even more obvious
and painful than in *Swann in Love* for the mediator has
come much nearer.

War has been declared; the account of the themes
which accompany the execution of the sentence is colored
by the atmosphere of the time. To the traditional terms
describing a "bore" is added "German spy." Microcosmic
and macrocosmic aspects of "chauvinism" are almost indistinguishable and Mme Verdurin is soon to blend them.
She announces to all her visitors that Charlus has been
"spying continuously" on her salon for two years.

The sentence reveals very clearly the systematic distortion of the real by metaphysical desire and hatred. This distortion provides the subjective unity of perception. Our immediate thought is that the sentence fits the patroness too well to fit her object too: the Baron de Charlus. If we have to find the individual essence in an irreducible difference, the sentence cannot reveal the essence of Mme Verdurin without falsifying the essence of the Baron de Charlus. It cannot contain the mutually incompatible essences of both.

Yet this is the miracle it accomplishes. When she declares that Charlus has for two years been a spy in her salon, Mme Verdurin depicts herself, but she also depicts the Baron. Charlus is not, of course, a spy. The patroness exaggerates wildly but she is very well aware of what she is doing; the barb pierces Charlus in the most vulnerable part of his being. Charlus is a terrible defeatist. He is not content to despise Allied propaganda in silence. He launches into subversive suggestions even in the streets. His Germanism chokes him.

Proust analyzes at length Charlus' defeatism. He gives many explanations but the most important of them is homosexuality. Charlus feels a hopeless desire for the handsome soldiers swarming all over Paris. These unattainable soldiers are "exquisite tormentors" for him. They are automatically associated with Evil. The war which divides the universe into two enemy camps provides nourishment for the instinctive dualism of the masochist. The Allied cause being that of the wicked persecutors, Germany must of necessity be associated with the persecuted Good. Charlus confuses his own cause with that of the enemy nation all the more easily that the Germans inspire in him real physical revulsion; he makes no distinction between their ugliness and his own, their military defeats and his own amorous defeats. Charlus is justifying himself when he justifies a crushed Germany.

These feelings are essentially negative. His love for Germany is not nearly as strong as his hatred of the Allies. The frenzied attention he pays to chauvinism is that of the subject to the mediator. Charlus' Weltanschauung is a perfect illustration of the masochistic scheme we described in the preceding chapter. The unity of Charlus' existence becomes even more obvious if we explore his social life, an intermediary zone between his sexual life and his defeatist opinions.

Charlus is a Guermantes. He is the object of an idolatrous cult in the salon of his sister-in-law, the Duchess of Guermantes. He never misses an opportunity, especially in front of his plebeian friends, of proclaiming the superiority of his background, but for him the Faubourg Saint-German has none of the fascination it holds for the bourgeois snobs. By definition, metaphysical desire is never aimed at an accessible object. Thus the baron's desires are not drawn by the noble Faubourg but by the lower "riff-raff." This "descending" snobbism explains his passion for the debauched character Morel. The prestige of baseness with which Charlus endows him extends to the whole Verdurin salon. The nobleman can scarcely distinguish this bourgeois hue from the more garish colors which are the normal background of his clandestine pleasures.

Chauvinist, immoral, and bourgeois, the Verdurin salon is a fascinatingly wicked place at the heart of that greater and equally chauvinist, immoral, and bourgeois place, France. The Verdurin salon offers a refuge for the seductive Morel; France at war is full of proud officers. The Baron feels no more "at home" in the Verdurin salon than he does in chauvinist France. But he lives in France and his desire draws him to the Verdurin salon. The Guermantes salon, aristocratic and insipidly virtuous, plays in the Baron's social system a role similar to that of the beloved but distant Germany in his political system. Love, social life, and war are the three circles of this existence which is perfectly unified, or rather perfectly double in its contradiction. All levels correspond and verify the obsessive logic of the Baron.

Thus the counterpart of Mme Verdurin's "chauvinist" obsession is the "antichauvinist" obsession of Charlus. The two obsessions do not isolate the two victims as common sense would expect. They do not close them into two incommensurable worlds; they bring them together in a communion of hatred.

These two existences combine the same elements but organize them inversely. Mme Verdurin claims to be loyal to her salon but her heart is with the Guermantes. Charlus claims to be loyal to the Guermantes but his heart is with the Verdurins. Mme Verdurin praises her "little clan" and scorns the "bores." Charlus praises the Guermantes salon and scorns the "nobodies." We need only reverse the signs to pass from one universe to the other. The disagreement of the two characters is a perfect negative agreement.

This symmetry enables Mme Verdurin to give grotesque but striking expression to the truth about herself and about the Baron in a single sentence. To accuse Charlus of being a spy is Mme Verdurin's secret protest against the scorn of the Guermantes. Common sense cannot see what good it would serve the German High Command to have "detailed reports of the organisation of the little clan." Thus common sense sees through the folly of Mme Verdurin but the more one fixes his attention on her folly the greater the risk that it will fail to see the corresponding folly of Charlus. It is precisely to the extent that she slips into the irrational that Mme Verdurin resembles the Baron. The madness of one joins the madness of the other in an insane unity, disregarding completely the barriers that common sense would presume to exist between society, life, and the war. Mme Verdurin's chauvinism is aimed at the Guermantes salon and Charlus' defeatism is aimed at the Verdurin salon. Each has only to yield to his madness to understand the Other with an acute but incomplete knowledge—acute because passion triumphs over the object-fetishism which paralyzes common sense; incomplete because passion does not perceive the triangle of desire, it fails to recognize the anguish behind the Other's pride and apparent mastery.

In a one-sentence reference of Mme Verdurin to Charlus' "spying" Proust lets us glimpse the complexity of the bonds hatred can weave between two individuals. Mme Verdurin's words reveal both understanding and blindness, a subtle truth and a glaring lie; they are as rich in associations and implications of all kinds as a line of Mallarmé but the novelist is not inventing anything. His genius draws directly on an intersubjective truth which is almost completely unknown to the psychological and philosophical systems of our time.

These words indicate that relationships on the level of the salons and of internal mediation are very different from those established, or rather which cannot be established, at the level of external mediation. As we have seen, Combray is the kingdom of misunderstanding. Since the autonomy is real, relationships with the outside world must of necessity be superficial; no lasting intrigue can be formed. The brief scenes of Combray, like Don Quixote's adventures, are independent of each other. The order in which they succeed each other is almost a matter of indifference for each adventure constitutes a significant totality whose essence is misunderstanding.

Communication would seem to be even more impossible on the level of internal mediation since individuals and salons clash with each other even more violently. As the differences become more acute, any relationship would seem to become impossible in the small worlds which are more and more closed to each other. The aim of all romantic writers is to convince us of precisely this. Romanticism seeks that which is irreducibly ours in that which opposes us most violently to others. It distinguishes two parts in an individual, that which is superficial and permits agreement with Others and a more essential part in which agreement is impossible. But this distinction is false and the novelist proves it. The heightening of onto-logical sickness does not throw the individual out of gear. Mme Verdurin's chauvinism and Charlus' antichauvinism fit each other perfectly for one is hollow where the other projects. The *differences* displayed by the romantic are the teeth of the gears; they and they alone cause the machine to turn, and they give birth to a *novelistic world* which did not exist before.

Combray was truly autonomous but the salons are not. They are only the less autonomous for their shrill claims to autonomy. At the level of internal mediation, the collectivity, like the individual, ceases to be an absolute reference point. The salons can now be understood only by contrasting them with rival salons, by fitting them into the totality of which each of them is no more than an element.

On the level of external mediation there are only "closed little worlds." The bonds are so loose that there is not as yet any real *novelistic world,* any more than there is a "concert of Europe" before the seventeenth century. That "concert" is a result of rivalry on the national scale. Nations are obsessed with each other. Every day their relationships become closer but they often assume a negative aspect. Just as individual fascination gives birth to individualism, so collective fascination spawns a "collective individualism" which is called nationalism and chauvinism. Individualist and collectivist myths are brothers for they always mask the opposition of the same to the same. The desire to be "among one's friends" just as much as the desire to be oneself hides a desire to be the Other.

The "small closed worlds" are neutral particles which have no action on each other. The salons are positive and negative particles which both attract and repel each other, like atomic particles. There are no more monads but semblances of monads which form one vast closed world. The unity of this world, as coherent as that of Combray, is based on an inverse principle. At Combray love still has the upper hand, but hatred generates the world of the salons.

In the hell of *Cities of the Plain* the triumph of hate is absolute. Slaves gravitate around their masters and the masters themselves are slaves. Individuals and collectivities are at once inseparable and completely isolated. Satellites gravitate around planets and planets around stars. This image of the world of the novel as a cosmic system recurs frequently in Proust and brings with it the image of the novelist astronomer who measures the orbits and derives the laws that govern them.

The world of the novel obtains its cohesion from these laws of internal mediation. Only knowledge of these laws makes it possible to answer the question of Vyacheslav Ivanov in his work on Dostoyevsky: "How," the Russian critic asks, "can separation become a principle of union, how can hatred keep the very ones who hate bound together?"

THE MOVEMENT from Combray to the universe of the salons is continuous, with no perceptible transitions. The opposition between *external* and *internal* mediation is not an opposition between Good and Evil, it is not an absolute separation. A closer examination of Combray will reveal, in a nascent state, all the features of the worldly salons.

The great-aunt's ridicule at Swann's expense is an early and faint sketch of the thunderbolts Mme Verdurin and Mme de Guermantes will unleash. The petty persecutions endured by the innocent grandmother prefigure the cruelty of the Verdurins toward Saniette and the frightful coldness of Mme de Guermantes toward her great friend Swann. Marcel's mother refuses, in true bourgeois fashion, to receive Mme Swann. Even the narrator profanes the sacred in the person of Françoise, whom he tries to "demystify." He continually tries to destroy her naïve faith in Aunt Léonie. Aunt Léonie herself abuses her supernatural prestige; she foments sterile rivalries between Françoise and Eulalie; she turns into a cruel tyrant.

The negative element is already present at Combray; thanks to it the closed little world is shut up in itself. It secures the elimination of dangerous truths. This negative element grows gradually larger and ends by devouring everything in the worldly salons. And, as usual, this negative element is rooted in pride and its mediated desire. Pride prevents the great-aunt from perceiving Swann's social position, pride prevents Marcel's mother from receiving Mme Swann. This is but a nascent pride but its essence will not change from one end of the novel to the other. It has scarcely started on its destructive work, but the decisive choice has already been made. The seed of *Cities of the Plain* can already be found in Combray. All that is necessary to move from one universe to the other is to give in to the incline of the slope, to that movement which increases steadily and takes us ever further from the mystic center. This movement is almost imperceptible in Aunt Léonie stretched out in her bed; it becomes more rapid in the child who gazes too hard at the gods of Combray and prepares to succumb to every kind of exoticism.

What is this center which is never reached, which is left

further and further behind? Proust gives no direct answer but the symbolism of his work speaks for him and sometimes against him. Combray's center is the church, "epitomising the town, representing it, speaking of it and for it to the horizon." At the center of the church is the steeple of Saint-Hilary, which is for the town what Léonie's room is for the household. The steeple "shaped and crowned and consecrated every occupation, every hour of the day, every point of view in the town." All the gods of Combray are assembled at the foot of this steeple:

> It was always to the steeple that one must return, always it which dominated everything else, summing up the houses with an unexpected pinnacle, raised before me like the Finger of God, Whose Body might have been concealed below among the crowd of human bodies without fear of my confounding It, for that reason, with them.

The steeple is visible everywhere but the church is always empty. The human and earthly gods of external mediation have already become idols; they do not fall in line vertically with the steeple. But they always remain near enough to it so that one glance can encompass Combray and its church. The nearer the mediator comes to the desiring subject the more remote transcendency becomes from that vertical. It is deviated transcendency at work. It drags the narrator and his novelistic universe further and further from the steeple, in a series of concentric circles entitled *Within a Budding Grove, The Guermantes Way, Cities of the Plain, The Captive* and *The Sweet Cheat Gone*. The greater the distance from the mystic center, the more painful, frenzied, and futile becomes the agitation, until we arrive at *The Past Recaptured*, which reverses this movement. This double movement of flight and return is prefigured in the evening pursuits of the crows of Saint-Hilary:

From the tower windows, it [the steeple] released, it let fall at regular intervals flights of jackdaws which for a little while would wheel and caw, as though the ancient stones which allowed them to sport thus and never seemed to see them, becoming of a sudden uninhabitable and discharging some infinitely disturbing element, had struck them and driven them forth. Then after patterning everywhere the violet velvet of the evening air, abruptly soothed, they would return and be absorbed in the tower, deadly no longer but benignant.

Does Proust's work have a sociological value? It is frequently said that *Remembrance of Things Past* is inferior in this respect to *The Human Comedy* or *The Rougon-Macquart*. We are told that Proust is interested only in the old nobility. His work therefore lacks "breadth and objectivity." Beneath these unfavorable comments we recognize the old realist and positivist conception of the art of the novel. Novelistic genius draws up a detailed inventory of men and things; it should present us with a panorama as complete as possible of economic and social reality.

If this idea were taken seriously, then Proust would be an even more mediocre novelist than they supposed. He is reproached with having "limited his inquiry to the Faubourg Saint-Germain," but that would be giving him credit for more than he attempts. Proust does not embark on any systematic exploration, even in the narrow area which the critics are willing to grant him. He tells us vaguely that the Guermantes are very rich, and that others have been ruined. Where the conscientious novelist would bury us under a heap of records, wills, inventories, accounts, bailiffs' procedures, portfolios of shares and bonds, Proust merely reports a few scraps of conversation over a cup of tea. And he never introduces them for their own sake but simply in relation to something else. There is nothing in all this which warrants the pompous title of *research*. Proust does not even try to suggest, by a definitive tone or an enumeration of unusual objects, that he has "exhausted the documentation."

None of the questions that interest the sociologist seem to attract Proust's attention. We conclude that this novelist is not interested in the problems of society. This indifference, whether it is blamed or praised, is always conceived as a negative element, a kind of mutilation in the service of a particular aesthetic, something similar to the proscription of plebeian words in classical tragedy.

We have learned enough to reject this narrow concept of the art of the novel. The novelist's truth is total. It embraces all aspects of individual and collective existence. Even if the novel neglects some of these aspects it is sure to indicate a perspective. Sociologists can recognize nothing in Proust which reminds them of their own approach because there is a fundamental opposition between the sociology of the novel and the sociology of sociologists. This opposition involves not only the solution and methods but also the data of the problem to be resolved.

In the eyes of the sociologist the Faubourg Saint-Germain is a very tiny but real sector of the social landscape. The frontiers seem to be so clearly fixed that no one questions them. But these frontiers become increasingly blurred the further one reads in Proust's novel. The narrator suffers a terrible let-down when he eventually gains admittance to the Guermantes'! He discovers that the conversation and thought in their salon does not differ from that to which he is accustomed. The essence of the Faubourg seems to vanish. The Guermantes salon loses its individuality and blends into the vague grey of already known milieux.

The Faubourg cannot be defined by tradition since that tradition is no longer understood by so considerable and vulgar a character as the Duke of Guermantes. The Faubourg cannot be defined by heredity since a member of the middle class like Mme Leroi can enjoy a more brilliant social position in it than a Mme de Villeparisis. Since the end of the nineteenth century the Faubourg has not really been a center of political or financial power despite the fact that wealth abounds there and men of influence frequent it in great numbers. Nor is the Faubourg distinguished by a peculiar mentality. It is reactionary in politics, snobbish and superficial in art and literature. There is nothing in all of this to distinguish the milieu of the Guermantes from those of the other idle rich of the early twentieth century.

The sociologist interested in the Faubourg Saint-Germain should not turn to *Remembrance of Things Past*. This novel is not only useless, it can be dangerous. The sociologist thinks he has hold of the object of his research and suddenly he finds it slipping between his fingers. The Faubourg is neither a class, nor a group, nor a milieu; none of the categories currently used by sociologists is applicable to it. Like certain atomic particles, the Faubourg vanishes when scientific instruments are brought to bear on it. This object cannot be isolated. The Faubourg ceased to exist a hundred years ago. And yet it exists because it excites the most violent desires. Where does the Faubourg begin, and where does it end? We do not know. But the snob knows; he never hesitates. It is as if the snob possessed a sixth sense which determined the exact social standing of a salon.

The Faubourg exists for the snob and does not exist for the nonsnob. We should say, rather, that it would not exist for the nonsnob were it not that the latter agrees to accept the snob's testimony in order to settle the question once and for all. Obviously the Faubourg exists only for the snob.

Proust is accused of confining himself to too narrow a milieu but no one recognizes and denounces that narrowness better than Proust. Proust shows us the insignificance of "high society" not only from the intellectual and human angle but also from the *social* point of view: "The members of the fashionable set delude themselves as to the social importance of their names." Proust pushes the demystification of the Faubourg Saint-Germain much further than his democratic critics. The latter, in fact, believe in the objective existence of the magic object. Proust constantly repeats that the object does not exist. "Society is the kingdom of nothingness." We must take this affirmation literally. The novelist constantly emphasizes the contrast between the objective nothingness of the Faubourg and the enormous reality it acquires in the eyes of the snob.

The novelist is interested neither in the petty reality of the object nor in that same object transfigured by desire; he is interested in the process of transfiguration. This has always been the fundamental concern of the great novelists. Cervantes is not interested in either the barber's basin or Mambrino's helmet. What fascinates him is that Don Quixote can confuse a simple barber's basin with Mambrino's helmet. What fascinates Proust is that the snob can mistake the Faubourg Saint-German for that fabled kingdom everyone dreams of entering.

The sociologist and the naturalistic novelist want only *one* truth. They impose this truth on all perceiving subjects. What they call *object* is an insipid compromise between the incompatible perceptions of desire and nondesire. This object's credibility comes from its intermediate position, which weakens all the contradictions. Instead of taking the edge off these contradictions the great novelist sharpens them as much as possible. He underscores the metamorphoses brought about by desire. The naturalistic writer does not perceive this metamorphosis because he is incapable of criticizing his own desire. The novelist who reveals triangular desire cannot be a snob but he must have been one. He must have known desire but must now be beyond it.

The Faubourg is an enchanted helmet to the snob and a barber's basin to the nonsnob. Every day we are told that the world is controlled by "concrete" desires: wealth, well-being, power, oil, etc. The novelist asks an apparently harmless question: "What is snobbism?"

In his probe of snobbism the novelist is asking himself in his own way just what might be the hidden springs that make the social mechanism tick. But the scientists shrug their shoulders. The question is too frivolous for them. If they are urged to give an answer they become evasive. They will suggest that the novelist is interested in snobbism for the wrong reasons. He himself is a snob. Let us say rather he was one. That is true; but the question remains. What is snobbism?

The snob seeks no concrete advantage; his pleasures and sufferings are purely *metaphysical*. Neither the realist, the idealist, nor the Marxist can answer the novelist's question. Snobbism is the grain of dust that finds its way into the gears of "science" and throws it out of kilter.

The snob desires nothingness. When the concrete differences among men disappear or recede into the background, in any sector whatever of society, abstract rivalry makes its appearance, but for a long time it is confused with the earlier conflicts whose shape it assumes. The snob's abstract anguish should not be confused with class oppression. Snobbism does not belong to the hierarchies of the past as is generally thought, but to the present and still more to the democratic future. The Faubourg Saint-

Germain in Proust's time is in the vanguard of an evolution that changes more or less rapidly all the layers of society. The novelist turns to the snobs because their desire
is closer to being completely void of content than ordinary desires. Snobbism is the caricature of these desires.
Like every caricature, snobbism exaggerates a feature
and makes us see what we would never have noticed in
the original.

The Faubourg Saint-Germain is a pseudo-object and
thus plays a privileged role in novelistic revelation. This
role can be compared to that of radium in modern physics. Radium occupies a position in nature as limited as
the Faubourg Saint-Germain in French society. But this
extremely rare compound possesses exceptional proper-
ties which contradict certain principles of the old physics
and gradually overthrows all the perspectives of an earlier "science." Similarly, snobbism gives the lie to certain
principles of standard sociology; it shows us motives for
action never suspected by scientific thought.

The genius of Proust's novel derives from snobbism
transcended. His snobbism takes the author to the most
abstract place in an abstract society, toward the most out-
rageously empty pseudo-object—in other words, to the
place most suited to novelistic revelation. In retrospect,
snobbism must be identified with the first steps of genius;
an infallible judgment is already at work, as well as an irresistible impetus. The snob must have been excited by
a great hope and have suffered tremendous let-downs, so
that the gap between the object of desire and the object
of nondesire imposes itself on his consciousness, and that
his consciousness may triumph over the barriers erected
each time by a new desire.

After serving the author, the caricatural force of snobbism should now serve the reader. In reading we relive
the spiritual experience whose form is that of the novel it-

self. After conquering his truth, the novelist can descend from the Faubourg Saint-Germain to the less rarefied regions of social existence, like the physicist who extends to "ordinary" compounds the facts he has learned from that "extraordinary" compound, radium. In most circles of middle- and even lower-class existence Proust discovers the same triangular structure of desire, the sterile opposition of contraries, hatred of the hidden god, the excommunications and destructive taboos of internal mediation.

This progressive broadening of novelistic truth entails the extension of the term snobbism to the most diverse professions and environments. In *Remembrance of Things Past*, we find a snobbism of professors, doctors, lawyers, and even servants. Proust's uses of the word snobbism define an "abstract" sociology, universal in its application, but whose principles are most active among the very rich and idle.

Thus Proust is far from indifferent to social reality. In a sense this is all he talks of, for to the novelist of triangular desire interior life is already social and social life is always the reflection of individual desire. But Proust stands in radical opposition to the old positivism of Auguste Comte. He is equally opposed to Marxism. Marx's *alienation* is analogous to metaphysical desire. But alienation has little correspondence with anything but external mediation and the upper stages of internal mediation. The Marxist analyses of bourgeois society are more penetrating than most but they are vitiated at the outset by yet another illusion. The Marxist thinks he can do away with all alienation by destroying bourgeois society. He makes no allowance for the extreme forms of metaphysical desire, those described by Proust and Dostoyevsky. The Marxist is taken in by the object; his materialism is only a relative progress beyond middle-class idealism.

Proust's work describes new forms of alienation that

succeed the old forms when "needs" have been satisfied and when concrete differences no longer control relationships among men. We have seen how snobbism raises abstract barriers between individuals who enjoy the same income, who belong to the same class and to the same tradition. Some of the intuitions of American sociology help us appreciate the fertility of Proust's point of view. Thorstein Veblen's idea of "conspicuous consumption" is already triangular. It deals a fatal blow to materialist theories. The value of the article consumed is based solely on how it is regarded by the Other. Only Another's desire can produce desire. More recently, David Riesman and Vance Packard have shown that even the vast American middle class, which is as free from want and even more uniform than the circles described by Proust, is also divided into abstract compartments. It produces more and more taboos and excommunications among absolutely similar but opposed units. Insignificant distinctions appear immense and produce incalculable effects. The individual's existence is still dominated by the Other but this Other is no longer a class oppressor as in Marxist alienation; he is the neighbor on the other side of the fence, the school friend, the professional rival. The Other becomes more and more fascinating the nearer he is to the Self.

The Marxists explain that these are "residual" phenomena connected with the bourgeois structure of society. Their reasoning would be more convincing if analogous phenomena were not observed in Soviet society. Bourgeois sociologists are only shuffling the cards when they claim, observing these phenomena, that "classes are forming again in the U.S.S.R." Classes are not forming again: new alienations are appearing where the old ones have disappeared.

Even in their boldest intuitions the sociologists do not succeed in completely throwing off the tyranny of the object. None of them has gone as far as novelistic reflection. They tend to confuse the old class distinctions, distinctions imposed externally, with the inner distinctions created by metaphysical desire. It is easy to make this confusion since the transition from one alienation to another covers a long period during which double mediation is proceeding underground without ever coming to the surface. The sociologists never get as far as the laws of metaphysical desire because they do not realize that even material values are finally swallowed up by double mediation. The snob desires nothing concrete. The novelist observes this and traces the symmetrical and empty oppositions of snobbism on all levels of individual and collective life. He shows us how the abstract triumphs in private, professional, national, and even international life. He shows that the First World War, far from being the last of the national conflicts, is the first of the great abstract conflicts of the twentieth century. In short, Proust takes up the history of metaphysical desire at the very point where Stendhal left it. He shows us double mediation crossing national frontiers and acquiring the planetary dimensions which we find that it has today.

After describing social rivalries in terms of military operations, Proust describes military operations in terms of social rivalries. What we considered a moment ago as an image now becomes an object and the object becomes an image. As in contemporary poetry, the two terms of the image are interchangeable. The same desire triumphs in both microcosm and macrocosm. The structure is the same, only the pretext changes. Proust's metaphors deflect our attention from the object and direct it to the mediator; they help us turn from linear desire to triangular desire.

Charlus and Mme Verdurin confuse social life with the First World War; the novelist goes beyond this madness as it in turn had outgrown "common sense." He no longer confuses the two areas, he methodically assimilates them to one another. The novelist for this reason runs the risk of appearing superficial in the eyes of *specialists*. He is accused of explaining big events by "little causes." Historians want history to be taken seriously and they will never forgive Saint-Simon for having interpreted some of Louis XIV's wars in terms of court rivalries. They forget that nothing which concerned Louis XIV's favor could be considered unimportant during his reign.

The distance between pure and simple futility and cataclysmic futility is imperceptible. Saint-Simon is aware of this and so are the novelists. There are, in any case, no "causes" great or small, there is only the infinitely active void of metaphysical desire. The First World War, like the war of the salons, is the fruit of this desire. To be convinced of this, we have only to consider the antagonists. We see the same indignation, the same theatrical gestures, on both sides. The speeches are all the same: to make them admirable or atrocious, depending on the listener, all that is necessary is to reverse the proper names. Germans and French slavishly copy each other. A comparison of certain texts gives Charlus an opportunity for some very bitter laughter.

Some years ago we could still smile at this universal snobbism. A prisoner of his own obsession with society, the novelist seemed to us far removed from contemporary horrors and anguish. But Proust should be reread in the light of recent historical development. Everywhere there are symmetrical *blocs* opposing each other. Gog and Magog imitate and hate each other passionately. Ideology is merely a pretext for ferocious oppositions which are secretly in agreement. The *Internationale* of nationalism and the nationalism of the *Internationale* blend and intersect in inextricable confusion.

In his book, *1984,* the English novelist George Orwell portrays directly certain aspects of this historical structure. Orwell clearly understands that the totalitarian structure is always *double.* But he does not show the connection between individual desire and the collective structure. We sometimes get the impression from his books that the "system" has been imposed from the outside on the innocent masses. De Rougemont in *Love In the Western World* goes still further; he is even closer to novelistic insight when he traces the source of collective wills to power and totalitarian structures to that individual pride which originally gave birth to the mystics of passion. "Unmistakably, when rival wills to power confront one another—and there were already *several* Totalitarian States!—they are bound to clash passionately. Each becomes for some other an *obstruction.* The real, tacit, and inevitable aim of the totalitarian elevation was therefore war, and war means *death.*"

We are told that Proust has neglected the most important aspects of modern social life, that he does no more than describe a relic of former times, a survival destined to disappear, and which at best is only slightly picturesque. In a way this is true. Proust's little world is rapidly receding from our life. But the great world in which we are beginning to live grows more like it every day. The setting is different, the scale is different, but the structure is the same.

A quarter of a century of this ambiguous historical evolution has made a relatively obscure and difficult work crystal clear. Critics have noticed the growing clarity of this masterpiece and they see in it the result of its own radiance. The novel itself is supposed to be training its own readers and shedding more and more light on the understanding of itself. This optimistic point of view is linked to the romantic idea of the artist as a creator of new values, another Prometheus refining the celestial fire in order to give it to a grateful human race. This theory certainly cannot be applied to the novel. The novel does not contribute new values; with great effort, it reconquers the values of previous novels.

Remembrance of Things Past no longer seems obscure but it is not necessarily better *understood*. The spiritual influence of great novels is weak, as we know, and it is very seldom exerted in the direction anticipated by the author. The reader projects into the work the same meanings he already projects into the world. With the passing of time this projection becomes easier since the work is "ahead" of society, which gradually catches up with it. The secret of this advance is in no way mysterious. In the first place, it is the novelist who feels desire the most intensely. His desire leads him into the most abstract regions and to the most meaningless objects. Thus his desire almost automatically leads him to the summit of the social edifice. As we have already remarked in connection with Flaubert, this is where the ontological sickness is most acute. The symptoms observed by the novelist will gradually spread to the lower layers of that society. The metaphysical situations portrayed in the novel will become familiar to a great number of readers; the oppositions in the novel will find their exact replicas in day-to-day existence.

The novelist who reveals the desire of the social elite is almost always *prophetic*. He is describing intersubjective structures that will gradually become banal. What is true of Proust is also true of other novelists. Almost all the great novelists yield to the temptation of an aristocratic background. In all of Stendhal's novels there is a double movement from the provinces to the capital and from middle-class life to fashionable life. Don Quixote's adventures gradually lead him toward the aristocracy. Stavrogin, the universal mediator of *The Possessed,* is an aristocrat. *The Idiot, The Possessed, The Raw Youth,* and *The Brothers Karamazov* are "aristocratic" novels. Dostoyevsky often explains the role of the Russian aristocracy in his novels. Its degeneracy and moral corruption act as a magnifying glass on Russian life, excluding the life of the peasant. If allowance is made for the differences of language and ethical outlook, that is precisely the role played by the aristocracy in the novels of Cervantes, Stendhal, and Proust.

The great novels end in the sterile abstraction of high society because the whole society gradually tends toward that abstraction. Such diverse minds as Paul Valéry and Jean-Paul Sartre have criticized Proust for the frivolity of his book. Everyone says that he does not understand France, that he confuses it with the Faubourg Saint-Germain. We must agree with the critics, but in this brilliant confusion lies one of the great secrets of Proust's creation. Those who portray the social elite are either very superficial or very profound depending on whether they reflect metaphysical desire or whether on the contrary they succeed in revealing it.

CHAPTER X

TECHNICAL PROBLEMS
IN PROUST AND
DOSTOYEVSKY

COMBRAY is not an object but the light with which all objects are suffused. This light is as invisible from "the outside" as it is from "within." The novelist cannot make us see things in this light. Even if he could, we should not see Combray, we would be part of it. Thus the novelist can only proceed through a series of suggestive contrasts between Combray's manner of perceiving and that of the "barbarians."

Proust shows us that an object never looks the same to Combray as it does to the outside world. The novelist does not examine objects with a "microscope" in order to analyze them and "split them into minute particles"; on the contrary, he recomposes *subjective* perceptions which our fetishism of the object decomposes into *objective* data. The Proust who "splits sensations into tiny particles" only exists in the imagination of certain contemporary critics. Their mistake is all the more astonishing when we consider that the atomic and sensationalist point of view, which enables an anonymous perception to be split into objective atoms, is refuted at the very beginning of the novel.

Even the simple act which we describe as "seeing some one we know" is, to some extent, an intellectual process. We pack the physical outline of the creature we see with all the ideas we have already formed about him, and in the complete picture of him which we compose in our minds those ideas have certainly the principal place. In the end they come to fill out so completely the curve of his cheeks, to follow so exactly the line of his nose, they blend so harmoniously in the sound of his voice that these seem to be no more than a transparent envelope, so that each time we see the face or hear the voice it is our own ideas of him which we recognize and to which we listen.

The quarrel of the critics is with Proust's words. They find an expression in his text which has recently become unfashionable and assert triumphantly that the whole work is out of date. But the great novelist's universality requires him to consider intelligibility of primary importance. He is not concerned with the various interdicts that trends in philosophy at various times place on the most diverse portions of the French language. Some readers are pained by certain inoffensive words in *Remembrance of Things Past* such as *habit, sensation, idea,* or *feelings.* If they would only forget their philosophical preciosity for a little while and set about examining the real substance of the novel they would discover that the most fruitful intuitions of phenomenological and structural analysis are already present in Proust's work. Thus it could be said that Proust is well *ahead* of his time. But we shall not be so foolish as to suggest that our era has discovered human truths which completely eluded our forebears. Proust's "phenomenology" merely clarifies and develops some intuitions that are common to all great novelists. But these intuitions were not the subject of didactic developments for former novelists. They are incorporated in novelistic situations whose essence can always be traced to a *quid pro quo*. But whereas the vaudeville type of *quid pro quo* is accidental, novelistic *quid pro quo* is essential. By contrasting two perceptions it reveals the specific quality of each. It defines two incompatible worlds, whether individual or collective, two perceptual empires so absolute that they are totally unaware of the gulf between them.

The *quid pro quo* between Don Quixote and the barber reveals at the outset a qualitative difference of perception. Don Quixote sees an enchanted helmet where the barber sees only a simple barber's basin. In the text we have just quoted, Proust describes the structures of perception which make the *quid pro quo* inevitable. He states the theoretical basis for the essential misunderstanding. As we have seen in the previous chapter, he supported this theory with numerous concrete illustrations. Combray's *quid pro quo*'s do not differ fundamentally from those of *Don Quixote*. Cervantes schematizes and magnifies the contrasts to create an extremely farcical effect. Proust's effects are in half-tones but the data of novelistic revelation has not changed much. The principle on which the comedy of errors is based in *Swann's Way* is identical with that of Don Quixote's adventures. The evening spent with Swann is the analogue of Don Quixote and Sancho's fantastic nights in the inn—the first in the realm of conversation, the second in the world of action.

The subjectivities who are prisoners of this metamorphic desire, that is, of pride, are doomed to misunderstanding. They are incapable of "putting themselves in another's place." The novelist is able to reveal their helplessness only because he has experienced it himself and overcome it. He has been victorious in his struggle with the imperialism of perception. The *quid pro quo* reveals the abyss separating two characters by causing them to fall into it. The novelist can create this misunderstanding only because he has seen the abyss and has one foot firmly planted on each side.

The two victims of the *quid pro quo* are the thesis and the antithesis; the novelist's point of view is the synthesis. These three moments represent successive stages of the novelist's spiritual evolution. Cervantes could not have written *Don Quixote* if the same object had not been for him first an enchanted helmet and then an ordinary barber's basin. The novelist is a man who has overcome desire and who, remembering it, can *make a comparison*. It is this process of comparison which the narrator defines at the beginning of *Swann's Way:*

> . . . I have the feeling of leaving some one I know for another quite different person when, going back in memory, I pass from the Swann whom I knew later and more intimately to this early Swann—this early Swann in whom I can distinguish the charming mistakes of my childhood, and who, incidentally, is less like his successor than he is like the other people I knew at that time, as though one's life were a series of galleries in which all the portraits of any one period had a marked family likeness.

Like all novelists, Proust's narrator moves freely from room to room in the "museum without walls" of his existence. The novelist-narrator is none other than Marcel cured of all his errors, who has overcome his desires and is rich with novelistic grace. The great Cervantes is also a Don Quixote who has overcome his desires, a Don Quixote who can see a barber's basin as a barber's basin but who nevertheless remembers that he once saw it as Mambrino's helmet. This clear-sighted Don Quixote is present in the book only for an instant; it is the dying Don Quixote of the conclusion. Proust's narrator too dies in *The*

Past Recaptured and he too is cured in death. But he comes to life again as novelist. He reappears *in person* in the body of his novel.

The novelist is a hero cured of metaphysical desire. The novelistic process works unseen before Proust and becomes visible in his work. The novelist is a metamorphosed hero. He is at once as far from the primitive hero as the transcendency of *The Past Recaptured* requires, and as close to him as the conditions of the novel's revelation demand. The creator is present in his novel and step by step comments on it. He intrudes at will, not, as so often has been said, to increase the number of "digressions" but to enrich immensely the novel's descriptions, to push them as it were to the second degree. For instance we have seen that Proust is not content merely to present revealing *quid pro quo*'s; he even develops the theory of them. The commentaries which some critics would like to cut out of Proust's work provide a marvelous introduction to *all* the great novels.

Remembrance of Things Past is a novel and it is also the exegesis of that novel. In it the subject-matter becomes the object of a reflection which transforms the narrow stream flowing from previous novels into an immense river. We are struck by this metamorphosis; the statement that Proust "divides sensation into minute particles" is a clumsy attempt to interpret that metamorphosis. The realists conceive of every novel as a photograph of reality and Proust's novel is seen as an *enlargement* of previous clichés, simply a magnification which enables us to distinguish extremely small details. If we are to determine the contribution of *Remembrance of Things Past* to the art of the novel we should not start from a realist or naturalist copy but from Cervantes and Stendhal. If Proust were a supernaturalist, perception would have an absolute value in his work; the novelist would not be aware of the role of metaphysical desire in his victims' varying interpretations of reality, and he would be incapable of constructing the essential *quid pro quo*'s. His work would be as void of novelistic humor as that of Emile Zola or Alain Robbe-Grillet.

THE PRESENCE of the novelist-narrator makes it possible for him to incorporate in his work a reflective element completely absent from the great novels prior to it. His presence also fulfills other needs, which this time are very closely dependent on the type of metaphysical desire revealed in Proust's novel.

After Combray comes Paris; the old country house gives way to the Champs-Elysées and the Verdurin salon. The mediator draws nearer and desire changes shape. Henceforth its structure is so complex that the novelist must take the reader by the hand and guide him through the labyrinth. None of the previous techniques of the novel can be used, since truth is no longer immediately present anywhere. The consciousness of the characters is as deceptive as the external appearances.

Mme Verdurin, for example, feigns an insurmountable disgust for the milieu of the Guermantes. There is nothing in either her conduct or her consciousness that contradicts that pretension. The patroness would die a thousand deaths rather than admit to others, and *admit to herself*, that she wants desperately to be received at the Guermantes'. We have reached the stage where *askesis* for the sake of desire is no longer voluntary. The lucid hypocrisy of Julien Sorel has been succeeded by this almost instinctive hypocrisy which Jean-Paul Sartre has named "bad faith."

Consequently it is no longer enough to break into the characters' consciousness. All the techniques previously used in novels are powerless when faced with this underground duplicity. Julien Sorel conceals his desire from Mathilde but he does not conceal it from himself. Thus Stendhal need only violate the intimacy of his heroes in order to reveal to us the truth about their desires. This expedient is no longer adequate; objective description no longer makes contact with reality even if the barriers between interiority and exteriority are suppressed and even if the novelist moves freely from consciousness to consciousness.

The present moment is a vast desert unequipped with signposts; it provides us with nothing. In order to understand that Mme Verdurin's hatred hides a secret adoration we have to turn to the future; we need to compare the ferocious patroness of the "little clan" with the future Princess of Guermantes, the hostess marvelling at all those "bores" whom she used to consider absolutely intolerable. The stages of this social career have to be brought together if we are to understand the real meaning; the observations have to cover a long period of time.

What is true of Mme Verdurin is equally true of all the other characters, and most of all of the narrator himself. When Marcel sees Gilberte for the first time he makes terrible faces at her. Only time can show us how much adoration there really was in his strange behavior. The child himself does not always understand what motivates him; we should not expect to find the truth in his obscure consciousness.

The problem of revelation in the novel can be solved only by adding a new dimension to the omniscience of the "realistic" novelist: the temporal dimension. "Spatial" ubiquity is no longer sufficient, there must also be temporal ubiquity. This dimension can be added only if the change is made from an impersonal to a personal style. The modalities peculiar to Proust's metaphysical desire necessitate the novelist-narrator's presence at the very heart of the book.

Stendhal and Flaubert never really needed the future or the past, since their characters were as yet neither divided within themselves nor split into several successive selves. Homais remains Homais and Bournisien remains Bournisien. It is enough to bring these two puppets together to settle their accounts once and for all. There they go back to back for an eternity of stupidity. They are transfixed forever in the pose in which the novelist has surprised them. The same scene occurs repeatedly, with minor variations, from one end of the book to the other.

Flaubert has no need to use the temporal dimension as a direct instrument of revelation in the novel. Marcel Proust, on the other hand, cannot do without it, for his characters are both inconstant and blind. Only an inventory of their successive about-faces makes the revelation of the truth about their desires possible. And only the narrator can compile this inventory.

When Mme Verdurin gains admittance to the Faubourg Saint-Germain the "bores" turn out to be "interesting" and the faithful are declared tedious. All the opinions that belong to the preceding period of her life are abandoned and replaced by contrary opinions. Sudden *conversions* are not the exception but the rule in Proust's characters. One fine day Cottard gives up his terrible puns; he takes up the "cool manner" of the great scientist. Albertine changes both her vocabulary and her manners from the moment she begins to move among cultured friends. Somewhat similar revolutions are strewn through the narrator's life. Gilberte withdraws and is replaced by another divinity. The whole universe is reorganized around the new idol. A new self replaces the old.

The duration of these Selves is long enough, the transitions are gradual enough for the subject himself to be the first to be deceived. He thinks he is eternally faithful to his principles and as stable as a rock. His own about-faces remain hidden from him by the protective mechanisms that work so well. Thus Mme Verdurin will never realize that she has betrayed her unfortunate followers. And those who belonged to the anti-Dreyfus group and became advocates of a "fight to the bitter end" during the war will never realize that they have contradicted themselves shamelessly. They solemnly reproach the "barbaric Germans" for faults which only yesterday they thought were virtues: a fighting spirit, fanaticism for traditions, scorn of "effeminate culture." Only the other day they had been accusing the Dreyfus traitors of wanting to sap France of these male virtues. If one were to draw the attention of those involved to these reversals in their ideas they would answer gravely, "that is not the same thing."

Indeed it is never the same thing. Marcel, the hero, is a little more lucid than the other characters; he foresees and dreads the death of his present self, but nevertheless he ends up by forgetting that self completely. Soon he has difficulty believing it ever existed.

Only the omniscient and omnipresent novelist can gather together and compare the fragments of duration in order to reveal contradictions that escape even the characters themselves. The increase in the number of mediators and the particular modalities of mediation require an essentially *historic* art.

In the first moment of Proust's revelation the character gives us the impression of permanence and "fidelity to principles" he is trying to give himself. This first moment is the moment of pure and simple appearance. It is followed by a second moment in which unity gives way to diversity, continuity to intermittence, fidelity to disloyalty. The shadow cast by the real gods can be seen behind the painted paper gods, which are the only ones acknowledged by the official cult.

But this second moment is followed in turn by a third. The impression of diversity and intermittence is in a sense as deceptive as the impression of unity and permanence from which we started. When Mme Verdurin is admitted to the Faubourg Saint-Germain everything seems to be changed but in reality nothing is changed. The patroness's ideas were subordinated to her snobbism, and they still are. The wind turns the weather vane but the weather vane does not change; it would be changed if it stopped turning. Proust's characters turn in the wind of their desire. Their changes in direction should not be taken for genuine conversions. They are always only the result of the changing data of the original mediation or, at the very most, of a change of mediator.

Thus beyond the diversity and intermittence a new form of permanence emerges. Every man has only one way of desiring women, of seeking love or success, in other words, of desiring divinity. But it is not the permanence of being on which middle-class consciousness prides itself, it is a permanence of nothingness. Desire never actually acquires its true object: it leads to failure, oblivion, and death.

In previous novelists there is no gap between subjective illusion and objective truth, between the illusory permanence of being and the actual permanence of nothingness. In most of *Remembrance of Things Past* Proust's revelation requires an intermediate moment of diversity and intermittence, of heterogeneity and chaos. The presence of this supplementary moment reveals the acute state of ontological sickness. This is the *modern* moment *par excellence;* it could even be called the *existentialist* moment by reason of the exclusive importance given to it by the literary school of the same name.

The stage of metaphysical desire we have just described determines Proust's technique in the novel since it occupies a central position in *Remembrance of Things Past*. But ontological sickness becomes increasingly serious as one progresses in the novel. This central stage was preceded by "Combray" and we shall see that it is followed, in the last volumes of the novel, by an even more acute stage. The effects of ontological sickness become at that point so radical that the conditions of revelation in the novel once more undergo fundamental changes.

A comparison between the Baron de Charlus and Mme Verdurin clearly reveals the difference between the two final stages of Proustian desire. Mme Verdurin makes no advances, even indirectly, to her mediator; she does not write any extravagant letters. When she moves, bag and baggage, into the camp of the "bores" she cannot be said to have capitulated; on the contrary, it is the enemy who lays down his weapons and surrenders unconditionally.

Mme Verdurin clings to her "dignity"; Charlus throws his to the wind. He is always to be found at the feet of the persecutor whom he adores. He does not hesitate to commit any baseness. It is, moreover, this lack of reserve, this inability to conceal his desire, which makes Charlus a perpetual slave, and a pitiful victim beneath the brilliant outward appearance of a great lord.

The mediator's attraction is now so strong that the Baron cannot remain faithful, even in appearance, to his domestic gods, to his Guermantes, to the image of himself he wants to impose on others. Charlus' mediator is closer than Mme Verdurin's. This is the explanation of the Baron's inability to regain what he believes to be his camp; it is this which brings about his perpetual exile in the "enemy" camp, whether the enemy is chauvinist France or the Verdurin salon.

In comparison with the deep-rootedness of Combray, Charlus is the embodiment of a rootlessness even more total than the Verdurin chauvinsim, a third stage of

Proustian metaphysical desire, which transcends the second just as the second transcends the first. Far from being a stabilizing factor, his social position alienates the Baron at least as much as proletarization would do. Proust is right in seeing in Charlus primarily an intellectual, for it is alienation that determines the intellectual.

Like many intellectuals tormented by metaphysical desire, Charlus is extremely perceptive when it comes to the types of mediation through which he has already *descended*. He perceives clearly, for example, that only their "bad faith" permits the Verdurin-type bourgeois to continue to worship dead gods. He is all the more irritated by the fact that mediocre people are still deceived by tricks which he has already seen through. Yet his extremely lucid intelligence cannot protect him against the fascination which beings less vulnerable than themselves always hold for those possessed by metaphysical sickness. The enchantment is all the more horrible now that the victim is able to penetrate the absurd secret. We can already see in this the futile clairvoyance of the underground man face to face with Zverkov. It is the impotent fury of many intellectuals when confronted with the *bourgeois*.

Charlus' very eloquence on the topic of his desired persecutor's nonentity is an attempt to convince himself. He is indeed an "intellectual" in that he attempts to use his intelligence as a weapon against his mediator and against his own desire; using his murderous lucidity he hopes to penetrate that arrogant thickness and insolent inertia. He has to keep proving that the radiant mastery which the mediator seems to enjoy is a blatant illusion. In order the better to demystify himself, Charlus spends his time demystifying others around him. He wants constantly to destroy "prejudices" which are indeed perfectly real but which all his talk cannot penetrate.

Thus Charlus understands Mme Verdurin much better than she understands him. The pictures he gives us of the patroness and his criticism of middle-class chauvinism are wonderfully true and vivid. His knowledge of the fascinating Other is penetrating because it is based on a knowledge of himself. It is a haughty caricature of genuine wisdom. Transcendence toward the nadir is a mirror likeness of transcendence toward the zenith. The analogy between deviated transcendency and vertical transcendency never fails.

When he reveals the truth about the bourgeois and the desires hidden by hypocrisy, Charlus is not unaware that he is also revealing his own desire. As always, lucidity is rewarded by a thickening of the shadows with respect to oneself. The psychological circle is now so small that Charlus cannot condemn the Other without condemning himself before the eyes of the world.

The contradictions which were hidden at the Verdurin stage of mediation are now brought out into the light. Charlus no longer tries to keep up *appearances;* he remains prostrate at the feet of his mediator, his eyes glued to him; every gesture, every sentence, every imitation proclaims the truth. After the walled-up silence of the bourgeois we now have a flood of words, sometimes truthful, more often mendacious, but whatever comes from this contorted mouth is always extremely revealing.

Charlus is luminous and sheds light all around him. No doubt there is some obscurity along with this light; it is the murky light of a smoking lamp but nevertheless we are brilliantly illuminated. The narrator therefore is no longer necessary for the novel's revelation. When Charlus occupies the foreground, Marcel discreetly disappears. The moment the Baron appears in *Within a Budding Grove* Proust's usual technique is replaced by a technique of pure description that is objective and almost behaviorist. Charlus is the only character whom the narrator allows to talk without interruption. The Baron's great monologues are unique in *Remembrance of Things Past*. They are self-sufficient. Some of the words of Mme Verdurin, Legrandin, or Bloch would take volumes to explain; in the case of Charlus all that is necessary is a little focusing, a slight smile, a simple wink.

We have distinguished three main stages of metaphysical desire in Proust's novel: Combray, the Verdurin salon, and Charlus. These three stages are obviously linked with the narrator's experience; they define his spiritual evolution up to but not including *The Past Recaptured*. All the characters except the grandmother and the mother are linked with this fundamental evolution. They are all the harmonics of the primordial desire. Some of them recede into the background when the novel goes beyond the stage of metaphysical desire in which they remain fixed. Others die or disappear with the desire characteristic of them; still others evolve along with the narrator; and finally others, when the time arrives, reveal an aspect of their personality invisible in the less acute stages of ontological sickness. This is the case with Saint-Loup, with the Prince de Guermantes, and many other characters who reveal their homosexuality in the last volumes of *Cities of the Plain*. Just as the damned and the elect in Dante are always surrounded by those who practiced the same vices or virtues as they themselves, so the narrator always seeks the company of the characters whose desire is most analogous to his own.

The third stage of Proustian desire, found in the last volumes, is not therefore the prerogative of Charlus alone. The narrator's passion for Albertine resembles very closely that of Charlus for Morel. Between these two passions there is the same analogical relationship as between Marcel's love for Gilberte and the bourgeois characters of the Verdurin type. In fact, during the period in which he is in love with Gilberte, the narrator makes use of dissimulation in his love life in a way that is very reminiscent of the strategy of Mme Verdurin in the social world. Marcel avoids Gilberte in the same way that Mme Verdurin avoids the Guermantes. The "principles" retain a certain efficacy, appearances are maintained. Middle-class order reigns. During the Albertine period there is complete disintegration of the will. The narrator is no more capable than Charlus of keeping up his role in the face of his mediator. His conduct continually contradicts his words, and the lie becomes more hyperbolical as it grows more transparent and loses all efficacy. Marcel does not fool Albertine for a minute; he becomes her slave just as Charlus becomes Morel's slave.

If the narrator evolves in the same direction as the Baron de Charlus, the technical observations made about the latter should apply equally to the former. But the desire the narrator experiences for Albertine, like all the preceding desires, is described for us from the point of view of *The Past Recaptured*—from the point of view of a truth grasped long after the event. If our analysis is correct, in this third stage it would be enough for the novelist to give an external description of words and behavior. The truth would leap out at us from the now glaring contradictions. Proust, however, has not modified his technique. This fact can easily be explained if we give a little thought to the disadvantages of such a modification in the eyes of a writer as careful about continuity and aesthetic unity as Proust. The fact remains, nevertheless, and the considerations we have just mentioned would seem very abstract and even venturesome were it not that Proust himself had confirmed their accuracy in an unequivocal statement. Proust did not make use of the possibility presented him but he considered it in a curious meditation on techniques of the novel which he inserts in the account of his unsuccessful attempts to delude Albertine as to his feelings about her:

> My words, therefore, did not in the least reflect my sentiments. If the reader has no more than a faint impression of these, that is because, as narrator, I reveal my sentiments to him at the same time as I repeat my words. But if I concealed the former and he were acquainted only with the latter, my actions, so little in keeping with my speech, would so often give him the impression of strange revulsions of feeling that he would think me almost mad. A procedure which would not, for that matter, be much more false than that which I have adopted, for the images which prompted me to action, so opposite to those which were portrayed in my speech, were at the moment extremely obscure; I was but imperfectly aware of the nature which guided my actions; at present, I have a clear conception of its subjective truth.

It is important to notice that the advantages of direct revelation occur to the novelist only in the most anguished pages of *The Captive*, in other words at the extreme point of development of metaphysical desire in the novel; the "strange revulsions" are already to be found in the regions of more moderate desire but their rhythm is much less rapid. The terms of the contradictions are very far from each other. If the author were content with an external and chronological presentation we should forget as we went along—just like the characters themselves— and we should not perceive the revelatory contradictions. In order to throw light on metaphysical desire at this stage of its development the novelist has to intervene personally; he becomes a professor proving a theorem.

In the last volumes, however, the ontological sickness has become so serious that, as we have said before, the hero's existence loses all stability. There is no longer even a semblance of permanence and homogeneity. From now on the existential moment, the moment of heterogeneity and intermittence, becomes one with appearance. Now and only now does the elimination of the author-narrator become at least conceivable. It is possible to imagine a novelistic art based on simple chronological presentation of contradictory attitudes and words.

This technique of "hiding feelings and revealing words" is not utilized by Proust but it is by Dostoyevsky in most of his works. It is Dostoyevsky's technique which the author of *Remembrance of Things Past* has defined in masterly fashion in the preceding quotation. Yet Dostoyevsky is not even mentioned. Proust did not seem to have the Russian novelist in mind when writing this text. Such an omission does not diminish but rather increases the value of Proust's reflections by making it impossible for us to attribute the Dostoyevskian echoes in the passage to literary reminiscences. It is almost too perfect that a meditation on the exigencies of his work should lead Proust toward Dostoyevsky's technique at the precise moment of his arrival at the dividing line between his own territory and that of his "successor." The connection cannot be fortuitous; it confirms our own assertion of the unity of novelistic genius. The study of techniques, instead of creating an abyss between the great novelists, reveals the same ability to adapt to the very diverse demands brought about by the variations of the same desire.

THE TECHNIQUE of "hiding feelings and revealing words" is no longer simply conceivable; it alone is adequate when the "strange revulsions" of which Proust speaks become even more rapid than at the end of *Remembrance of Things Past*, and all the images which cause the action of the characters become so obscure and confused that any analysis would falsify their nature. This is indeed the situation in most of Dostoyevsky's work.

Fundamentally Dostoyevsky's method is to bring about confrontations which exhaust all possible relationships between the different characters in the novel. The work is divided into a series of scenes which the author hardly bothers to connect by suitable transitions. During these scenes the characters reveal to us one or more facets of their interior kaleidoscope. No one scene can reveal the whole truth about a character. The reader can grasp that truth only after having made the necessary comparisons, a task which the author leaves entirely up to him.

The reader is supposed to recollect; it is not the author who does the remembering for him, as in Proust. The development of the novel can be compared to a game of cards. In Proust the game proceeds slowly; the novelist constantly interrupts the players to remind them of previous hands and to anticipate those to come. In Dostoyevsky, on the contrary, the cards are laid down very rapidly and the novelist lets the game proceed from beginning to end without interfering. The reader must be able to remember everything himself.

The complexity in Proust is on the level of the sentence, in Dostoyevsky it is on the level of the whole novel. One can turn to any page of *Remembrance of Things Past* and understand it immediately. But one must read a book of Dostoyevsky's from beginning to end without skipping a line. One must give to the novel the attention which Veltchaninov gives to the "eternal husband," the attention of a witness who is not sure he understands and is afraid of missing the slightest detail that might enlighten him.

Of the two novelists obviously Dostoyevsky runs the greater risk of not being understood. Obsessed by this fear, he stresses the revealing gestures, emphasizes the contrasts, increases the number of contradictions. But these precautions work against him, at least in the mind of a Western reader whose immediate reaction is to begin talking in terms of "Russian temperament" and "oriental mysticism." Proust very clearly anticipated this danger in the passage from *The Captive* we quoted immediately above. If he hides his feelings, he tells us, and meanwhile repeats his words and actions to the reader, he will be considered *almost mad*. In fact it is precisely an impression of madness that Dostoyevsky left with his early Western readers. Today, through a misunderstanding which may be even more serious, we have taken a liking to "strange revulsions" and we praise in Dostoyevsky the creator of characters who are *freer* than those of other novelists. We contrast Dostoyevsky with the "psychological" novelists who emprison their characters in a maze of laws.

The contrast is false, for Dostoyevsky has not dispensed with the laws; they secretly control the chaos; it is the advance of ontological sickness which destroys the last semblance of stability and continuity. The moment of permanence, whether real or illusory, from which other novelists depart has now been suppressed. All that remains are the second and third moments of the Proustian revelation. Like those of Stendhal and Flaubert, Dostoyevsky's revelations are confined to two moments. But the first moment is not the same as theirs; it is not the moment of stability but of intermittence and chaos. It is Proust's second moment. There is no break between this "existential" moment and the permanence of nothingness.

Contemporary neoromantic schools are happy to make this existential moment an absolute. So long as the contradictions of the mediated individual are still somewhat hidden it is possible to see in them the emergence of a mysterious "unconscious," the source of deep and "authentic" life. As soon as these same contradictions become obvious they are considered the supreme expression of a "freedom" which is also "negativity" and which, in practice, becomes confused with the sterile oppositions of double mediation. Faithful to the teachings of the early Rimbaud, our contemporaries declare their mind's disorder "sacred."

We should not judge novelists by the part which the "existential" moment plays in their work. Obviously its role is greater in Proust than in novelists before him, and even greater in the work of Dostoyevsky. The existential moment actually first appears in Proust but it is hidden and mediate. Most of Dostoyevsky's characters have reached the paroxysmal stage of metaphysical desire and the existential moment becomes immediate. It is the third moment which introduces the conclusion and the moral and metaphysical point to the lives in the novel. If it is systematically overlooked then it is understandable that present-day neoromantic critics consider Proust a rather timid precursor of so-called existential literature and Dostoyevsky its true founder. The only characters in Proust they consider entirely satisfactory are obviously those who are closest to the Dostoyevskian stage of desire, especially Charlus. As for Dostoyevsky, they feel no one can equal him, not because of his genius but because of the tremendous instability of his characters. He is honored for that which formerly made him suspect; in short, the nature of the error has not changed. It is never seen that the "existentialism" of the underground characters does not depend on the author but on the spread of ontological sickness, on the proximity and multiplication of the mediators.

No distinction is made between the setting of the novel and the personal contribution of the novelist. The existential moment, whatever its position in a novel, is never the final stage of a truly novelistic revelation. Far from making it an absolute the novelist sees in it yet another illusion and a particularly vicious one. He denounces a lie in the chaotic existence of the underground character which is as monstrous as middle-class hypocrisy and more directly destructive. The neoromantic prides himself on his revolt against that hypocrisy, but on the foundation of his "unconscious" or his ineffable "freedom" he erects aspirations very similar to those which the bourgeois had based on "loyalty to principle." The individual has not renounced his goal of autonomy and glorious mastery; he has not renounced his pride. Instead of sharing his faith, the great novelist is trying desperately to disclose its vanity. The neoromantic of our time thinks he is "liberated" because he is onto the game of the middle class and clearly sees its bankruptcy. But he has no inkling of the failure which awaits him, a failure far more sudden and disastrous than that of the middle class. Blindness as usual increases with "lucidity." The victims of metaphysical desire are caught up in a whirlwind of increasing velocity and narrowing circumference. Dostoyevsky tries to attain this impression of a whirlwind in each of his novels, and especially in *The Possessed*.

VARIATIONS in the novel's technique depend essentially on metaphysical desire. They are functional. The paths are always different, for the illusions are always different; but the end is the same: the revelation of metaphysical desire. We have seen that Proust tends toward Dostoyevskian solutions in the Dostoyevskian parts of his work. We shall now see how Dostoyevsky tends toward Proustian solutions in the least "underground" part of his work.

The characters in *The Possessed* belong to two different generations, that of the parents and that of the chil-

dren; it is the latter who are the "possessed" in the proper
sense of the term. The parents' generation is represented
by the governor and his wife, by the "great writer" Karmazinov, by Varvara Petrovna and, most of all, by the un-
forgettable Stepan Trofimovitch. The parents are further
from their mediator than are the children and their universe constitutes what we should like to call the "Proustian side" of Dostoyevsky's novel. The reference to the
French novelist is valid, at least in the sense that the
"parents" maintain the same illusionary certainty of permanent being as Proust's middle class. During twenty-two
years of *heroic silence* Varvara Petrovna nurses her amorous hatred of Stepan Trofimovitch. Stepan too leads an
existence of "mute protestation"; he pictures himself as
a part of the "eternal truths" of "Russian liberalism." In
full view of the kaleidoscopic political life of St. Petersburg, and despite the fact that he spends most of his time
reading Paul de Kock and playing cards, Stepan Trofimovitch sets himself up as an "incarnate reproach." It is apparent that he is playing a part but his acting is perfectly
sincere, like Mme Verdurin's devotion to the little clan, to
art, and to the fatherland. The being of Stephan Trofimovitch and Varvara Petrovna, like that of Proust's bourgeois, is already deeply divided and disintegrated by a
sterile pride, but the disease remains hidden. An unshake-
able "loyalty to principles" hides the work of decomposition. A serious crisis is needed to bring the truth out into
the open.

The parents' generation still keeps up *appearances.*
Thus it presents Dostoyevsky with problems of novelistic
revelation similar to those which face Proust in those
areas central to his work. We should not be surprised that
the Russian novelist resolves his problem with a solution
parallel to Proust's. Dostoyevsky uses a narrator. This narrator returns through the past like Proust's narrator, and

compares facts that are far removed from one another in order to reveal the contradictions that are the result of metaphysical desire. Dostoyevsky tends toward a narrative, explanatory, and historical technique because at this point he cannot do without narration, explanation, and history. When the children are on the stage, the mediator is much closer, the rhythm of reversals grows faster, and Dostoyevsky reverts to direct presentation; he forgets the narrator whose role is purely utilitarian. He does not even seem to notice the question of "credibility" raised by the disappearance of this official intermediary between the reader and the universe of the novel.

When dealing with the "parents," especially the most perfect representative of that generation, Stepan Trofimovitch, Dostoyevsky cannot do without an observing consciousness. He needs its testimony to destroy the tenacious pretentions of these "parents" and to reveal metaphysical desire. Many contemporary critics, following the lead of Jean-Paul Sartre, see the presence of the novelist himself or of an omniscient narrator within the novel as an "obstruction" to the "freedom" of the characters. These critics praise Dostoyevsky as the liberator of the novelistic character, that is, as the creator of the underground character; if they were true to their theories these critics should then criticize the Russian novelist for his creation of Stepan Trofimovitch. This character, who nevertheless rings marvelously true, should seem to them lacking in "freedom" for he is constantly observed and analyzed by a narrator who is external to the action of the novel. In all that concerns Stepan Trofimovitch, Dostoyevsky's technique is very close to that of Proust.

The objection will be made that Dostoyevsky's narrator is very different from Proust's. It is true he does not give us the author's reflections on the art of the novel. He *is* not the novelist in the way that Proust's narrator is. Do-

stoyevsky's narrator possesses only one of the functions of
Proust's narrator: the "psychological" function; he helps
us understand what makes certain of the characters tick.
We will be told that he is more naïve than Proust's narrator. He never knows as much about the characters as the author does. He never follows out all the implications of the
facts and gestures he puts before us. All of this is true but
the difference remains very superficial; it cannot change
in general the metaphysical status of the character being
analyzed and in particular it cannot restore his "freedom"
—if one can talk of freedom in connection with a fictional
character!—for the facts and gestures which Dostoyevsky's narrator assembles are always those which the
reader needs in order to arrive at a full and complete understanding of the character. The reader must go beyond
the somewhat elementary interpretation of the narrator
to a more profound truth, the metaphysical truth. The in-
experience and relative short-sightedness of the narrator
ensures a unity of tone with the technique of direct revelation. The enigmatic atmosphere favored by Dostoyevsky is preserved throughout.

This enigmatic atmosphere, moreover, does not war-
rant the importance given it today. It is certainly not the
result of a "margin of freedom" and an unknowable element left to the character. Freedom is there, without a
doubt, but not in the form the existentialist critics suppose. Freedom can be affirmed only in the form of a genuine conversion such as Stepan Trofimovitch undergoes at
the novel's conclusion. What cannot be determined is the
degree of culpability or innocence of a character. It is
never any more than this. To suppose that Dostoyevsky
allows the reader's imagination free play, that there is in
his work an area of freedom, a sort of void which we can
fill in as we like, would be a profound misunderstanding
of his genius. The novelist's primary aim is to reveal the

truth; the area of silence in his work is that of fundamental truths, the area of first principles which are not formulated because the novel itself must suggest them to the reader.

THE DOMAINS of the novel are "welded" to one another; each has a more or less extensive stretch of the total structure, each is defined by the two extremes of distance between mediator and desiring subject. Thus there is a total novelistic duration of which the various works are fragments. The pre-Dostoyevskian characters and desires do not appear at the end of *Remembrance of Things Past* by chance. The Proustian characters and desires do not appear by chance at the *beginning* of that Dostoyevskian *summa* which is *The Possessed*. There is always the same meaning behind the adventure of the hero of a novel; it takes us from the upper to the lower regions of a particular novelistic domain. The career of the hero is a descent into hell which almost always ends in a return to the light, by means of a metaphysical, nontemporal conversion. Novelistic durations overlap but there is always a descent into hell which begins where the previous one breaks off. There are a hundred heroes and yet there is a single hero whose adventure spreads over the whole of novelistic literature.

Dostoyevsky had a far clearer idea of this falling movement than the novelists before him. In *The Possessed* he tries to make it visible. The transition from one generation to another makes clear the dynamism of the underground. The successive illusions seem to be independent of each other, and even contradictory, but as they unfold they form an implacable history. The mediator's approach is the source of the novel's temporal span and gives the latter its meaning.

Each generation embodies one stage of ontological sickness. The truth about the parents remains hidden for a long time but it breaks out with incredible force in the feverish agitation, the violence, and the debauchery of the children. The parents are amazed to discover that they have brought forth monsters; in their children they see the opposite of themselves. They do not see the connection between the tree and its fruit. The children, on the contrary, are fully aware of the histrionics in their parents' indignation. "Loyalty to principles" does not impress them. They fully understand that middle-class dignity is a form of "bad faith." In Dostoyevsky even more than in Proust descending transcendence is a caricature of ascending transcendence. It consists of elements of wisdom mixed with obscuration. But the results of underground lucidity are always injurious; they drag the characters down, not up. The victim of ontological sickness is always excited to fury at the sight of others less sick than himself and he always chooses his mediator from among them. He tries constantly to bring his idol down to his own level.

We shall know the tree by its fruit. Dostoyevsky places great emphasis on the connection between the generations and on the parents' responsibility. Stepan Trofimovitch is the father of all the possessed. He is Pyotr Verhovenski's father; he is the spiritual father of Shatov, of Daria Pavlovna, of Lizaveta Nikolaevna, and especially of Stavrogin, since he taught them all. He is the father of Fedka, the assassin, since Fedka was his serf. Stepan Trofimovitch abandoned Pyotr, his blood son, as well as Fedka, his son in the eyes of society. His noble rhetoric and romantic aesthetics do not prevent Stepan from failing in all his own concrete responsibilities. Romantic liberalism is the father of destructive nihilism.

Everything in *The Possessed* starts with Stepan Trofimovitch and ends with Stavrogin. The children reveal

the truth about Stepan but in his turn Stavrogin reveals
the truth about the children, the truth about all the characters. The parents' generation embodies the first moment of Proustian revelation, as we defined it earlier. The
children's generation embodies the second moment. Stavrogin alone embodies the third. Beneath middle-class
"loyalty to principles" is the furious agitation of the possessed, and beneath this furious agitation is immobility
and nothingness, the frigid *acedia* of Stavrogin.

Beneath the modern phantasmagoria, beneath the
whirl of events and ideas which lies at the end of the ever
more rapid development of internal mediation, lies nothingness. The sound has reached the zero point. And
Stavrogin is the incarnation of that zero point, the pure
nothingness of absolute pride.

Stavrogin is the axis for all the characters of *The Possessed* and equally for all the heroes in previous novels
and all the victims of metaphysical desire. This monster
does not belong to a third generation for he is the incarnation of a spirit as atemporal as God the Spirit; the spirit
of disorder, of decay, and of nothingness.

In *The Possessed* Dostoyevsky rises to the level of an
epic of metaphysical sickness. The characters of that
novel acquire a quasi-allegorical significance. Stepan
Trofimovitch is the Father, Stavrogin the son, and the
muddle-headed conspirator, Pyotr Verhovenski, is none
other than the absurd Spirit of a demoniacal Trinity.

CHAPTER XI

THE DOSTOYEVSKIAN
APOCALYPSE

EXISTENTIALISM has made the word "freedom" fashionable. After the war we were constantly told that the novelist cannot reach the heights of genius unless he "respects" the freedom of his characters. Unfortunately we were never told in what form such "respect" should be. The notion of freedom is inevitably ambiguous when applied to the novel. If the novelist is free it is hard to see how his characters would be. Freedom cannot be shared even by created and creator. This is a fundamental dogma and Jean-Paul Sartre uses it to try to prove the impossibility of a God the Creator. What is impossible for God could not be possible for a novelist. Either the novelist is free and his characters are not, or else the characters are free and the novelist, like God, does not exist.

These logical contradictions do not seem to embarrass the theoreticians of contemporary fiction. Their "freedom" derives from a hopeless confusion of a philosophical usage of the term with its daily usage. For most critics freedom is synonymous with spontaneity. The novelist should pay no attention to "psychology"; in other words he should create characters whose actions are never *predictable*. Strangely enough Dostoyevsky is considered the originator of the spontaneous character. *Notes from the*

Underground has been particularly highly praised. It has almost become the breviary of the new school.

The first part receives most attention and scarcely any of the second part, which is the only truly novelistic part, is noticed except the astonishing freedom—i.e., spontaneity—of the underground character. This fantastic independence evidently produces such "surprising effects" that we are told we should find in them the greatest aesthetic pleasure.

The critics do not seem to be aware of either the insolent officer or Zverkov. The mediator is simply suppressed. The laws of underground desire, analogous to Proust's but still more rigorous, are completely overlooked. They are dazzled by the horrible convulsive spasms of the underground man; they are pleased by the irrationality of these spasms. They admire these free spasms and almost go so far as to suggest their hygienic use to the reader.

The underground man is bound to be surprising if the means of understanding him are removed. If metaphysical desire is suppressed then mechanism becomes spontaneity and slavery becomes freedom. The character's obsessions are not perceived, nor is the fierce passion which takes hold of him the moment he is rejected. The grotesque spasms disappear and a "glorious rebellion" against society and the "human condition" takes their place.

Thus the underground man who is presented for our admiration has nothing in common with Dostoyevsky's creation, but he does bear a considerable resemblance to the type of hero tirelessly reproduced in contemporary fiction. Neither Roquentin in *Nausea* nor Meursault in *The Stranger* nor Samuel Beckett's tramps desire metaphysically. These characters are overwhelmed by many different ailments but the worst of all—metaphysical desire—is spared them. Our contemporary heroes never imitate anyone. They are all perfectly autonomous and they could repeat in chorus with Valéry's M. Teste: "We may look like just *anyone* but we are completely self-sufficient."

Many superficial resemblances can be traced between Dostoyevsky and recent fiction. In both there is the same hatred of Others, the same radical disorder, the same "polymorphism" in the collapse of all bourgeois values. But the differences are far more essential. Our contemporary heroes always keep their precious freedom intact; the underground man relinquishes his to his mediator. We cannot distinguish between our alleged free spontaneity and underground slavery. How can we make such a glaring confusion?

It is for one of two reasons: either we are innocent of all metaphysical desire or else that desire possesses us so completely that we are entirely unaware of it. The first hypothesis is not very likely since it is incessantly repeated that the Russian novelist gives us an accurate translation of the truth of our time. We must therefore accept the second hypothesis. Dostoyevsky describes us better than our contemporary writers because he reveals a metaphysical desire which we have succeeded in hiding from ourselves. We have even managed to keep the mediator hidden from ourselves while reading Dostoyevsky; we admire the Russian novelist without understanding the nature of his art.

If Dostoyevsky is right, our heroes are false. They are false because they flatter our illusion of autonomy. Our heroes are just new romantic lies destined to prolong the Promethean dreams to which the modern world desperately clings. Dostoyevsky reveals a desire that our fiction and criticism have only reflected. Our fiction hides from us the presence of the mediator in our daily existence.

Our criticism hides that same mediator from us in a work expressly written to reveal his presence. By quoting Dostoyevsky this criticism is unwittingly introducing a ravenous wolf into the existentialist sheepfold.

Beneath the superficial resemblances there is an irreducible opposition between Dostoyevsky and contemporary fiction. It is always remembered that Dostoyevsky repudiated the *psychological* unity of the characters in his novels and this is thought to prove that he is in agreement with our novelists. But our novelists denounce that psychological unity only in order to lay a better foundation for metaphysical unity. It was this same metaphysical unity that the bourgeois sought through psychological unity. The middle-class illusions of permanence and stability have vanished but the aim has not altered. Under the guise of freedom this same aim is pursued doggedly amid the anguish and chaos.

Dostoyevsky rejects both psychological and metaphysical unity. He rejects psychological illusion only in order to dissipate more completely the metaphysical illusion. The will to autonomy gives rise to slavery but the man from the underground is not aware of it and does not want to be. We are equally unaware of it, or do not wish to be aware of it. Thus it is true that we are like the underground man but not for the reasons given by the critics.

It would be impossible for the critics to make this mistake about *Notes from the Underground* were it not for a typical romantic identification of creature with creator. It is assumed that Dostoyevsky shares all the opinions of his underground hero. Emphasis is placed on the first part of the story because it constitutes a formidable attack on modern scientism and rationalism. It is true that Dostoyevsky shares his hero's disgust for the mediocre utopias of the end of the nineteenth century. But we should not mistake this partial agreement for total agreement. We should not confuse the novelist with his character, especially if he has drawn the character from himself. The underground Dostoyevsky is not Dostoyevsky, the genius, but rather the romantic Dostoyevsky of earlier works. The underground Dostoyevsky never talks about the underground; he tells us about "the beautiful and the sublime," about a tragic or sublime suffering after the fashion of Victor Hugo. The Dostoyevsky who describes the underground for us is in the process of leaving it; he will continue his rough uphill road from one masterpiece to the next until he reaches the peace and serenity of *The Brothers Karamozov*.

The underground is the truth hidden behind the rationalistic, romantic, and "existential" abstractions. The underground is the aggravation of an already existent evil, the cancerous spread of a metaphysics thought to be destroyed. The underground is not the individual's revenge on the cold rationalist mechanism. We must not plunge into it as if it brought us salvation.

The underground hero in his own way bears witness to the individual's true vocation. And he testifies more vigorously, in a way, than he would if he were less sick. As metaphysical desire grows more acute, the testimony becomes more insistent. The underground is the inverse image of metaphysical truth. This image becomes increasingly clear as one plunges deeper into the abyss.

An attentive reading makes it impossible to confuse author and character. Dostoyevsky is not writing a lyrical confession but a satirical text of undoubtedly bitter but prodigious farce.

I am alone and they are everyone—this is the underground motto. The hero wants to express the pride and suffering of being unique, he thinks he is about to grasp absolute particularity but ends up with a principle of universal application; he emerges with a formula which is almost algebraic in its anonymity. The greedy mouth closing on nothingness, the Sisyphean effort perpetually renewed, do indeed sum up the history of contemporary individualism. Symbolism, surrealism, existentialism are successive attempts to give content to the underground formula. But these attempts succeed only to the extent that they fail. They have to fail in order for the multitudes to repeat in chorus their particular version of: *I am alone and they are everyone*. The romantic has put into circulation a group of symbols and images intended not for communion but for universal separation. Like other contemporary social forces, our literature has a tendency toward conformity even when it thinks it is fighting it, since the path of leveling is a *via negativa*. Think, for example, of an American industry which "personalizes" what it mass produces. An entire youth "personalizes" its anonymous anguish at small expense by identifying with the *same* hero *against* all other men.

The underground man is never closer to the Others than when he thinks he is most cut off from them. *I am alone and they are everyone*. The interchangeability of the pronouns is obvious and brutally brings us back from the individual to the collective. Petty bourgeois individualism has become completely devoid of content. The image of Sisyphus is not accurate. Each of us is his own cask of the Danaïdes, which he tries in vain to fill. The existentialists assure us that they have given up this futile game. But they have not renounced the cask. They find it wonderful that it should be empty.

DOSTOYEVSKY and his character are thought to be the same because he never interrupts him. But the underground man is taken in by his motto and Dostoyevsky is not. The hero is incapable of laughing for he cannot see through the individualism of opposition. Our contemporaries are as sad as he. That is why they do not give Dostoyevsky credit for his tremendous humor. They do not see that Dostoyevsky is laughing at his hero. *I am alone and they are everyone.* Dostoyevsky's irony pours out in marvelous aphorisms, demolishing "individualist" pretentions, disintegrating the "differences" which appear so monstrous to offended consciousness. We do not know how to join in Dostoyevsky's laughter because we do not know how to laugh at ourselves. Today many people praise *Notes from the Underground* without any idea that they are unearthing a caricature of themselves written a century ago.

Since the First, and especially since the Second World War, there has been an acceleration in the decomposition of middle-class values; the Western world becomes daily more like that from which Dostoyevsky drew his great works. To restore to *Notes from the Underground* all its bite and that cruelty for which the Russian novelist used to be reproached, it is usually enough to make a few slight transpositions. Transport the underground man from the banks of the Nevsky to the banks of the Seine. For his petty official's existence substitute a writer's career and you will recognize in almost every line of this great text a ferocious parody of the intellectual myths of our time.

Doubtless one remembers the letter which the underground man was going to write to the officer who insulted him. This letter is a disguised appeal to the mediator. The hero turns to his "beloved persecutor" as the faithful toward his god but he wants us to think, and he convinces himself, that he is turning away from him in horror. Nothing can be more humiliating to underground pride than this appeal to the Other. For this reason the letter contains only insults.

This dialectic of appeal which denies that it is an appeal can be found in contemporary literature. To write and especially to publish a work is to appeal to the public, to sever by a unilateral gesture the bond of indifference between Self and Other. Nothing is as humiliating to underground pride as that initiative. The aristocrats of former times had already sensed that there was something common and low in a literary career which did not go well with their pride. Mme de la Fayette had her work published by Segrais. The Duke de la Rochefoucauld may have had his stolen by one of his valets. The somewhat bourgeois glory of the artist thereby reached these aristocratic writers without their having sought it in any way.

Instead of disappearing with the Revolution this point of literary honor became even sharper in the middle-class era. Starting with Paul Valéry, there is a *reluctance* to become famous. After twenty years of scorn, the creator of M. Teste yielded to universal supplication and charitably offered the gift of his genius to the enjoyment of Others.

The proletarianized writer of our times has neither influential friends nor valets at his disposal. He has to help himself. Thus the content of his works is entirely devoted to denying that the container has any meaning. We have reached the stage of the underground letter. The writer makes an anti-appeal to the public in the shape of anti-poetry, anti-novel, or anti-play. One writes in order to prove to the reader that one does not care about him. The main thing is to make the Other taste the rare, ineffable, and fresh quality of one's scorn for him.

Never before has so much been written but it is all to prove that communication is neither possible nor desirable. The aesthetics of "silence" with which we are overwhelmed are quite obviously an outcome of the underground dialectic. For a long time the romantic tried to convince society that he gave to it much more than it gave to him. Since the end of the nineteenth century, any idea of reciprocity, however imperfect, in the relationship with the public has become unbearable. The author still publishes his works, but to cover up this crime he does everything he can to avoid being read. For a long time he has claimed to be speaking only to himself; today he claims to be speaking without anything to say.

But he is not telling the truth. The writer talks in order to seduce us just as he did in the past. He constantly watches our eyes to see in them the admiration aroused by his talent. It is objected that he does everything to make us loathe him. This may be true, but the reason is that he is no longer able to pay court to us openly. First he has to convince himself that he is not trying to flatter us. Thus he courts us negatively like Dostoyevsky's tortured characters.

The writer is mistaken if he thinks that he is thereby protesting against "class oppression" and "capitalist alienation." The aesthetics of silence is the last of the romantic myths. Musset's pelican and Baudelaire's albatross make us laugh, but like the fabled phoenix, they keep rising again from their ashes. Within ten years we will see in "l'écriture blanche" and its "degré zéro" yet more abstract, yet more ephemeral and stunted transformations of the pompous romantic birds.

This calls to mind another scene from *Notes from the Underground*, that of the banquet for Zverkov at which the man from the underground finally shows up, but behaves in a very strange manner:

> I smiled contemptuously and walked up and down the other side of the room, opposite the sofa, from the table to the stove and back again. I tried my very utmost to show them that I could do without them, and yet I purposely made a noise with my boots, thumping with my heels. But it was all in vain. They paid

no attention. I had the patience to walk up and down in front of them from eight o'clock till eleven, in the same place, from the table to the stove and back again.

Many contemporary works resemble this endless walking up and down. If we really could "do without them" we would not stamp up and down on the floor with our heels but we would go back into our room. We are not *strangers*, but rather *bastards* in the Sartrean sense. We pretend we are free but we are not telling the truth. We are hypnotized by ridiculous gods and our suffering is doubled by the knowledge that they are ridiculous. Like the man from the underground we gravitate around these gods in a comfortless orbit fixed by the balance of contrary forces.

This is true too of Alceste, standing with his arms crossed, eyes blazing, behind the chair in which Celimène sits and gossips with her petty little marquises. Alceste is ridiculous so long as he does not leave. Rousseau the romantic takes sides with Alceste. He reproaches Molière for making us laugh at the misanthrope. Our own romantics would treat Dostoyevsky the same way if his humorous intentions did not escape them. They also take it seriously but their angle of vision has narrowed still more. In order to share the laughter of Molière and Dostoyevsky one must have got over romantic fascinations. It must be understood that desire and desire alone keeps Alceste behind Celimène's couch. And it is desire which keeps the underground man in the banquet room. It is desire which puts into the mouths of the romantics exclamations of revenge and curses against God and men. The misanthrope and the coquette, the underground man and his beloved persecutor are always the two sides of the same metaphysical desire. True genius transcends these deceptive oppositions and makes us laugh at one as much as the other.

Metaphysical desire drags its victims toward the ambiguous point of fascination situated exactly at equal distances from both true detachment and intimate contact with the desired object. This is the strange area explored by Franz Kafka: "the frontier between solitude and communion," equidistant from both, and excluding both equally. The fascinated person who wants to hide his fascination from us and from himself must pretend to live according to one or the other of these modes of existence which alone are compatible with the freedom and autonomy he prides himself on enjoying. Since these two poles of genuine freedom are at equal distances from his own position, the fascinated person has no reason to choose one rather than the other. He is as near and as far from proximity as from distance; he can claim either with as much and as little verisimilitude. Thus we can predict that fascination will hide behind the mask of "involvement" as often as it hides behind the mask of "detachment." This is precisely what is confirmed by the history of modern and contemporary romanticism. The myths of solitude—sublime, contemptuous, ironic, and even "mystic"—alternate regularly with the contrary and just as deceptive myths of complete surrender to the social and collective forms of historical existence. We can also predict that when the fascinated being reaches the paroxysmal stage of his sickness he will be completely incapable of maintaining his original pose and will constantly change roles. The underground man has reached this stage; that is why there are no romantic attitudes which do not find an echo in his brief confession.

We have already seen the underground man in "solitude" and "detachment." Let us now trace his *engagement*. Zverkov and his friends have got up from the table; they are going to bring the evening to a close at a house of ill-repute. Now there is no point to his contemptuous walking up and down. Will the underground hero finally give up the siege and return to his room to take up the thread of his earlier reveries? Will he go back to dancing "on Lake Como" and "exiling the Pope to Brazil"? Will he once again turn his attention to the "beautiful and the sublime"? Not a chance. He hurries off after his mediator.

As long as the mediator is immobile it is not difficult to feign "serene contemplation" but as soon as the idol moves away the mask of indifference falls to the ground. We seem to break into the dangerous light of truth. The underground man cannot completely protect himself from this light but he can shade its glare. We see him driven by his obsession, hurrying in pursuit of the absurd Zverkov, but that is not how he sees himself. He repudiates the sterile dreams of art for art's sake; he declares that he prefers hard contact with reality. In other words, he invents a doctrine of involvement for himself. He always has to make what was not the object of a choice appear as if he had chosen it. From the heights of his new-found "truth" the underground man looks with scorn on "the beautiful and the sublime" of former times; he ridicules the romantic dreams which but a moment before were his own justification:

> "So this is it, this is it at last—contact with real life,"
> I muttered as I ran headlong downstairs. "This is
> very different from the Pope's leaving Rome and go-
> ing to Brazil, very different from the ball on the
> shores of Lake Como! You are a scoundrel," a thought
> flashed through my mind, "if you laugh at this now."

The last idea is particularly pungent: the underground man accuses himself of being too hard on his own mistakes; Dostoyevsky cannot unveil the soul of his hero without shedding an equally pitiless but salutary light on all the excuses which help us to live. There is plenty of "existentialism" in the underground; there is surrealism in the early Stavrogin, who kisses the wives of functionaries at the subprefecture balls. The novelist forgets neither those who sanctify terror nor those who sanctify debauchery, neither the disciples of Saint-Just nor the pupils of the Marquis de Sade.

The tricks of a pride constantly involved in denying its gods are embodied in Dostoyevsky's fictitious characters; in our day we find them in the shape of philosophical and aesthetic theories. These theories never do more than reflect desire; they conceal it deep within that very reflection; Dostoyevsky reveals it.

In the writing of *Notes from the Underground* Dostoyevsky rises for the first time to the level of novelistic revelation. He escapes egotistic indignation and justification; he foregoes the literary fruits of the underground, renounces the "beautiful and the sublime" of *White Nights* and ceases to wallow in the misery of *Poor Folk*. He stops giving the name of involvement or noninvolvement to the fixed distance of fascination. And he describes all the lies of which he is in the process of ridding himself. The man's health and the novelist's genius are indistinguishable.

Only a radical misinterpretation of the message of his work would enable us to annex Dostoyevsky to our own lies and renew the paradox of the romantic critic who appropriates for himself *Don Quixote* or *The Red and the Black*. We should not be surprised by the analogy between all these misinterpretations: the same need gives rise to the same confusion of the novelistic work with the romantic work. Metaphysical desire itself suggests these aberrant interpretations of all novelists. Once more we must point out how easily ontological sickness transforms obstacles into resources and adversaries into allies.

THE CORRECT interpretation of Dostoyevsky's work is the discovery in it of the revelation of metaphysical desire in its supreme phase. To do this successfully we must first free ourselves of the illusion which accompanies that desire, for it is precisely that illusion which permeates our world. Dostoyevskian desire triumphs among us, and the Russian novelist's popularity is a paradoxical proof of the fact. Thus Dostoyevsky presents a particularly complex problem. His truth is neither stronger nor less scorned than that of other novelists; but the illusions he is denouncing are incomparably more powerful in our day than the illusions denounced by Cervantes, Stendhal, Flaubert, and even Marcel Proust. As usual these illusions find their best expression in literature. Thus to reveal the novelist's truth is to uncover the falsity of our own literature and vice versa. We have established this fact before and we will establish it again.

The moment we are no longer impressed by its prestige, contemporary neoromanticism seems even more abstract and fanciful than previous romanticisms. The latter without exception exalted the strength of desire. Right up to Gide's *The Immoralist* and *The Fruits of the Earth* the hero is always he who desires most intensely. This intense desire is the only spontaneous desire. It is opposed to the desires of Others which are always weaker because they are *copied*. The romantic cannot any longer hide from himself the role played by imitation in the genesis of desire but that role in his opinion is bound up with a weakening of the original desire. The copy of the desire appears to be a rather crude carbon copy; copied desires are always *more blurred* than the original. This is the same as saying these desires are never our own; in fact our own desires always seem the most intense of all. The romantic thinks he can save the authenticity of his own desire by claiming that it is the most violent.

Contemporary romanticism starts from the inverse principle. Now it is Others who desire intensely, and the hero—oneself—has little or any desire at all! Roquentin desires less than the citizens of Bouville and what he does desire he desires less intensely; he desires less than Annie. He is the only character in *Nausea* who knows that "adventures" do not exist, in other words, that exotic desire, metaphysical desire, always ends in disappointment. Similarly Meursault has only "natural" and spontaneous desires, in other words, limited, finite, and without any future. He too refuses adventure in the shape of a journey to Paris. He knows perfectly well that faraway places are transfigured by metaphysical desire.

The early romantic wanted to prove his spontaneity—his divinity—by desiring more intensely than Others. The latter-day romantic tries to prove exactly the same thing by totally opposite means. This complete reversal is necessitated by the closing-in of the mediator and the constant progress of metaphysical truth. Nobody today believes in noble spontaneous desires. Even the most naïve recognize the mediator's shadow behind the frantic passion of early romanticism. Thus we enter what Mme Nathalie Sarraute, quoting Stendhal, calls "the era of suspicion."

The violence of desire is no longer a criterion of spontaneity. The *lucidity* of our time is able to recognize the presence of the sacred in desires that would appear to be most natural. Contemporary reflection discovers "myths" and "mythology" in everyone of our desires. The eighteenth century demystified religion, the nineteenth century demystified history and philology, our era demystifies daily life. Not a single desire escapes the demystifier who is patiently occupied in constructing on top of all the dead myths the greatest myth of all, that of his own detachment. He alone, it seems, never desires. In short it is a question of convincing Others and especially of convincing oneself that one is completely and divinely autonomous.

Thus once more we have seen that lucidity and blindness increase side by side. Henceforth the truth is so brilliantly clear that it has to be taken into account if only in order to escape it. This frightful truth forces the subject into ever more delirious lies. The early romantics disguised their desire but they never denied its existence. *Askesis* for the sake of desire raged only in the public parks, in the salon, and in the bedroom. Now it triumphs even in the secret recesses of one's conscience and in the interior monologue.

The hero who experiences the greatest desire is succeeded by the hero who experiences the least desire. But the Manichean division between Self and Other has not disappeared; it secretly controls the metamorphoses of the romantic hero. The exception is always opposed to the norm as Good is opposed to Evil. Meursault alone is innocent in a sea of guilt; he dies the victim of the Others, as Vigny's Chatterton died. He is the judge of his judges, like all the romantics before him. The hero always escapes the curse which his creator hurls at the rest of mankind. There is always someone who comes out on top of the romantic game unscathed and that someone has to be *I*, the author, before it is *I*, the reader.

It is the truth about contemporary neoromanticism which Camus reveals under the veil of a transparent allegory in that admirable and liberating work, *The Fall*. Transcending the romanticism of *The Stranger* and *The Plague* the writer denounces the twin attempts at self-justification in the literature of involvement and the literature of noninvolvement. Like Dostoyevsky's *Notes from the Underground* this work does not achieve reconciliation; like *Notes from the Underground* it has already gone beyond romanticism. Albert Camus died at the moment when a whole new career was probably opening up before him.

Whereas romantic readers used to identify with the hero who felt the strongest desire, today they identify with the hero who feels least desire. They are always docile in their identification with heroes who provide with *models* their passion for *autonomy;* Don Quixote, driven by the same passion, identified with Amadis of Gaul. The mythology that nourishes contemporary fiction corresponds to a new stage of metaphysical desire. We think we are anti-romantic because we loudly repudiate previous romanticisms. We are like Don Quixote's friends who are busy trying to cure the poor man of his madness because they themselves are the victims of it in an aggravated form.

As SOON AS the subject who desires recognizes the role of imitation in his own desire he has to renounce either this desire or his pride. Modern *lucidity* has shifted the problem of *askesis* and broadened it. It is no longer a question of renouncing the object temporarily in order the better to possess it but of renouncing the desire itself. The choice is between pride and desire since desire makes slaves of us.

Nondesire once more becomes a privilege as it was for the wise man of old or the Christian saint. But the desiring subject recoils in terror before the idea of absolute renunciation. He looks for loopholes. He wants to create a personality in which the absence of desire has not been won with difficulty out of the anarchy of instincts and metaphysical passion. The somnambulist hero of American writers is the "solution" to this problem. Nondesire in this hero has nothing to do with the triumph of the mind over evil forces, nor with the self-discipline extolled by the great religions and higher humanisms. It makes one think rather of a numbing of the senses, of a total or partial loss of vital curiosity. In the case of Meursault this "privileged" state is merged with the pure individual essence. In Roquentin's case, it is a sudden gift of grace, which, without any apparent reason, descends on the hero in the form of *nausea*. In many other works the metaphysical structure is less apparent; it has to be disengaged from the fiction which at once expresses and conceals it. Alcohol, narcotics, extreme physical pain, erotic abuses can destroy or deaden desire. In the end the hero reaches a stage of *lucid stupefaction* which constitutes the final romantic pose. This nondesire of course has nothing in common with abstinence and sobriety. But the hero claims that in his indifference he accomplishes by caprice and almost without being aware of it, what Others accomplish by desire. This somnambulist hero lives on "bad faith." He tries to resolve the conflict between pride and desire without ever clearly formulating it. Perhaps a more radical pride is needed to present the problem frankly. At the time of writing *The Evening with M. Teste* Paul Valéry was a man with that sort of pride. Valéryism contrasts the *vaniteux* who desires through the Other and for the Other with the proud man who no longer desires anything but his own nothingness. The only individualist worthy of the name, the proud man is no longer looking for escape from his nothingness in desire; rather after a radical mental *askesis* he makes that nothingness the very object of his adoration. His aim is still divine autonomy but the direction of his effort is reversed. To found the whole of existence on that nothingness which one carries inside himself is to transform impotence into omnipotence, to inflate the inner desert island of Robinson Crusoe to the dimensions of infinity

"Remove everything that I may see," exclaims M. Teste

in his log-book. At the extreme limit of interior destitution, pride must finally arrive at the point where it sees itself in the original light of a pure Self. The passage from vanity to pride is a passage from the comparable to the incomparable, from division to unity, from masochistic anguish to "sovereign disdain."

The Nietzschean meditation takes place in the same dimension of individualism as M. Teste's undertaking. Superhumanity will be based on a double renunciation of both vertical and deviated transcendency. Zarathustra tries to enter into the sanctuary of his own existence through a purifying *askesis* analogous to religious *askesis* but differently oriented. This analogy is continually underscored by style and Biblical images. *Thus Spoke Zarathustra* is a new gospel which should mark the end of the Christian era.

In this dimension pride is no longer seen as man's natural bent but the highest and most austere of all vocations. Pride is always shown surrounded by its theological virtues. Mme Teste's confessor recognizes in this retinue all the Christian virtues except one, charity. The thinker sets up for our admiration an ideal of quasi-saintliness well suited to seducing the noblest and strongest minds.

What would Dostoyevsky think of this supreme temptation which Nietzsche and Valéry murmur in the ears of twentieth-century men? Zarathustra and M. Teste seem to be a thousand leagues away from the disorder of the underground. Will these heroes escape the condemnation of Promethean ambitions pronounced by the Russian novelist, and the whole of novelistic literature before him? Again we must turn to *The Possessed* for the answer to this supreme question. This inexhaustible work contains the real dialogue between Nietzsche and Dostoyevsky. When the engineer, Kirillov, decides out of pride to commit suicide he enters at the decisive point the decisive game which has been side-stepped up to this point.

Kirillov's thought, like Nietzsche's, takes its point of departure from a meditation on Christ and the destiny of Christianity. Christ sent men in search of God; he gave them a glimpse of eternity. Man's feeble efforts fail and turn back on humanity, bringing about the excruciating universe of deviated transcendency. If there was no resurrection, if Christ, that incomparable being, was not exempt from the laws of nature, then Christianity is evil. We must renounce the madness of Christ, we must renounce the infinite. The post-Christian universe must be destroyed. Man must be firmly established here on earth by proving to him that his light is the only light. But one cannot get rid of God merely by denying him with one's lips. Men cannot forget the law of the gospel, the law of superhuman love which in their weakness they transform into a law of hatred. When he sees the infernal merry-go-round of the possessed, besmirched as they are with crime and shame, Kirillov recognizes the mark of the divine.

The Christian's desires are transfigured by his thirst for immortality. Neither science nor humanism can quench that thirst. Neither philosophical atheism nor social utopias can stop this mad pursuit in which each one tries to steal a phantasmal divinity from his neighbor. To annul Christianity the current of desire must be reversed, it must be deflected from the Other to the Self. Men waste their energy pursuing God anywhere but within themselves. Like Zarathustra, like M. Teste, Kirillov wants to worship his own nothingness. He wants to worship what each of us considers most miserable and despicable in our own depths

But for Kirillov the undertaking does not remain merely an idea. Kirillov does not want to write a particularly original book, he wants to make his idea incarnate in a decisive act. Desiring one's own nothingness is desiring oneself at the weakest point of his humanity, desiring to be mortal, desiring to be dead.

Kirillov hopes by committing suicide to grasp himself in a moment of vertiginous possession. Why does he expect this conquest from death? According to some, death should not bother us since it is never more than an idea, since it is always outside of our individual experience.

Kirillov agrees: eternity naturally dwells within us—that is the whole idea but it is not enough to affirm this idea, it must be proved. The proof must convince a man corrupted by two thousand years of Christianity. All the philosophic talk has never prevented anyone, not even philosophers, from dreading death.

Strange as it seems, before Kirillov, suicide was committed out of fear of death. A person killed himself not in order to renounce infinity but out of fear of the finiteness to which he thinks he is condemned by the failure of desire. Kirillov, however, is going to kill himself simply in order to be dead and to be himself in death.

One man has to take the first step in daring to desire his own nothingness, in order that future humanity may base its whole existence on that nothingness. Kirillov is dying for others as much as for himself. In wanting his own death and only that, Kirillov is engaging in a duel with God which he hopes will be decisive. He wants to show the Almighty that his best weapon, the dread of death, has lost its power.

If the hero succeeds in dying the way he wishes, he will have won that gigantic fight. It will force God—whether God exists or not—to give up his millennial ascendency over men. Kirillov dies to destroy fear in one blow with hope, he dies to enable man to renounce immortality, not on the superficial level of belief but on the essential level of desire.

But Kirillov fails. Instead of the serene apotheosis he imagined, his death is indescribably horrible beneath the gaze of the most ignoble of them all, Verhovenski, the

Mephistopheles of the possessed. The divinity Kirillov so desires grows nearer as death approaches. But the nearer it comes the more inaccessible it becomes. One can commit suicide in order to become God but one cannot become God without renouncing suicide. In the face of death the desired omnipotence becomes one with extreme impotence. And Kirillov discovers his grinning demon, Verhovenski, hovering over him.

Kirillov is hurled from the summit of pride into the abyss of shame. If he ends by killing himself it is in scorn of himself and hatred of his finiteness, like other men. His suicide is an ordinary suicide. In Kirillov the oscillation between pride and shame, those two polarities of the underground consciousness, is constantly present, but in him it is reduced to one single movement of extraordinary amplitude. Thus Kirillov is the supreme victim of metaphysical desire. But by whom is the engineer mediated in his desire of those dizzy heights and depths?

Kirillov is obsessed with Christ. There is an icon in his room and in front of the icon, burning tapers. In the eyes of the *lucid* Verhovenski, Kirillov is "more of a believer than a Pope." Kirillov makes Christ a mediator not in the Christian, but in the Promethean, the novelistic, sense of the word. Kirillov in his pride is imitating Christ. To put an end to Christianity, a death in the image of Christ's is necessary—but it must be a reversed image. Kirillov is imitating the redemption. Like all proud people he covets Another's divinity and he becomes the diabolic rival of Christ. In this supreme desire the analogies between vertical and deviated transcendency are clearer than ever. The satanic side of the arrogant mediation is plainly revealed.

Kirillov is imitating Christ through Stavrogin, who is the very incarnation of the modern spirit. The idea which consumes Kirillov comes to him through Stavrogin. Thus the idea is evil but the man is good and pure. Kirillov could not incarnate the supreme dimension of the meta-physical revolt if he were completely lacking in grandeur. He is a match for the ultimate stage of the sickness as Dostoyevsky sees it.

In the opinion of some critics Kirillov's qualities contradict the apparent, and, as it were, accepted sense of Dostoyevsky's novel. They look for a "deeper" meaning which, they suppose, Dostoyevsky sometimes succeeds in "repressing" but which crops up in this crucial episode. Their reasoning is that the writer ends up making his character "likeable" because he is secretly in sympathy with his cause.

Kirillov's suicide is a demonstration whose whole significance depends upon his virtue. Kirillov has to be good the way Stavrogin has to be rich and handsome. This is the way it has to be, so that his own arguments against Christianity turn on him and defeat him. If this hero cannot die in peace, if the laws of transgression and redemption are not suspended for this saint of pride, then they will be suspended for no one. Men will go on living and dying in the shadow of the cross.

Dostoyevsky is the prophet of the whole series of deifications of the individual which have been proclaimed since the end of the nineteenth century. The fact that he was the first to treat certain themes tends to lend support to romantic interpretations. His foresight is so astounding it is thought that Dostoyevsky must himself be secretly committed to the development he foresees. Dostoyevsky is seen as a remarkable but inevitably timid precursor of the Promethean thinkers. The Dostoyevskian novel is supposed to present an early embodiment of the modern hero, not quite freed from his orthodox swaddling clothes. Everything in Dostoyevsky which goes beyond revolt is attributed to not-yet-dispelled mists of feudalism and religion, and the critics thus cut themselves off from the highest levels of novelistic genius. Bit by bit, with the help of history, one gets used to denying the most glaring evidence and Dostoyevsky is enrolled under the banner of "modernity."

We must clearly proclaim the elementary truths to which the inverted conformity of our time has succeeded in giving a scandalous air. Dostoyevsky does not justify Promethean ambitions, he expressly condemns them, and prophesies their failure. In his eyes Nietzsche's superhumanity would have been merely an underground dream. It can be seen in the dreams of Raskolnikov, of Versilov, and of Ivan Karamazov. As for M. Teste, from Dostoyevsky's point of view he is hardly any more than a dandy in the realm of intelligence. He abstains from desire in order that we should desire his mind. In Valéry, *askesis* for the sake of desire has invaded the territory of pure thought. His distinction between vanity which makes comparisons and incomparable pride is a new kind of comparison and therefore a new kind of vanity.

THE ONTOLOGICAL sickness grows more and more serious as the mediator approaches the desiring subject. Its natural end is death. The power of pride cannot but end in the fragmentation and ultimately in the complete disintegration of the subject. The very desire to unify oneself disperses, and here we have arrived at the definitive dispersion. The contradictions caused by internal mediation end by destroying the individual. Masochism is followed by the last stage of metaphysical desire, that of self-destruction, physical self-destruction in all Dostoyevsky's characters who are dedicated to evil: Kirillov's suicide, the suicides of Svidrigailov, Stavrogin, and of Smerdiakov; and finally spiritual self-destruction, whose agony has been constituted by all the forms of fascination. Inevitably the fatal outcome of ontological sickness is, directly or indirectly, a form of suicide, since pride has been freely chosen.

As the mediator approaches, the phenomena connected with metaphysical desire tend to be of a collective nature. This is more apparent than ever in the supreme stage of desire. Thus in Dostoyevsky along with the individual suicide we find a quasi-suicide of the collectivity.

The cosmos of internal mediation is still intact in Proust. Even in *The Past Recaptured* the threat hanging over the nocturnal and frenzied city of Paris is still very distant. But in Dostoyevsky the great chaotic scenes of his master-pieces are a real dislocation of the world of hatred. The balance between the forces of attraction and repulsion is broken, the social atoms no longer gravitate around each other.

The collective aspects of this will to die are particularly developed in *The Possessed*. One whole town, shaken by increasingly violent shocks, finally succumbs to the dizzi-ness of the void. There is a metaphysical bond between the absurd party of Julie Michaïlovna, the fires, the mur-ders, and the wave of scandals which engulfs the com-munity. It is all one disaster and the muddle-headed activ-ity of the mediocre Verhovenski would never have pro-voked it had it not been for the demoniacal contagion and the secret complicity with the spirit of evil in the upper and middle layers of society. "We will proclaim destruc-tion," yaps Verhovenski, "why is this idea so fascinating?"

This unleashing of the possessed is prefigured in the preceding novels. Most of the great collective scenes in Dostoyevsky end in visions of chaos. In *Crime and Pun-ishment* it is the extraordinary funeral feast in honor of Marmeladov. In *The Idiot* it is the great scenes at Lebe-deff's villa, the public concert interrupted by the entrance

of Nastasia Philipovna and the slap in the face to Prince
Myshkin. Dostoyevsky is always haunted by the same
spectacle, but even at the height of his genius he seems
incapable of translating its horror. It is not his imagination but rather the literary genre which is not capable of
the task. Dostoyevsky cannot transgress the limits of credibility. The scenes we have just mentioned seem timid beside the nightmare that haunts Raskolnikov during his
sickness. This torment is visited upon the hero at the
lowest point of his descent into hell, just before the release of the conclusion. This vision of terror must be compared with other great novelistic scenes in order to gain a
glimpse of the abyss in which Dostoyevsky's universe is
always on the point of being engulfed:

> He seemed to see the whole world laid waste by a
> terrible and unparalleled plague which had swooped
> down on Europe from the heart of Asia. Everyone ex-
> cept a very few elect perished. Microscopic trichina
> of a hitherto unknown variety penetrated the human
> organism. But these corpuscles were spirits endowed
> with intelligence and will-power. Individuals in-
> fected with them immediately became unbalanced
> and mad. Yet by a strange paradox never before had
> men thought they were so wise, so sure of knowing
> the truth. They had never had such confidence in the
> infallibility of their judgment, of their scientific theo-
> ries and of their moral principles. . . . Everyone
> was a prey to anguish and beyond understanding
> each other. Yet each one believed he alone knew the
> truth and was grieved at the thought of the others.
> Each person at the sight of the other beat his breast,
> and wrung his hands and wept. . . . They could not
> agree on the measures to be taken for good and evil
> and they did not know whom to convict and whom to
> acquit. They killed each other in a kind of absurd
> fury.

This sickness is contagious and yet it isolates individuals; it turns them one against the other. Each believes he alone knows the truth and each is miserable when he looks at his neighbors. Each condemns and acquits according to his own law. None of these symptoms is unfamiliar to us. Raskolnikov is describing ontological sickness at the paroxysmal stage which triggers this orgy of destruction. The reassuring vocabulary of microbic medicine and technology emerges in the apocalypse.

THE TRUTH of metaphysical desire is death. This is the inevitable end of the contradiction on which that desire is based. Novels are full of signs announcing death. But the signs remain ambiguous so long as the prophecy is not fulfilled. As soon as death is present it lights up the path behind it; it enriches our interpretation of the mediated structure; it gives their full meaning to many aspects of metaphysical desire.

In the experience which originates the mediation the subject recognizes in himself an extreme weakness. It is this weakness that he wants to escape in the illusory divinity of the Other. The subject is ashamed of his life and his mind. In despair at not being God, he searches for the sacred in everything which threatens his life, in everything which thwarts his mind. Thus he is always oriented toward what will debase and finally destroy the highest and most noble part of his being.

This orientation can already be seen in Stendhal. Julien's intelligence and sensitivity are a disadvantage in the universe of the *Black*. As we have seen, the game of internal mediation depends on hiding what one feels. The cleverest at the game will always be the one who feels the least. Thus he can never be the genuinely "passionate" hero. The struggle between master and slave requires coldness and "English phlegm," qualities which in the end amount to insensibility. Everything which procures mastery is by definition incompatible with the "Italian temperament"—that is, with the greatest intensity of life.

Once the stage of masochism has been reached it becomes very obvious that metaphysical desire tends toward the complete destruction of life and spirit. The obstinate search for an *obstacle* gradually assures the elimination of accessible objects and benevolent mediators. Let us recall the adolescent Dolgorouki who rejects the old servant who brings him food. The masochist feels the same disgust for those who "wish him well" as he feels for himself, rather he turns eagerly toward those who seem to despise his humiliating weakness and thus reveal to him their superhuman essence. Admittedly the masochist usually meets only an apparent scorn but that is all his gloomy soul requires. Beneath this apparent scorn there can be, as we have seen, the mechanical obstacle of a rival desire. But there can also be something else. It is not a rival's desire which presents the biggest, most inert, and most implacable obstacle; it is rather the total absence of desire, pure and simple apathy, the lack of spirit and intelligence. The individual who is spiritually too limited to respond to our advances enjoys, in his relationships with everybody, an autonomy which inevitably appears *divine* to the victim of metaphysical desire. This individual's very insignificance confers on him the only virtue the masochist demands in his mediator.

Swann is attracted sexually by qualities completely contrary to those which make him admire women in society or fictional creations in art and literature. He is drawn to vulgar people, who are incapable of appreciating his social position, his culture, and his refined distinction. He is fascinated by people who are insensitive to his very real superiority; thus in his amorous life he is doomed to mediocrity.

The narrator's tastes are no different. Albertine's health

and plumpness excite his desire but this is not on account
of any Rabelaisian sensuality. As always in double mediation, the apparent materialism hides an inverse spiritual-
ism. Marcel remarks that he is always drawn to that
which seems "the most contrary to [his] extreme and painful sensibility and intellectuality." Albertine clearly illustrates this law. Her animal passivity, her middle-class ignorance of aristocratic hierarchies, her lack of education,
her inability to share Marcel's values make her the inaccessible, invulnerable, and cruel person who alone can
arouse desire. In this connection we should recall that
profound axiom of Alain's: "The amorous person desires
the soul, that is why the coquette's stupidity looks like
cunning."

Snobbism, too, bows before stupidity. This is the structure of desire which is exaggerated to the point of caricature in the Baron de Charlus. But in order to grasp the orientation of Proustian desire it is not necessary to bring in
the "blackguards" and "petty brutes" whom the Baron
chases. It is enough to re-read the first description of the
"little band" in *Within a Budding Grove:*

> perhaps these girls (whose attitude was enough to
> reveal their nature, bold, frivolous and hard), ex-
> tremely sensitive to everything that was ludicrous or
> ugly, incapable of yielding to an intellectual or moral
> attraction, had naturally felt themselves, among com-
> panions of their own age, repelled by all those in
> whom a pensive or sensitive disposition was betrayed
> by shyness, awkwardness, constraint, by what, they
> would say, "didn't appeal" to them and from such
> had held aloof.

The mediator is the mediator only because he seems
"incapable of yielding to an intellectual or moral attraction"; the girls owe their prestige to their apparent
baseness. It seems that the little band *must* feel "repulsion"

for all who betray "a pensive or sensitive disposition." The narrator feels he is obviously the object of their scorn; he imagines that it would be completely out of the question for these adolescents ever to have anything to do with him. That is all he needs to determine his desire. Marcel's instantaneous desire amounts to supposing that Albertine is insensible and brutal. Baudelaire already had affirmed that "stupidity" is a necessary adornment of *modern* beauty. One must go further; the very essence of what is sexually desirable is to be found in spiritual and moral insufficiency, in all the vices which, were it not for the desire, would make it intolerable to be around the desired person.

Let it not be said that Proust is an "exceptional" person. In revealing his hero's desire the novelist as always reveals the sensibility of his epoch or of the epoch to follow. The whole of our contemporary world is permeated by masochism. Proustian eroticism is today the eroticism of the masses. For proof we need only glance at the least "sensational" of our illustrated magazines.

The masochist is constantly running up against the blind wall of stupidity, and it is against this wall that he finally smashes himself to bits. Denis de Rougemont draws the same conclusion at the end of *Love in the Western World:* "Thus this preference for the desired obstruction was a progress towards death." The various stages of this progress can be traced on the level of literary images. Common to all modern writers, the imagery of deviated transcendency is as strict, despite its richness, as the imagery of vertical transcendency in the writings of the Christian mystics. We can only touch on this inexhaustible theme. First there is a group of images starting with the animal in its most inhuman aspects, continuing through elementary decay to the purely organic. One might study, for example, the role played by vermin in the jungle scenes of André Malraux's novel *The Royal Way*.

Spiders and snakes haunt the dreams of Svidrigailov, Hyppolithe, and Stavrogin. A writer like Dostoyevsky recognizes the malignant nature of the fascinations controlling his heroes. Our contemporary writers, on the other hand, surrender to their attraction, and the more they are tainted with neoromanticism, the more willingly they do so. In *Notes from the Underground* the mediator bears an eminently symbolic name: Zverkov, which signifies "animal," "beast." All of the Proustian desires already bore the mark of that beast. Mme de Guermantes' charms are those of a "bird of prey." In *Within a Budding Grove* the novelist compares the movements of the girls to that of a "school of young fish," in other words to the least individualized part of animal life. Later the comings and goings of the "little band" make Marcel think of "a flight of gulls which performed with measured steps upon the sands . . . a movement the purpose of which seems obscure." This obscure universe is again that of the mediator. The Other is more fascinating the less accessible he is; and the more despiritualized he is, the more he tends toward an instinctive automatism, the more inaccessible he is. And the absurd project of self-divinization ends up by going beyond the animal to the automatic and even the mechanical. The individual becomes increasingly bewildered and unbalanced by a desire which nothing can satisfy and finally seeks the divine essence in that which radically denies his own existence: the inanimate.

The tireless pursuit of what negates him leads the hero into the most parched deserts, into those "metallic kingdoms of the absurd" through which wander the most significant work of neoromantic art today. Maurice Blanchot accurately remarks that novelistic fiction—in our terms romantic—since Kafka describes an endless circular movement. There would seem to be no end to the pursuit. The hero is no longer alive but he is not yet dead. Moreover the hero knows that the end of his search is death, but this knowledge does not turn him from metaphysical desire. The greatest lucidity is also the most total blindness. In a contradiction at once more subtle and more blatant than those which have gone before, the hero decides that death is the meaning of life. Henceforth the mediator is identified with the image of death which is always close by yet always denied. It is this image that fascinates the hero. Death is the supreme goal of desire and a final mirage

"They were seeking death but it will flee before them," announces the angel of the apocalypse. "Nothing ends in this world," Stavrogin picks up as an echo. But Stavrogin is wrong; it is Dacha who is right when she answers: "There will be an end here."

That end is found in the mineral world, the world of a death which the absence of all movement, of all quivering, has made complete and definitive. The horrible fascination ends in the density of lead, the impenetrable immobility of granite. This is the inevitable termination of that ever more effective negation of life and of spirit, deviated transcendency. The affirmation of the self ends in the negation of self. The will to make oneself God is a will to self-destruction which is gradually realized. De Rougemont perceived this very clearly and expressed it masterfully in *Love in the Western World:* "The same movement which makes us worship life hurls us into its negation."

Ever since Hegel, the modern world has boldly and openly presented this same negation as the supreme affirmation of life. The exaltation of the negative is rooted in that *blind lucidity* which characterizes the last stages of internal mediation. This negativity, which it is easy to see is woven all through contemporary reality, is never anything other than a reflection of human relationships at the level of double mediation. This superabundant "annihilation" should be regarded not as the true substance of the spirit but as the noxious by-product of a fatal evolution. The massive and dumb *en-soi* which the *pour-soi* always denies, is actually the obstacle that the masochist avidly seeks and on which he remains fixed. The *Negative* which so many modern philosophers identify with freedom and life is in reality the herald of slavery and death.

IN AN earlier chapter we compared the structure of metaphysical desire with a falling object whose shape changes as the speed of its fall increases. Henceforth we know the end of that fall. Dostoyevsky is nearer to that fatal end than the other novelists. Thus he is not novelist *and* metaphysician; he is the metaphysical novelist. Dostoyevsky has an acute awareness of the mortal dynamism which animates desire. His work does not tend toward disintegration and death because he is a "pessimist," he looks like a pessimist because his work tends toward disintegration and death.

To perceive the metaphysical structure of desire is to foresee its catastrophic conclusion. Apocalypse means development. The Dostoyevskian apocalypse is a development that ends in the destruction of what it has developed. Whether one sees it as a whole or isolates a part of it, the metaphysical structure can always be defined as an apocalypse. All the previous novels are, therefore, also apocalypses. The minor catastrophes which conclude these works prefigure the Dostoyevskian terror. One could doubtless trace various influences that affected Dostoyevsky and furnished certain details of the apocalyptic structure. The Russian novelist's interpretation is always enclosed in the framework of a national and religious tradition. But the essential is nonetheless dictated to the author by his novelistic situation.

Previous novelists are usually only implicitly metaphysical. The full significance of their psychology, their sociology, and their imagery can be understood only if they are extended in the direction of Dostoyevsky's metaphysics. On the level of Dostoyevskian observation there is no longer any distinction between novel and metaphysics. All the threads we have connected, all the tracks we have followed converge toward the Dostoyevskian apocalypse. The whole of novelistic literature is carried along by the same wave, all its heroes obey the same call to nothingness and death. Deviated transcendency is a giddy descent, a blind plunge into the shadows. It ends in the monstrosity of Stavrogin, and in the infernal pride of all the possessed.

The novelist discovers in the episode of the demons of Gerasa the scriptural translation of the novelistic vision. A man lives alone among the tombs. The unclean spirit which inhabits him is exorcised by Christ. The spirit has a name: it is called Legion, it is both unique and many and it begs to take refuge in a herd of swine. No sooner is the permission granted than these animals hurl themselves into the sea until every last one of them drowns.

THE CONCLUSION

THE ULTIMATE meaning of desire is death but death is not the novel's ultimate meaning. The demons like raving madmen throw themselves into the sea and perish. But the patient is cured. Stepan Trofimovitch on his deathbed recalls the miracle: "But the sick man will be healed and 'will sit at the feet of Jesus,' and all will look upon him with astonishment."

These words are applicable not only to Russia but to the dying man himself. Stepan Trofimovitch is this sick man who is healed in death and whom death heals. Stepan let himself be carried away by the wave of scandal, murder, and crime which engulfed the town. His flight has its roots in the universal madness but as soon as it is undertaken its significance changes—it is transformed into a return to the mother earth and to the light of day. His roaming finally leads the old man to a wretched bed in an inn where a gospel woman reads him the words of St. Luke. The dying man sees the truth in the parable of the swine of Gerasa. Out of supreme disorder is born supernatural order.

The closer Stepan comes to death, the more he withdraws from lying: "I've been telling lies all my life. Even when I told the truth I never spoke for the sake of the truth, but always for my own sake. I knew it before, but I only see it now." In these words Stepan *clearly contradicts his former ideas*.

The apocalypse would not be complete without a positive side. There are two antithetical deaths in the conclusion of *The Possessed:* one death which is an extinction of the spirit and one death which is spirit; Stavrogin's death is only death, Stepan's death is life. This double ending is not unusual in Dostoyevsky. We find it in *The Brothers Karamazov* where the madness of Ivan Karamazov is contrasted with the redeeming conversion of Dmitri. We find it in *Crime and Punishment* where Svidrigailov's suicide is contrasted with the redeeming conversion of Raskolnikov. The gospel woman who watches at Stepan's bedside plays a similar role to Sonia's, though less pronounced. She is the mediator between the sinner and the Scriptures.

Raskolnikov and Dmitri Karamazov do not die a physical death but they are nonetheless restored to life. All Dostoyevsky's conclusions are fresh beginnings; a new life commences, either among men or in eternity.

But perhaps it would be better not to push this analysis any further. Many critics refuse to accept Dostoyevsky's religious conclusions. They find them artificial, ill-considered, and superficially imposed on the novel. The novelist is supposed to have written them when he ran out of novelistic inspiration, in order to give his work an appearance of religious orthodoxy.

So let us leave Dostoyevsky and turn to the conclusions of other novels, such as *Don Quixote.* The hero's death is very like that of Stepan Trofimovitch. His passion for chivalry is portrayed as an actual possession of which the dying man sees himself fortunately, though somewhat belatedly, delivered. The clarity of vision that he regains enables Don Quixote, like Stepan Trofimovitch, to reject his former existence.

At this time my judgment is free and clear and no longer covered with a thick blanket of ignorance woven by my sad and constant reading of detestable books of chivalry. I recognize their extravagance and trickery. My only regret is that my disillusionment has come too late and that I do not have time to make up for my mistake by reading other books which would help to enlighten my soul.

The Spanish *desengaño* has the same meaning as Dostoyevsky's conversion. But again there are many writers who advise us not to dwell on this conversion in death. The conclusion of *Don Quixote* is almost as unappreciated as Dostoyevsky's conclusions, and strangely enough the same faults are found in it. It is considered artificial, conventional, and superimposed on the novel. Why should two such great novelists both consider it proper to disfigure the final pages of their masterpieces? As we have seen, Dostoyevsky is considered the victim of self-imposed censure. Cervantes, however, is supposed to have succumbed to external censure. The Inquisition was hostile to books of chivalry. The critics remain convinced that *Don Quixote* is a book of chivalry. Cervantes therefore was obliged to write a "conformist" conclusion which would allay ecclesiastical suspicions.

Let us then leave Cervantes, if we must, and turn to a third novelist. Stendhal was not a slavophile and had no reason to fear the Church, at least during the period when he wrote *The Red and the Black*. But the conclusion of that novel is nevertheless a third *conversion in death*. Julien also utters words which *clearly contradict* his former ideas. He repudiates his will to power, he makes a break with the world which fascinated him; his passion for Mathilde disappears; he flies to Mme de Rênal and refuses to defend himself.

All these analogies are remarkable. But again we are asked not to attach any importance to this conversion in death. Even the author, who seems ashamed of his own lyricism, conspires with the critics to discredit his own text. He tells us we should not take Julien's meditations seriously for "the lack of exercise was beginning to affect his health and give him the exalted and weak character of a young German student."

Let Stendhal say what he likes. We can no longer be put off the scent. If we are still blind to the unity displayed in novelistic conclusions, the unanimous hostility of romantic critics should be enough to open our eyes.

It is the hypotheses of the critics that are insignificant and artificial, not the conclusions. One would have to think very little of Dostoyevsky to see in him the censor of his own novels. One would have to have little esteem for Cervantes to think him capable of betraying his own thought. The hypothesis of self-censure is not even worth discussing, for the beauty of the text alone is enough to demolish it. The solemn adjuration of the dying Don Quixote is addressed to us, the readers, just as much as to his friends and relatives gathered about him: "In the extremity which I have reached I must not make light of my soul."

It is easy to understand the hostility of the romantic critics. All the heroes, in the conclusion, utter words which *clearly contradict their former ideas,* and those ideas are always shared by the romantic critics. Don Quixote renounces his knights, Julien Sorel his revolt, and Raskolnikov his superhumanity. Each time the hero denies the fantasy inspired by his pride. And it is that fantasy which the romantic interpretation always exalts. The critics do not want to admit that they have been mistaken; thus they have to maintain that the conclusion is unworthy of the work it crowns.

The analogies between the conclusions of the great novels destroy *ipso facto* all interpretations that minimize their importance. There is a single phenomenon and it must be accounted for by one principle.

The unity of novelistic conclusions consists in the renunciation of metaphysical desire. The dying hero repudiates his mediator: "I am the enemy of Amadis of Gaul and of all the infinite battalions of his kind . . . today, through God's mercy, having been made wise at my own expense, I loathe them."

Repudiation of the mediator implies renunciation of divinity, and this means renouncing pride. The physical diminution of the hero both expresses and conceals the defeat of pride. One sentence with a double meaning in *The Red and the Black* expresses beautifully the link between death and liberation, between the guillotine and the break with the mediator: "What do *Others* matter to me," exclaims Julien Sorel, "my relations with others are going to be abruptly cut off."

In renouncing divinity the hero renounces slavery. Every level of his existence is inverted, all the effects of metaphysical desire are replaced by contrary effects. Deception gives way to truth, anguish to remembrance, agitation to repose, hatred to love, humiliation to humility, mediated desire to autonomy, deviated transcendency to vertical transcendency.

This time it is not a false but a genuine conversion. The hero triumphs in defeat; he triumphs because he is at the end of his resources; for the first time he has to look his despair and his nothingness in the face. But this look which he has dreaded, which is the death of pride, is his salvation. The conclusions of all the novels are reminiscent of an oriental tale in which the hero is clinging by his finger-tips to the edge of a cliff; exhausted, the hero finally lets himself fall into the abyss. He expects to smash against the rocks below but instead he is supported by the air: the law of gravity is annulled.

ALL NOVELISTIC conclusions are conversions; it is impossible to doubt this. But can one go further? Can one maintain that all these conversions have the same meaning? Two fundamental categories seem to be distinguishable from the outset: those conclusions which portray a solitary hero who rejoins other men and those which portray a "gregarious" hero gaining solitude. Dostoyevsky's novels belong to the first category, Stendhal's to the second. Raskolnikov rejects solitude and embraces Others, Julien Sorel rejects Others and embraces solitude.

The opposition seems insurmountable. Yet it is not. If our interpretation of the conversion is correct, if it puts an end to triangular desire, then its effects cannot be expressed either in terms of absolute solitude or in terms of a return to the world. Metaphysical desire brings into being a certain relationship to others and to oneself. True conversion engenders a new relationship to others and to oneself. The mechanical oppositions of solitude and gregariousness, involvement and noninvolvement are the result of romantic interpretations.

If we examine Stendhal's and Dostoyevsky's conclusions more closely we find that the two aspects of true conversion are always present but that they are not equally developed. Stendhal places more emphasis on the subjective aspect and Dostoyevsky more on the intersubjective aspect. The neglected aspect is never completely suppressed. Julien wins solitude but he triumphs over isolation. His happiness with Mme de Rênal is the supreme expression of a profound change in his relationship with Others. When the hero finds himself surrounded by a crowd at the beginning of his trial, he is surprised to find that he no longer feels his old hatred for Others. He wonders whether Others are as bad as he once thought them. When he no longer envies people, when he no longer wishes to seduce or dominate them, then Julien no longer hates them.

Similarly Raskolnikov, in the conclusion, triumphs over his isolation but he also gains solitude. He reads the Gospel; he recovers the peace which has so long escaped him. Solitude and human contact exist only as functions of each other; they cannot be isolated without lapsing into romantic abstraction.

The differences between novelistic conclusions are negligible. It is less a question of opposition than of a shift of accent. The lack of balance between the various aspects of the metaphysical cure reveal that the novelist has not rid himself entirely of his own "romanticism"; he remains the prisoner of formulas whose function of pure justification he does not perceive. Dostoyevsky's conclusions are not completely purified of the tendency to wallow in misery. In Stendhal's conclusions can be found traces of the middle-class romanticism which was rampant in the Delécluze salon. In the process of underlining these *differences* it is easy to lose sight of the unity of novelistic conclusions. The critics ask no better, for unity in their language means banality and banality is the worst charge of all. If the critics do not reject the conclusion outright they try to prove that it is *original,* that it contradicts the conclusions of other novels. They always trace the author back to his romantic origins. They think they are doing his work a good service. And this is doubtless true according to the romantic taste of the educated public. But on a more profound level they are doing it a disservice. They are exalting that in it which is contrary to novelistic truth.

Romantic criticism rejects what is essential; it refuses to go beyond metaphysical desire to the truth of the novel which shines beyond death. The hero succumbs as he achieves truth and he entrusts his creator with the heritage of his clairvoyance. The title of hero of a novel must be reserved for the character who triumphs over metaphysical desire in a tragic conclusion and thus becomes *capable of writing the novel.* The hero and his creator are separated throughout the novel but come together in the conclusion. Approaching death, the hero looks back on his lost existence. He sees it with the "breadth and depth of vision" which suffering, sickness, and exile gave to Mme de Clèves and which is that of the novelist himself. This "breadth and depth of vision" is not so different from the "telescope" mentioned by Marcel Proust in *The Past Recaptured*, and from the supereminent position which Stendhal's hero attains in his prison. All these images of distance and elevation are the expression of a new and more detached vision, which is the creator's own vision. This ascending movement must not be confused with pride. The aesthetic triumph of the author is one with the joy of the hero who has renounced desire.

Therefore the conclusion is always a memory. It is the eruption of a memory which is more true than the perception itself. It is a "panoramic vision" like Anna Karenina's. It is "revivification of the past." The expression is Proust's but he is not speaking of *The Past Recaptured*, as one would immediately imagine, but of *The Red and the Black*. The inspiration always comes from memory and memory springs from the conclusion. Every novelistic conclusion is a beginning.

Every novelistic conclusion is a *Past Recaptured*.

Marcel Proust in his own conclusion merely uncovered a meaning that had previously been hidden by a transparent veil of fiction. The narrator of *Remembrance of Things Past* makes his way to the novel through the novel. But all the heroes of previous novels did the same. Stepan Trofimovitch moves toward the gospel which summarizes the meaning of *The Possessed*. Mme de Clèves moves toward the "breadth and depth of vision," that is, toward novelistic vision. Don Quixote, Julien Sorel, and Raskolnikov have the same spiritual experience as Marcel in *The Past Recaptured*. Proust's aesthetics do not consist of a number of formulas and percepts; they are indissolubly united with the escape from metaphysical desire. All of the characteristics of novelistic conclusions mentioned above may be found in *The Past Recaptured,* but here they are represented as exigencies of creation. The novel's inspiration springs from the break with the mediator. The absence of desire in the present makes it possible to recapture past desires.

In *The Past Recaptured* Proust emphasizes that *self-centeredness* is a barrier to novelistic creation. Proustian self-centeredness gives rise to *imitation* and makes us live *outside ourselves.* This self-centeredness is other-centeredness as well; it is not one-sided egotism; it is an impulse in two contradictory directions which always ends by tearing the individual apart. To triumph over self-centeredness is to get away from oneself and make contact with others but in another sense it also implies a greater intimacy with oneself and a withdrawal from others. A self-centered person thinks he is choosing himself but in fact he shuts himself out as much as others. Victory over self-centeredness allows us to probe deeply into the Self and at the same time yields a better knowledge of Others. At a certain depth there is no difference between our own secret and the secret of Others. Everything is revealed to the novelist when he penetrates this Self, a truer Self than that which each of us displays. This Self imitates constantly, on its knees before the mediator.

This profound Self is also a universal Self. The dialectic of metaphysical pride alone can help us understand and accept Proust's attempt to reconcile the particular and universal. In the context of the romantic's mechanical opposition between Self and Others, such an attempt would be absurd.

This logical absurdity no doubt struck Proust and he occasionally gives up his attempt at reconciliation and slips back into the clichés of twentieth-century romanticism. In a few isolated passages of *The Past Recaptured* he declares that the work of art must permit us to grasp our "differences" and makes us delight in our "originality."

These scattered passages are the result of Proust's lack of a theoretic vocabulary. But the attempt at logical coherence is quickly swept away by inspiration. Proust knew that in describing his own youth he was describing ours as well. He knew that the true artist no longer has to choose between himself and Others. Because it is born of renunciation, great novelistic art loses nothing and regains everything.

But this renunciation is very painful. The novelist can write his novel only if he recognizes that *his* mediator is a person like himself. Marcel, for example, has to give up considering his beloved a monstrous divinity and seeing himself in the role of an eternal victim. He has to recognize that his beloved's lies are similar to his own.

This victory over a self-centeredness which is other-centered, this renunciation of fascination and hatred, is the crowning moment of novelistic creation. Therefore it can be found in all the great novelists. Every novelist sees his similarity to the fascinating Other *through the voice of his hero.* Mme de la Fayette recognizes her similarity to the women for whom love has been their undoing. Stendhal, the enemy of hypocrites, recognizes at the end of *The Red and the Black* that he is also a hypocrite. Dostoyevsky, in the conclusion of *Crime and Punishment,* gives up seeing himself alternately as a superhuman and as a subhuman. The novelist recognizes that he is guilty of the sin of which he is accusing his mediator. The curse which Oedipus hurls at Others falls on his own head.

This is the meaning of Flaubert's famous cry: "Mme Bovary, c'est moi!" Flaubert first conceived Mme Bovary as that despicable Other whom he had sworn to deal with. Mme Bovary originally was Flaubert's enemy, as Julien

Sorel was Stendhal's enemy and Raskolnikov Dostoyev-sky's enemy. But while remaining that Other, the hero of the novel gradually merges with the novelist in the course of creation. When Flaubert cries, "Mme Bovary, c'est moi," he is not trying to say that Mme Bovary has become one of those flattering doubles with whom romantic writers love to surround themselves. He means that the Self and the Other have become one in the miracle of the novel.

Great novels always spring from an obsession that has been transcended. The hero sees himself in the rival he loathes; he renounces the "differences" suggested by ha-tred. He learns, at the expense of his pride, the existence of the psychological circle. The novelist's self-examination merges with the morbid attention he pays to his mediator. All the powers of a mind freed of its contradictions unite in one creative impulse. Don Quixote and Emma Bovary and Charlus would not be so great were they not the re-sult of a synthesis of the two halves of existence which pride usually succeeds in keeping separate.

This victory over desire is extremely painful. Proust tells us that we must forego the fervent dialogue endlessly carried on by each one of us at the superficial levels of our being. One must "give up one's dearest illusions." The novelist's art is a phenomenological *epochē*. But the only authentic *epochē* is never mentioned by modern phil-osophers; it is always victory over desire, victory over Promethean pride.

Some texts written shortly before Marcel Proust's great creative period throw a brilliant light on the connection between *The Past Recaptured* and classical novelistic conclusions. Perhaps the most important of them is an article published in *Le Figaro* in 1907 entitled "The Filial Sentiments of a Parricide." The article is devoted to the drama of a family whom the Prousts knew slightly. Henri Van Blarenberghe had killed himself after murdering his mother. Proust gives a short account of this double tragedy concerning which he seems to have no special information. At the conclusion there is a widening of the perspective and the tone becomes more personal. The Van Blarenberghe affair becomes a symbol of the mother-son relationship in general. The vices and ingratitude of children make their parents age prematurely. This theme is already present in the conclusion of *Jean Santeuil*. After describing in his article how terribly decrepit a mother, worn-out by suffering, seems to her son, Proust writes:

> perhaps women who could see that, *in that belated moment of lucidity which may occur even in lives completely obsessed by illusions, since it happened even to Don Quixote,* perhaps that someone, like Henri Van Blarenberghe after he stabbed his mother to death, would recoil from the horror of his life and snatch up a gun, in order to put an immediate end to his existence. [Italics added.]

The parricide recovers his lucidity in the course of expiating crime, and expiates his crime in the course of recovering his lucidity. His terrifying vision of the past is a vision of truth; it stands in direct opposition to his life "obsessed by illusions." The "Oedipal" atmosphere of these lines is quite striking. It is the year 1907. Proust has just lost his mother and is obsessed with remorse. In this brief paragraph we are given a glimpse of the process which enables a Stendhal, Flaubert, Tolstoy, or Dostoyevsky to give expression to his experience as a man and a writer in an ordinary news item.

In his "belated moment of lucidity" the parricide joins the ranks of all the heroes of previous novels. How can we deny this *when Proust himself compares this death to that of Don Quixote?* "The Filial Sentiments of a Parricide" provides the missing link between classical conclusions and *The Past Recaptured*. This attempt will have no immediate sequel. Proust will discard the classical method of transposition in the novel. His hero will not kill himself; rather he will become a novelist. But nevertheless the inspiration will come from death, that death which Proust is in the process of living in 1907, and whose horror is reflected in all his writing of that period.

Is this giving too much importance to a few forgotten lines? Perhaps it will be objected that the text has no literary value, that it is written in a hurry for a daily newspaper, and that its conclusion wallows in melodramatic clichés. That may be, but such considerations carry little weight in the face of Proust's own evidence. In a letter of Calmette, which accompanied the article, Proust gave *Le Figaro* full permission to edit and cut his text— except for the last paragraphs, which he demanded should be published in their entirety.

The allusion to Don Quixote's belated lucidity is all the more precious since it reappears in the notes which were published in an appendix to *Contre Sainte-Beuve,* and this time in a purely literary context. The many comments on Stendhal, Flaubert, Tolstoy, George Eliot, and Dostoyevsky in these same notes show us Proust's awareness of the unity of novelistic genius. Proust notes that all Dostoyevsky's and Flaubert's works could be entitled *Crime and Punishment.* The principle of the unity of all the great works is clearly stated in the chapter on Balzac: "All the writers come together at certain points and they seem like different and sometimes contradictory elements of a single genius."

There can be no question that Proust was aware of the connection between *The Past Recaptured* and the classical novelistic conclusions. He could have written the one book on the unity of novelistic genius which would have been worthy of such a great topic.

Under the circumstances it is surprising that Proust

never broached the theme of novelistic unity in his own conclusion, *The Past Recaptured,* which broadens into a meditation on novelistic creation. His silence on the topic of other novels is all the more surprising when we consider the number of literary references he makes. He acknowledges forerunners of the "affective memory" in Jean-Jacques Rousseau, Chateaubriand, and Gérard de Nerval. But he does not mention a single novelist. The intuitions of *Contre Sainte-Beuve* are never taken up and developed. What happened?

In Proust, as in all persons who experience a very intense and solitary spiritual experience, the fear of appearing extravagant is superseded only by that of seeming ridiculous by repeating universally accepted truths. The wish to avoid both of these opposite dangers would seem to have suggested to Proust the compromise he finally adopted. Fearing that he would be accused on the one hand of leaving the royal paths of literature, and on the other of plagiarizing the great novels, Proust picks out some literary ancestors but scrupulously avoids the novelists.

Proust, we know, lived only for his work. Léon-Pierre Quint has demonstrated the forces he could marshal in the art of literary strategy. This final "idolatry" does not blemish the perfection of *The Past Recaptured,* but it somewhat limits its universality. The author of *Remembrance of Things Past* is not interested in indicating similarities of structure among the great novels. He is afraid of putting his critics on a track that would lead to too many discoveries. He knows the importance given to *originality* in his time, and he is afraid of having some of his literary glory taken from him. He emphasizes and brings into relief the most "original" elements of his novel's revelation, especially the affective memory which we discover upon examination to play a much less central role in the works which precede *The Past Recaptured* than that assigned to it in this final novel.[1]

What explanation other than "literary strategy" can be given for Proust's silence? How are we to explain the omission, in his reflections on the art of the novel, of Stendhal's conclusion whose every characteristic he had pointed out in his *Contre Sainte-Beuve*, characteristics which can be found in *The Past Recaptured:* "An exclusive taste for sensations of the soul, revivification of the past, detachment from ambition and lack of interest in intrigue." How can we not be impressed by the fact that Proust is the only one to have seen the part played by memory in Julien's death, and that he perceived this role at the very moment he was preparing to write *The Past Recaptured?*

Proust was also very interested, at the same time and in that same conclusion, in the visit paid to Julien by the Abbé Chélan, very much weakened by age. "The weakening of a great intelligence and a great heart linked to that of the body. The old age of a virtuous man: moral pessimism." Julien's lucid death stands out marvelously against the background of this slow and terrible decomposition of the flesh.

Again the attention given by Proust to this episode is not disinterested. He builds the whole of *The Past Recaptured* on a similar contrast between two antithetical deaths. The hero is lucid when he dies to be reborn in the work but around him people continue to die without hope of resurrection. The spiritually fertile death of the narrator is contrasted with the cruel spectacle of the

[1] We are far from seeing in that central position given to the affective memory a "fault" of the novelist or a betrayal of the original experience. This position is justified by reasons of economy in the novel. We wish only to note that Proust managed to combine very cleverly the superior demands of revelation in the novel with the practical demands of "literary strategy."

Guermantes' soirée, with the horrible and useless aging of the members of high society. This contrast is already to be found in "The Filial Sentiments of a Parricide" but from now on it gains its classically novelistic meaning, and achieves unity with the Dostoyevskian apocalypse. In fact we must see in *The Red and the Black* and *The Past Recaptured* the two inseparable and opposed faces of the novelistic apocalypse as they were first revealed in the work of Dostoyevsky. In all genuine novelistic conclusions death as spirit is victoriously opposed to death of the spirit.

Are we being carried away by our imagination? To dispel any doubts we will introduce a final witness in favor of the unity of novelistic conclusions: Balzac. This novelist has not been included in our group but his creative experience is just as close in certain points to those which we have been considering. For proof of these analogies we need only look at the following passage taken from the conclusion of *Cousin Pons*. Balzac is describing his hero's death and in doing so he defines the double face of the novelistic apocalypse:

Ancient and modern sculptors have often placed on either side of the tomb genies holding flaming torches. These flames illuminate for the dying their faults, their errors, as they light up the paths of Death. Sculpture there represents great ideas, it formulates a human fact. Death has its wisdom. Often simple girls, at a very tender age, are found to have the wisdom of old men, become prophets, judge their family and not be taken in by any deception. This is the poetry of Death! But it is a strange thing and should be noticed that one dies in two different ways. This poetry of prophecy, this gift of penetration, whether before or after, is only found in those who are merely dying in the flesh, who are dying though the destruction of the organs of carnal life. Thus people suffering, like Louis XIV, from gangrene, consumption, people who die of fever like Pons, or of a stomach ailment like Mme de Mortsauf, enjoy this sublime lucidity, and achieve amazing and admirable deaths; whereas people who die of intellectual sicknesses, as it were, where the trouble is in the brain, in the nervous system which serves as an intermediary for the body to provide it with the brain's fuel; these die in entirety. In them, body and mind founder together. The first, souls without bodies, become Biblical spirits; the others are corpses. This virgin, this unascetic Cato, [Pons, the hero] this just and almost innocent man eventually penetrated the pockets of gall which made up the heart of the magistrate's wife. He understood the world as he was about to leave it. Several hours before he had resigned himself to the inevitable, like a joyful artist for whom everything is a pretext for caricature and raillery. The last ties binding him to life, the chains of admiration, the powerful knots which link the connoisseur to the masterpieces of art had been broken in the morning. When he saw that he had been robbed by the Cibot woman he made a Christian farewell to the pomp and vanity of art.

We must not begin from reality as we see it and subject novelistic creation to the standards of this vision. In this conclusion, historical figures like Louis XIV are put side by side with fictional creation like Pons and Mme de Mortsauf. Behind the veil of pseudo-physiology, as elsewhere beneath phrenology, Martinism, or magnetism, Balzac is incessantly telling us about his novelistic experience. Here in a few sentences he sums up the essential characteristics of the novelistic conclusion: the double face of death, the role of suffering, the detachment of passion, the Christian symbolism, and that *sublime lucid-*

ity which is both memory and prophecy, and which throws an equal light on the soul of the hero and the soul of the other characters.

In Balzac, as in Cervantes, Stendhal, and Dostoyevsky, the tragic event expresses the advent of a new vision, the novelist's vision. This is why Balzac compares the dying man's state of soul to that of a "joyful artist." The conclusion of *Cousin Pons* is a *Past Recaptured*.

It is easy to prove the unity of novelistic conclusions if we compare texts. But in theory, at least, this last proof is not necessary. Our analyses inevitably lead to the message unanimously proclaimed by all the great conclusions. When he renounces the deceptive divinity of pride, the hero frees himself from slavery and finally grasps the truth about his unhappiness. There is no distinction between this renunciation and the creative renunciation. It is a victory over metaphysical desire that transforms a romantic writer into a true novelist.

Up to this point this truth had only been hinted at, but at last we have reached it; we can grasp and possess it here in the last pages of the novel. All we needed was the author's permission, and this we now have: "I loathe Amadis of Gaul and all the infinite number of his kind." The novelists themselves, through the medium of their heroes, confirm what we have been asserting all the way through this book: the sickness is rooted in pride and the universe of the novel is a universe of people possessed. The conclusion is the stationary axle around which the wheel of the novel turns. The whole kaleidoscope of appearances depends on it. The conclusion of novels is also the conclusion of our present investigation.

Truth is active throughout the great novel but its primary location is in the conclusion. The conclusion is the temple of that truth. The conclusion is the site of the presence of truth, and therefore a place avoided by error. If error cannot destroy the unity of novelistic conclusions it tries to render it powerless. It attempts to sterilize it by calling it a *banality*. We should not deny that banality but loudly proclaim it. In the body of the novel novelistic unity is mediate, but it becomes immediate in the conclusion. Novelistic conclusions are bound to be banal since they all quite literally repeat the same thing.

This banality of novelistic conclusions is not the local and relative banality of what used to be considered "original" and could again be given oblivion followed by a "rediscovery" and a "rehabilitation." It is the absolute banality of what is essential in Western civilization. The novelistic dénouement is a reconciliation between the individual and the world, between man and the sacred. The multiple universe of passion decomposes and returns to simplicity. Novelistic conversion calls to mind the *analusis* of the Greeks and the Christian rebirth. In this final moment the novelist reaches the heights of Western literature; he merges with the great religious ethics and the most elevated forms of humanism, those which have chosen the least accessible part of man.

The theme of reconciliation has been so constantly harped on by unworthy authors that it is easy to become convinced, in this time given to indignation and scandal, that it never did and never could have any concrete content. It seems to emanate from the most superficial areas of novelistic consciousness. To put reconciliation in its proper perspective we must look on it as the conquest of a possibility that has long been denied the writer. The conclusion must be considered as a successful effort to overcome the inability to conclude. The criticism of Maurice Blanchot can help us in this task. Maurice Blanchot portrays Franz Kafka as the exemplary representative of a literature doomed to inconclusiveness. Like Moses, Kafka's hero will never see the promised land. This inability to conclude, Blanchot tells us, is an inability to die in the work and to free oneself in death.

The impossible conclusion defines a "literary space" which is not beyond but this side of reconciliation. The fact that this space is the only one accessible to our own time of anguish is disquieting but not surprising to anyone who bears in mind the evolution of the structure of the novel. The fact would not have surprised Dostoyevsky who has already given us characters doomed to inconclusiveness and was traversing Maurice Blanchot's "literary space" at the time he wrote *Notes from the Underground*. This story, like so many of Kafka's and those of writers after Kafka, has no conclusion:

> The notes of this paradoxalist do not end here, however. He could not refrain from going on with them, but it seems to us that we may stop here.

Notes from the Underground is the turning point between romanticism and the novel, between the preceding inauthentic reconciliations and the authentic reconciliations which follow. The great novelists cross the literary space defined by Blanchot but they do not stay there. They push beyond that space toward the infinity of a liberating death.

In contrast to the incompleteness of the contemporary narrative, an incompletion which in the best writers reflects not a passing fashion but a particular historical and metaphysical situation, the conclusion of the novelistic work embodies not only a historical but an individual possibility finally and triumphantly actualized.

The great novelistic conclusions are banal but they are not conventional. Their lack of rhetorical ability, even their clumsiness, constitute their true beauty and clearly distinguish them from the deceptive reconciliations which abound in second-rate literature. Conversion in death should not seem to us the easy solution but rather an almost miraculous descent of novelistic grace.

The truly great novels are all born of that supreme moment and return to it the way a church radiates from the chancel and returns to it. All the great works are composed like cathedrals: once again the truth of *Remembrance of Things Past* is the truth of all the great novels.

WE CARRY within us a whole hierarchy of the superficial and the profound, the essential and the subordinate, and we apply it instinctively to the novel. This hierarchy, which is often "romantic" and "individualist" in character, conceals from us certain essential aspects of artistic creation. For example, we are in the habit of never taking Christian symbolism seriously, perhaps because it is common to many works both mediocre and sublime. We attribute a purely decorative function to this symbolism when the author is not a Christian, and a purely apologetic function when he is a Christian. Truly "scientific" criticism would discard all these a priori judgments and would note the amazing points of similarity among all the different novelistic conclusions. If only our prejudices *pro* and *con* did not erect a water-tight barrier between aesthetic experience and religious experience we would see the problems of creation in a new light. We would not cut off Dostoyevsky's work from all its religious meditations. In *The Brothers Karamazov*, for example, we would discover texts as important for the study of novelistic creation as those of *The Past Recaptured*. And we would at last realize that Christian symbolism is universal for it alone is able to give form to the experience of the novel.

We must therefore look at this symbolism from the point of view of the novel. The task is all the more difficult since the author himself sometimes tries to throw us off the

scent. Stendhal attributes Julien Sorel's "German mysticism" to the extreme dampness of his prison cell. But the
conclusion of *The Red and the Black* remains a meditation
on Christian themes and symbols. In it the novelist reaf-
firms his skepticism but the themes and symbols are nonetheless present in order to be clothed in negations. They
play exactly the same role as in Proust or Dostoyevsky. We
shall see everything which touches on these themes, including the monastic vocation of Stendhal's heroes, in a
fresh light which the author's irony cannot hide from us.

Here, as before, we must interpret the novelists by com-
paring them to one another. We should not treat the religious question externally but if possible look on it as a
purely novelistic problem. The question of Christianity in
Stendhal, the question of "mysticism" in Proust and in
Dostoyevsky can be understood only through comparisons.

*If the seed does not die after it has been sown, it will
remain alone, but if it dies it will bear much fruit.* The
verse from St. John reappears in several crucial episodes
of *The Brothers Karamazov*. It expresses the mysterious
connections between the two deaths in the novel, the link
between the convict prison and Dmitri's spiritual healing,
the link between the mortal sickness and the redeeming
confession of the "unknown visitor," the link between
Ilusha's death and the charitable work of Alyosha.

Proust has recourse to the same verse from the Gospel
of St. John when he wants to explain to us the part played
by sickness, that younger sister of death, in his own creation. "When sickness, like a harsh spiritual director,
caused me to die to the social world, it did me a good
service for if the seed does not die after it is sown it will
remain alone and will not bear much fruit."

Mme de la Fayette too could have quoted St. John, for
one finds in *The Princess of Clèves* the sickness of Proust's

narrator. This sickness comes at the same point in the novel's development as in Proust and has exactly the same spiritual consequences: "The necessity of dying, which she saw was very near, made her used to detachment and the length of her illness made it a habit. . . . Worldly passions and activities appeared to her in the same way as to people who have broader and deeper vision." This *breadth and depth of vision* belongs to the new being who is literally born of the death.

The verse from St. John serves as an epigraph for *The Brothers Karamazov* and it could serve as an epigraph for all novelistic conclusions. Repudiation of a human mediator and renunciation of deviated transcendency inevitably call for symbols of vertical transcendency whether the author is Christian or not. All the great novelists respond to this fundamental appeal but sometimes they manage to hide from themselves the meaning of their response. Stendhal uses irony. Proust masks the true face of novelistic experience with romantic commonplaces but he gives the stale symbols a profound and secret brilliance. In his work symbols of immortality and resurrection appear in a purely aesthetic context and only surreptitiously do they transcend the banal meaning to which romanticism reduces them. They are not operetta princes; they are true princes disguised as operetta princes.

These symbols make their appearance long before *The Past Recaptured*, in all the passages which are both an echo and annunciation of the original experience. One of these passages is devoted to the death and funeral of the great writer, Bergotte:

> They buried him, but all through the night of mourning, in the lighted windows, his books arranged three by three kept watch like angels with outspread wings and seemed, for him who was no more, the symbol of his resurrection.

Bergotte is famous and Proust obviously is thinking of his posthumous glory, to that *"consolatrice affreusement laurée"* which so irritated Valéry. But this romantic cliché is no more than a pretext in this passage: it is merely an excuse to introduce the word *resurrection,* without disturbing the external positive and "realist" order. The death and resurrection of Bergotte foreshadow the death and resurrection of the author himself, the second birth from which *Remembrance of Things Past* springs. The true resonance of the sentence just quoted is derived from the expectance of that resurrection. Along with the images of deviated transcendency we can discern the outlines of the symbolism of vertical transcendency. Contrasted with the demoniacal idols who drag the narrator down into the abyss are angels with outspread wings. We must interpret this symbolism in the light of *The Past Recaptured:* "The greatness of Proust," André Malraux correctly notes, "became evident when the publication of *The Past Recaptured* revealed the significance of a literary achievement which, up to that point, did not seem to surpass that of Dickens."

It was *The Past Recaptured,* to be sure, which gave Proust's creation its meaning, but other novelistic conclusions contributed to that meaning as well. *The Brothers Karamazov* makes it impossible for us to consider the resurrection of Bergotte simply a romantic commonplace. And in the same way, *The Past Recaptured,* which Proust first entitled *Perpetual Adoration,* makes it impossible for us to see in the religious meditations of *The Brothers Karamazov* merely religious propaganda, external to the novel itself. If Dostoyevsky suffered so much while writing those pages it is not because he found it a boring task but because he considered them of prime importance.

In the second part of *The Brothers Karamazov* little Ilusha dies for the sake of all the heroes of Dostoyevsky's novels and the communion which springs from that death is Balzac's and Proust's *sublime lucidity* shared by many. The structure of crime and redeeming punishment transcends the solitary consciousness. Never did a novelist make such a radical break with romantic and Promethean individualism.

The conclusion of *The Brothers Karamazov* is borne on the highest crest of Dostoyevsky's genius. The last distinctions between novelistic and religious experience are abolished. But the structure of experience has not changed. It is easy to recognize in the words *memory, death, love,* and *resurrection* found in the mouths of the children of this novel the themes and symbols that inspired the creative ardor of the agnostic author of *The Past Recaptured:*

> "We love you, we love you!" they all caught it up. There were tears in the eyes of many of them.
> "Hurrah for Karamazov!" Kolya shouted ecstatically.
> "And may the dear boy's memory live for ever!" Alyosha added again with feeling.
> "For ever!" the boys chimed in again.
> "Karamazov," cried Kolya, "can it be true what's taught us in religion, that we shall all rise again from the dead and shall live and see each other again, all, Ilusha too?"
> "Certainly we shall all rise again, certainly we shall see each other and shall tell each other with joy and gladness all that has happened!" Alyosha answered, half laughing, half enthusiastic.

INDEX

Alain, 284
Aragon, Louis, 133
Aristotle: catharsis, 187n
Assemblée constituante, 127n

Balzac, Honoré de, 67, 119–20,
122, 138, 167–68, 302, 305, 306,
307, 315; *Cousin Pons*, 305–7;
The Human Comedy, 216
Barrès, Maurice, 133, 205
Baudelaire, Charles, 162, 264, 285
Beckett, Samuel, 257
Berlin, Isaiah: *The Hedgehog and
the Fox*, 166
Béroul, 109
Blanchot, Maurice, 286, 308–9
Breton, André: *Discours sur le Peu
de Réalité*, 151

Calmette, Gaston, 302
Camus, Albert, 271, 272; *The Fall*,
271; *The Plague*, 271; *The
Stranger*, 257, 270, 271, 273
Cato, 306
Cervantes, Miguel de: *The Curious
Impertinent*, 49–50, 51, 52, 99,
103; *Don Quixote*, 1–4, 10, 17,
52, 92, 97, 100, 102–4, 141, 231,
232, 268, 291–92
Chamisso, Adelbert von, 98
Charles X, 119
Chateaubriand, François-René de,
303; *Mémoires d'outre-Tombe*,
17n; *René*, 17n
Comte, Auguste, 222
Congrégation, 129, 132, 157
Corneille, Pierre, 19, 175
Cousin, Victor, 133

Dandyism, 162–64, 166–68; M.
Teste as dandy, 279
Dante Alighieri, 242
Diderot, Denis, 118
Dos Passos, John, 168

Dostoyevsky, Fyodor: *An Author's
Notebook*, 190; *The Brothers
Karamazov*, 187n, 190, 228, 259,
291, 310, 311, 312, 313–14;
Crime and Punishment, 280,
281–82, 291, 299, 302; *The
Eternal Husband*, 45–47, 50, 51,
69, 99; *The Idiot*, 55, 69, 94,
148, 163–64, 228, 280–81; *Notes
from the Underground*, 54, 57,
67–69, 185–86, 256–61, 262,
264–65, 266–68, 271, 286, 309;
Poor Folk, 268; *The Possessed*,
59–61, 158, 162–63, 172, 189–
90, 228, 249–53, 254–55, 274–
78, 280, 290–91, 297; *A Raw
Youth*, 44, 45, 156–57, 228;
White Nights, 268
Double Mediation, 101–4, 106, 109,
122, 124, 132, 138, 139, 158,
159, 167, 168–73, 203, 206, 224,
248, 284, 288
Dreyfus, Alfred, 237
Durry, Marie-Jeanne: *Flaubert et
Ses Projets Inédits*, 108n2

Eliot, George, 302

Ferrero, Louis: *Désespoirs*, 59
Flaubert, Gustave: *Bouvard and
Pécuchet*, 125, 151; *Madame
Bovary*, 8, 10, 63–64, 148–49;
The Sentimental Education,
135–36
Freud, Sigmund, 186n

Gaultier, Jules de, 24, 35–37, 63;
Bovaryism, 5
Gide, André: *The Counterfeiters*,
172; *The Fruits of the Earth*,
269; *The Immoralist*, 20, 269;
Lafcadio's Adventures, 21
Goncourt, Edmond and Jules:
Journal, 31

315